CW01670014

Coasters

An Illustrated History

OXBIRD

Coasters

An Illustrated History

Roy Fenton

Seaforth
PUBLISHING

Half-title: In July 2011 the steam coaster *Robin* arrives in the Royal Docks, London, near to where she was built in 1890. She will become a museum, remaining on her floating pontoon. *(Author)*

Title page: Now better known as a holiday resort, Torquay was one of many small ports receiving its coal supplies by coaster before the Second World War. R. & W. Paul's *Oxbird* of 1916 calls in the 1930s. *(David Eeles)*

Copyright © Roy Fenton 2011

First published in Great Britain in 2011 by
Seaforth Publishing,
Pen & Sword Books Ltd,
47 Church Street,
Barnsley S70 2AS

www.seaforthpublishing.com

British Library Cataloguing in Publication Data
A catalogue record for this book is available from the British Library

ISBN 978 1 84832 087 1

All rights reserved. No part of this publication may be reproduced or transmitted in any form or by any means, electronic or mechanical, including photocopying, recording, or any information storage and retrieval system, without prior permission in writing of both the copyright owner and the above publisher.

The right of Roy Fenton to be identified as the author of this work has been asserted by him in accordance with the Copyright, Designs and Patents Act 1988.

Typeset and designed by Ian Hughes
Printed and bound in China by 1010 Printing International Ltd

Contents

Preface

For much of the half century during which I have been an enthusiastic observer of, and researcher into, shipping, my particular passion has been coasters. Although lacking the grandeur of bigger ships, their modest scale is easier to relate to. Coasters are also associated with the more interesting and often picturesque smaller harbours, although it is debatable whether a landscape *aficionado* would consider my favourite ports of Runcorn and Goole as in any sense charming. A further attraction to the researcher is that coasters, together with their owners and builders, have been far less troubled by historians than have larger ships. Indeed, there is no overall history of the coaster, although there are admirable accounts of certain important types. This was an important attraction of Seaforth's proposal, because it allowed use to be made of some of the photographs, research, books and documents I have accumulated over many years.

Whether the finished product passes muster as a history of the coaster I must leave to the judgement of reader and reviewer, because there are some important limits to the book's coverage. It concentrates on coasters powered by steam or oil engines, the majority being of western European design and build, and which are designed mainly for cargo carrying. Each of these criteria require explanation.

First, the restriction to powered vessels. The sailing coaster died out in the twentieth century and it is almost one hundred years since the last were built in Europe. The skills and practices required to build ships in wood and navigate them by wind and tide differed greatly from those needed with their powered, iron and steel successors. The latter required the mastery of the new and different technologies of hull and engine building, of a new operating regime for its owner and manager, and new skills and disciplines for its crews. The differences are such that a single volume can hardly encompass both sail and powered coasters, hence the concentration on the latter.

Why western Europe? The United Kingdom in particular, but also the Netherlands, is where the powered coaster originated, is the area the author knows best and has the most accessible literature. Vessels of basically western European design have been used in most parts of the world. The notable exceptions have been the Americas and, to a

lesser extent, Australia, where distances are so great that vessels that elsewhere would be regarded as sea-going have been used for coastal voyages. Only in recent years have countries outside western Europe produced a significant number of ships recognisable as coasters. These show no radical departure in design from European vessels, but are typified by efficient building methods in the case of Japan and Korea, and by cheapness in the case of most yards in other emergent shipbuilding countries.

Although several vessels described herein had some passenger accommodation, the book concentrates on the vast majority of coasters designed to carry cargo. Passenger ships are a different field, with interest focused on speed and the standard and extent of accommodation and facilities for passengers. In contrast, cargo ships are designed to carry the largest quantity of goods as economically as possible, and a recurring theme of the book is how this is achieved. Nor will the book venture into the specialist field of roll-on, roll-off vessels, even though these and the trucks and trailers they carry have taken much of the cargo once carried by coasters.

This still leaves a vast field and one only lightly trodden by previous authors. Indeed, it would be quite possible to compile an entire book on, for instance, the coastal tanker, and the bibliography is witness to how individual owning companies, purely local trades and subtypes of coaster have provided enough material for substantial volumes. Readers must therefore forgive the author if he has omitted their favourite craft or neglected a much-respected fleet, as the choice of ship has been driven both by the availability of good images and the ships' typicality. The book attempts the widest coverage within its size constraints, but – with room for just over 300 examples from the tens of thousands of powered coasters ever built – it has had to ignore many fine ships and interesting operators. Originating in the early nineteenth century, the powered coaster is older than photography, and the earliest vessels were never recorded on camera. In order not to betray the photographic philosophy of the book, I have decided not to use paintings or drawings of these early vessels. As typical early vessels survived to be photographed in their dotage, it is believed that a representative selection of photographs is shown.

Unlike Ambrose Greenway's illustrated history of the cargo liner published by Seaforth, this book cannot tell its story in a strictly chronological sequence. The types of coaster that emerged followed sufficiently different evolutionary trends that each needs to be traced individually. For instance, the long chapter devoted to the coastal tanker covers a period of almost 120 years, and discusses trends, such as specialisation, not germane to dry cargo craft.

That is enough about the author's plans. Now it is time to attempt to define and describe a coaster.

Roy Fenton Wimbledon, 2011

Background photograph: The *Bessie* of 1901 at Goodwick, Pembrokeshire discharging coal into carts some time before the First World War. Taking the ground like this was a regular event for small steamers, and probably meant the crew of the 95 ft coaster would be required to work her cargo out. *(National Museums and Galleries of Wales)*

Introduction

Although in common use, the term 'coaster' is unsatisfactory. If it simply means 'a ship which trades on a coast' it covers a range from the smallest craft to the very large bulk carrier or tanker, as vessels of all sizes have from time to time been employed between ports on the same land mass. The term 'coaster and short-sea trader' is more accurate but clumsy. For the purpose of this book, 'coaster' is understood to mean a sea-going craft largely intended for operation over modest distances. It works between two or more ports either on the coast of one land mass or requiring a sea passage of anything from hours to a few days. The dimensions of length, beam, water and air draught of coasters are usually strictly limited by the ports, harbours and waterways likely to be used and by the sizes of shipments expected to be carried.

The size of a coaster and its short range should not be taken as an indication of its lack of seaworthiness. Conditions on the short sea passages that coasters routinely undertake – such as on the Irish, North, Baltic or Mediterranean seas – can be hostile. In certain circumstances, coasters can and do make successful ocean crossings, for instance on delivery voyages or when operators seize an opportunity to carry a particular cargo to or from a distant port. Nevertheless, cargo capacity, crew size, habitability, and capability for carrying fuel bunkers, fresh water and crew provisions usually restrict a coaster to voyages of hundreds rather than thousands of miles, certainly in European waters.

The British definition of home trade limits, enshrined in the Merchant Shipping Act 1894 and in force until the 1970s, is useful in illustrating the typical range of a coaster, and how it has been extended. Home trade limits were set as the coasts of the British Isles, and the coast of continental Europe between Brest to the south and the River Elbe to the north. Within this range, ships could trade with uncertificated officers, which in practical terms meant men who had grown up in coastal vessels.

After the Second World War the growing size of coasters and new trading opportunities led to the introduction of middle trade limits. These extended from Bergen to Santander and required officers to have foreign-going certificates, although the crew size was not greatly increased compared to ships in the home trade. Beyond middle trade, ships of whatever size had to be fully manned. From the mid-1970s, and influenced partly by international conventions, these limits were amended, and certification of officers became mandatory for all vessels. It is apparent that, in the eyes of authority, the certification of its officers and the size of its crew are of more importance than its physical size in deciding where a coaster can trade.

Even within sight of land, coastal vessels can encounter hostile conditions, as witness Stephenson Clarke's small bulk carrier *Washington* experiencing boisterous weather in the English Channel.

WASHINGTON

Types of coaster

There are two distinct categories of cargo-carrying coaster, liners and bulk carriers, and these and their subtypes largely determine how this book is organised.

The earliest powered coasters were developed for the regular or liner trades in which a wide variety of individual packets of cargo were conveyed. These ships, the prototype coastal liners, typically ran on predetermined routes, often maintaining a schedule that meant they sailed on an appointed day, whether full or not. Where there was a timetable to be followed, extra speed was desirable and engines were typically more powerful than in other coasters. Cargo gear was often augmented to speed turnaround in port, although increasingly these ships relied on shoreside equipment and their own gear simply got in the way. Some of these ships had accommodation for passengers, although this book considers only those for which conveying cargo was at least as important as carrying people. Some coastal liners had part or even all of their cargo space devoted to a particular cargo, such as livestock or refrigerated goods. Some were equipped to handle heavy lifts, although specialist vessels have also been developed for indivisible loads. The past tense is used because the trades of these liners have been largely lost to container ships and roll-on, roll-off vessels.

The second distinct category of coaster, and numerically the largest, is the bulk carrier. It is intended to carry dry or liquid cargoes in bulk, and its design aims to maximise capacity and economy of operation. On each voyage, bulk carrying coasters usually load just one commodity to the full extent of their capacity and deliver it to just one customer.

Dry cargo bulk carriers can usefully be split into two categories. The most common type is that designed to carry a range of cargoes, the most common of which are coal, grain, stone, ore, bagged cement, salt, fertilisers and timber. Their design has to be a compromise: their holds have to be large enough for lighter cargoes such as wheat, but equally able to handle denser cargoes, such as stone, where the ship is down to its marks well before the hold is filled. For those regularly carrying coal, the ability to load a full cargo without the need for manual adjustment, or trimming, of the cargo is important, as a 'self trimmer' obtains the best freight rates. The bulk carriers just described are the archetypal coaster and tend to go wherever a cargo offers. The somewhat pejorative term 'tramp' could be applied to these because consecutive voyages might well be very different in terms of what is carried and the ports served.

The other category of dry cargo coaster runs regularly between a restricted number of ports with just one commodity. Historically, coal was overwhelmingly the most

One of the last generation of ships built for the coastal and short-sea liner trades, and almost certainly the last with engines amidships, was *Tuskar* of Clyde Shipping Co Ltd, Glasgow; her cargo gear comprised solely of deck cranes. After only six years, the 1962-built motor ship was sold to Yugoslav owners. *(Laurence Dunn)*

common such commodity, encouraging the design of specialist colliers which would run, say, from the coal rivers of the Tyne and Wear to serve customers on the Thames or in south coast ports of the United Kingdom, or from Newcastle, New South Wales to Sydney. In extreme cases, the draught and other dimensions of a collier might be finely calculated to make it suitable to serve one particular berth, perhaps at a power station or gas works.

Another subtype of the bulk carrier, albeit very important and varied, is the coastal tanker. Within this group there is considerable specialisation to cope with the large range of liquids carried by sea, although vessels intended for carrying petroleum products predominate. Some tankers may carry a range of products in separate compartments.

Whatever their employment, bulk carrying coasters need substantial water ballast capacity. For up to half of their time at sea they are not carrying a cargo, and are fitted with tanks to be filled with seawater in order to provide stability and ensure the screw is immersed. In older and smaller coasters, water ballast was carried in fore and aft peak tanks, but larger vessels have tanks in their double bottoms. With certain light cargoes, especially timber, a certain amount of water ballast is necessary to ensure stability.

To complicate the above divisions, there is considerable crossover between types of coasters and their trades. During shortages of tonnage, the bulk carrier might be found on charter to a liner company, but its ability to carry general cargo is limited by how high the cargo can be stacked without damaging the lower layers. Superannuated or otherwise unemployed liner tonnage may be found carrying bulk cargo even when intermediate decks make stowage inconvenient or inefficient. 'Tween decks were a particular problem when grabs are used for discharge, and such ships can more easily be damaged in the rough and tumble of the bulk trade. A ship intended as a tramp might spend its entire life shuttling between just two ports. Conversely, changes in industrial circumstances may necessitate a collier roving the seas as a tramp. It must be borne in mind that a coaster designed for one particular trade may well end up running in another.

Photographed leaving Swansea and down to her marks with coal is a classic British steamer built for the bulk trades, *The Countess* of 824 grt. Built in 1928 she worked until 1960 for owner John Hay & Sons Ltd, Glasgow, a company related to the Clyde puffer owners J & J Hay Ltd. *(World Ship Society Ltd)*

Handling and stowing cargo

The simplest mechanical device for loading and unloading a ship is the derrick, essentially a long pole hinged to a mast, kingpost or to the superstructure. A rope or wire running from a winch on deck through sheaves on the mast and at the free end of the derrick is used to hoist cargo into and out of the hold. The end of the derrick also has ropes or wires that allow it to be raised, lowered and slewed from side to side. The derrick has proved incredibly durable, and for over one hundred years has given many coasters the basic ability to load or unload, albeit slowly, in ports with no shoreside gear. A major development was the replacement of wood with steel to increase the safe working load of a derrick. The application of steam power to the ship meant that the winches that operated the derricks could be steam powered rather than manually operated. Later, as diesel replaced steam in the engine room, electrical, hydraulic and diesel winches were introduced.

While a single derrick at each mast suffices for the basic, bulk-carrying coaster, vessels in the liner trade usually need to handle cargo more quickly to maintain schedules, which often involve calls at several ports. One answer is to provide multiple derricks at each mast. Those with adjacent heels can be used independently providing both sides of the ship was being worked, or a pair can work together using a union purchase rig to move heavier items of cargo. Faster are deck cranes, steam powered from donkey boilers that were initially placed on deck and later moved

Steam colliers running to power stations or gas works that had unloading equipment were some of the first coastal vessels to be built without cargo gear. At this power station the shoreside gear would unload a large collier such as *Sir John Snell* much quicker than on-board gear.

to the engine room. Later, cranes were driven by diesel, hydraulic or electrical power.

A trend that is apparent in the later chapters of this book is for cargo gear to be omitted from coasters and short-sea traders. By the 1950s, derricks and other on-board equipment had become an anachronism in most north European ports. Eventually their major use was merely to lift hatch boards and possibly a small boat. Provision of cargo gear essentially depends where and how a ship is expected to trade: although containers are generally handled by dedicated shoreside gantries, a few of today's container ships are fitted with cranes for use in unmechanised ports or perhaps for special deck cargoes.

The ease of stowing cargo has had a profound effect on coaster design. Early steamers had small hatches, as a hangover from their wooden sailing ship predecessors. With wooden hulls, hatches were kept as small as practically possible as any aperture in the deck seriously reduced the vessel's strength. But it soon became apparent to steamer designers that this need not apply to much stronger iron hulls, and key features of early colliers were the large hatches that made loading faster, facilitated the use of mechanical discharging methods and required less manual trimming of the coal cargo.

Originally hatches were closed with wooden boards placed on removable beams, mostly handled manually, and sealed against rain and sea with tarpaulins. Change came slowly, and only after the Second World War were mechanically handled, steel hatch covers generally introduced. In addition to their strength, they were a factor in reducing crew requirements, and also permitted a further enlargement of hatches that can now extend almost to the full width of the hold.

The hold of the earliest bulk-carrying steamer was essentially a box. It had a flush wooden floor (perversely known as a ceiling) but the sides were punctuated by the vertical frames and longitudinal stringers, which made it difficult to remove the last vestiges of a bulk cargo. For reasons of strength, vertical pillars were needed in holds of a certain size, again inhibiting efficient discharge. Gradually, these disadvantages were removed. Improvements in the structure of hulls introduced in the 1890s allowed pillars to be reduced or eliminated. Many vessels dedicated to the coastal coal trades had holds which were hopper-shaped at the bottom to facilitate discharge by grabs. Eventually, the box-hold concept has become universal, where the walls of the hold are perfectly flush, facilitating the stowage of unitised cargo and of cleaning after a bulk cargo.

Most bulk-carrying coasters have a single deck with one or more holds extending almost the full depth of the hull, but this was not ideal for ships in the regular, liner trades. Coastal liners routinely carried many small consignments of different cargoes that needed to be segregated and readily accessed if discharge at an intermediate port was required. The usual solution was to compartmentalise the hull by adding a 'tween deck at about half the depth of the hold. To work cargo in the lower part of the hold, hatches had to be fitted in the 'tween deck. In these ships, the mate had to ensure that parcels of cargo were stowed in such a way that they could be discharged without first moving other items.

A further elaboration was to increase capacity by fitting a shelter or spar deck above the main deck. These decks were typically lighter than the main deck. In the case of the shelter deck the space beneath it was technically unenclosed but had small, so-called tonnage openings left, although these were often secured by watertight washports.

Gross and net tonnages are not measures of weight, but of capacity, where 100 cubic feet equals one ton. Gross tonnage is the total enclosed volume of the ship, while net tonnage is the revenue-earning space. Historically, the space created beneath a shelter deck or spar deck did not count when tonnage was measured, and so improved the ship's carrying capacity without increasing the net tonnage on which harbour and other dues were paid.

Shipbuilders and designers have always been at pains to keep the declared tonnage to an absolute minimum with these and other stratagems. As a result, tonnage has long been an unsatisfactory way of indicating size: a 500-ton coaster of 1980 would accommodate much more cargo than a 500-tonner of 1880. These practices came to an end with the introduction of the international tonnage convention (ITC 69), which applied to new ships from 1982 and existing ships from 1994. Tonnage is now calculated by computer, and gives a much more accurate indication of a ship's size. In a historical survey such as this, figures for length (registered or overall) are quoted alongside the more familiar gross tonnage because they tend to give a better indication of true size.

As the steamer *T P Tilling* approaches her berth, her hatch boards have been taken off, exposing the beams, in anticipation of loading as soon as she arrives.

Steam machinery

The earliest marine steam engines drove paddle wheels, and worked at a relatively slow speed to suit the rotation of these wheels. In the oscillating engine, well established by the time the earliest screw steamers were built in the 1840s, the piston drove the crankshaft directly, and the cylinders oscillated from side to side. For efficiency, a screw needs to be turned at a higher speed than paddle wheels, at least 60 rpm compared with 20 rpm. The increase in rotational speed required by a screw meant that the vibration associated with oscillating cylinders was unacceptable. An alternative emerged in the inverted or vertical steam engine, which as early as 1846 was fitted by Caird & Company to the coastal steamer *Northman*. 'Inverted' refers to the cylinders being placed above rather than below the crankshaft. The cylinders were attached vertically one behind the other to a casting known as the bedplate, which also supported the crankshaft bearings. The advantages included compactness plus a simple, robust design that was relatively easy to build, maintain and develop. It became almost universal in coastal steamers and indeed most other cargo-carrying vessels.

The screw collier arrived before the inverted engine had become established, and early examples were fitted with a variety of machinery, including oscillating engines in *Lady Berriedale* and two single-cylinder engines fitted side by side and geared to a single shaft in *John Bowes*. It is a measure of the success of the inverted engine that almost all of the early colliers were eventually re-engined with this type of machinery, as was *John Bowes* in 1864.

In parallel with the development of steam machinery was an improvement in the design, materials, techniques and workmanship of boilermaking, with the aims of increasing efficiency of combustion, safety and working pressure. In a marine engine, steam is simply a medium for

For relatively small coasters such as *Jane Rowland*, photographed running trials on the Clyde in October 1905, the compact, two-cylinder compound engine was specified even when triple-expansion machinery offered better efficiency. *Jane Rowland* had a single boiler producing steam at 150 psi. *(Glasgow University Archives)*

conveying the energy released by burning coal to a point where it can do useful work by moving a piston in a cylinder, which in turn rotates the screw shaft. This process is accompanied by enormous waste of energy, with heat lost in turning the boiler water into steam, through the walls of cylinders and pipework, in the exhaust gases and in condensers. The overall efficiency of the steam engine is lamentably low, and in the 1880s it was estimated that as little as 5 per cent of the energy from the burning fuel was translated into propulsive power. The best way to improve efficiency was to increase working pressure, as the higher the pressure at which steam is generated, the smaller the proportion of energy lost in the ways listed above.

Early boilers, including those fitted into screw colliers of the 1850s, were primitive, with working pressures as low as 12 pounds per square inch (psi). Of particular significance to the development of the coasting steamer was the introduction of the Scotch boiler, dating from about 1862. It was designed so that hot gases from the coal were led through fire tubes in a cylindrical drum that was situated directly above the furnace. The boiler water was heated not only by conduction from the gases passing through the tubes, but also by direct convection and radiation from the fire. With some improvements in detail, and further modest increases in working pressure, the Scotch boiler proved remarkably long-lived, and saw out the life of the coastal steamer. Boiler pressures of 80 psi were not uncommon in coasters of the 1880s, and the last steam colliers built in the 1950s had Scotch boilers working at 220 psi.

However, increased boiler pressures brings its own problems. A high degree of steam expansion is theoretically possible in a single cylinder, but heat losses are severe. By expanding the steam in stages, the compound engine reduces these losses. Steam first enters the high-pressure cylinder and expands to a certain pressure and temperature, pushing out the piston. Valves then admit this steam to a low-pressure cylinder where it expands further until it reaches the temperature of the condenser. The two cylinders in a compound engine work at a narrower range of temperatures and pressures than a single cylinder, and so reduce heat losses. Patented in 1853, compounding was first used in the *Brandon* of 1854 and reduced fuel consumption by 30 to 40 per cent, with an approximately 20 per cent increase in first cost of the engine.

With further increases in boiler pressure, the logical development was to move from the two-stage expansion of the compound engine to the triple-expansion engine, which had high-, intermediate- and low-pressure cylinders. The latter became standard in medium-sized steam coasters, say over 150 feet in length, but in smaller vessels where space considerations became important, the more compact (and less expensive) two-cylinder compound engine remained the first choice. The step beyond triple-expansion, to a quadruple-expansion engine, was rarely taken in coastal ships, the extra cost and complexity not being considered worthwhile for a modest increase in efficiency. However, some of the last steamers built (especially in Germany) had double compound engines, with two low- and two high-pressure cylinders.

As a result of the robustness of the steam engine, and its familiarity to engine room personnel, it persisted in coastal craft long after it had been overtaken in efficiency by the internal-combustion engine.

Oil engines

The energy losses inescapable with the steam engine led to the investigation of ways in which energy from liquid fuel could be released inside the cylinder itself, and two of the solutions are relevant to coastal vessels. In one solution, the hot-bulb engine, fuel is ignited by a heated element in the cylinder head. Initially, the element is heated by an electrical current or even by a blowlamp, but once the engine has fired and warmed up, the burning fuel keeps the element hot. In the second type, the diesel or compression-ignition engine, the air in the cylinder is compressed to such an extent that the accompanying increase in temperature ignites the fuel when it is forced in. Such an engine can run on heavy oil, which is cheaper than lighter fuels such as petrol or paraffin, and is also easier and safer to handle and store because it is much less volatile. Hot-bulb engines were used in the earliest oil-engined coasters, but the compression-ignition type quickly gained favour, and eventually became universal in ships. The search for higher power output, for fuel economy and especially for reliability has seen the marine diesel engine evolve through several different forms, including two- and four-stroke types, double- and single-acting types.

In a four-stroke diesel engine, as the piston moves away

Today's coaster will benefit from refinements to increase speed and manoeuvrability such as a controllable pitch propeller. The symbols on the hull of the Dutch *Veersedijk* notify observers that she also has a bulbous bow and a bow thruster. This 2001-built cellular container ship has a four-stroke, eight-cylinder main engine of US design built in Germany, giving her a service speed of 18.4 knots. *(Author)*

from the cylinder head, inlet valves open and air is drawn into the cylinder. On the second stroke, the piston compresses the air, and fuel is injected. The high temperature and pressure ignites the fuel, driving back the piston and giving the third or power stroke. During the fourth stroke the exhaust valves in the cylinder head open and the burnt gases are pushed out by the returning piston. The cylinder thus fires once for every two rotations of the crankshaft.

In a two-stroke diesel engine, every second stroke is a power stroke, so that each cylinder fires once for every rotation of the crankshaft. Air is compressed as the piston moves towards the cylinder head, and at the top of the stroke fuel is introduced and begins to burn. The crucial difference to the four-stroke engine is that, towards the end of the power stroke, the piston uncovers exhaust ports, which are basically holes in the cylinder wall. Further movement of the piston uncovers another set of holes, the scavenge ports, which admit compressed air that expels the burnt gases though the exhaust ports.

The two-stroke diesel is inherently more efficient than the four-stroke, in which energy has to be expended moving the piston four times for every power stroke compared with just twice. The two-stroke engine is also simpler, as the use of exhaust valves is unnecessary. It is, however, more highly stressed, and hence was initially considered less reliable. The need for efficient scavenging also limits the speed at which a two-stroke engine can operate. In the early development of the oil engine, the greater robustness of the four-stroke diesel meant that it was preferred. However, as the reliability of the two-stroke engine improved, its lightness, simplicity and economy increased its popularity.

The engines described above are single-acting, meaning that the fuel is burnt on one side of the piston only. In a double-acting engine the lower half of the cylinder is enclosed and a combustion cycle also takes place below the piston. In a double-acting two-stroke, for example, every stroke is a power stroke. Double action has important advantages, since in theory twice as much power per cylinder can be delivered at the expense of slightly heavier and – especially in the case of a four-stroke – considerably more complex machinery.

Although oil engines offer greater efficiency than steam engines, engineers have been anxious to increase this still further by reducing the energy lost in exhaust gases. The most successful approach has been the development of supercharging to use the exhaust to force air into the cylinder to enhance fuel combustion. Also referred to as turbocharging, this uses the waste gases to turn a turbine coupled to a fan that blows air into the cylinder at higher than atmospheric pressure. Turbocharging has become routinely used in marine diesels, boosting engine power by around a third. This increase in output has helped to restore the popularity of the single-acting engine.

Coastal ship owners

Owning even a small coaster requires capital, confidence and – above all – knowledge and experience. It is not something to be undertaken lightly, and thus the ranks of owners are drawn from men who are familiar with the sea and its trades, or those who have the funds necessary to hire others with such knowledge and experience. Thus, the great majority of individuals and organisations who have owned coasters have come to it by just four routes.

The coaster is small enough that an enterprising master mariner can, with thrift and diligence, accumulate enough capital, interest sufficient investors, or convince enough bankers to fund his own ship. If the ship is traded successfully, and periodic financial storms ridden out, this can lead to further ships resulting in a whole fleet to be left to the founder's successors. The latter tend to become professional ship owners, often with an expansive lifestyle funded by their business. Sadly, it is sometimes observed

The captain-owner was much rarer in British practice than in the Netherlands. One of the last and best-known was Captain Kenneth Shaw, who went to sea on his father's auxiliary schooner in 1931. His last ship was the former Dutch coaster *Zanzibar*, built 1954, and which was sold when Captain Shaw retired at the age of 75 in 1991. *(World Ship Society Ltd)*

that interest in the shipping business tends to wane after the third or fourth generation, although in some cases the family has simply received an offer for their business too good to refuse. As a result, even the largest and most successful of coaster owning companies have a life expectancy which is rarely beyond a century.

The second route into ship owning involves shipbrokers and others who, in intimate contact with customers for coasters, are tempted to enter ship owning themselves if confident that a continuing flow of profitable cargo can be assured. Shipping companies that begin in this way tend to come and go, because their principals have more than one string to their bow, and can turn to another aspect of their business in the periodic downturns that characterise shipping.

Merchants that trade in commodities brought to them by sea may also found shipping companies, because they realise that their supplies can be assured and profits increased through owning their own ships. Some of the best-known owners of bulk-carrying coasters (and most of the collier owners) entered shipping by this route. Fleets that originate in this way may be among the most stable, in that ship owning is not an end in itself but a means to a greater and more reliably profitable end. Nevertheless, the fashion for accountants and consultants to encourage management to 'become vertically integrated' at one time and in a later decade to 'concentrate on core activities' has closed down the activities of a number of long-lived and respected coastal ship owners, nowhere more so than in the United Kingdom.

Many coastal liner companies were founded in a similar way by groups of merchants (perhaps in conjunction with existing small ship owners and even shipbuilders) who saw benefits in improving trade to their home port. The dangers they faced were acquisition by a larger shipping group such as Coast Lines or P&O, and competition from the railways. Most purely coastal liner services that survived the First World War soon succumbed to competition from a combination of rail and road transport. In the case of Tyne-Tees Steam Ship Co Ltd, its well-patronised passenger services from the north-east of England to London disappeared almost overnight when motor coaches were put on the Great North Road, although the shipping company's cargo services proved much more durable.

The fourth route to ship owning is with the large manufacturing or utility company that decides to ease fluctuations in freight rates by buying ships. The commonest examples of these are the power and energy companies, especially gas and electricity suppliers, coal or oil companies. These undertakings often have the financial muscle to rapidly acquire a substantial fleet, but equally quickly such fleets may be disposed of seemingly at the whim of a manager or his accountant.

There are good reasons why almost all ship owners specialise in either the liner trades or bulk carrying, because each requires a different type of organisation. Liner companies need a network of agencies or offices at the ports served, and they often also have a marketing organisation to advertise and promote their services. In contrast, the bulk carrying or tramp operator has a small, centralised operation, occasionally with a subsidiary office at one of his commonly used ports, but relying on an efficient information network and, especially in the coastal trade, the good offices of local shipbrokers who find the ship owner his cargoes day in, day out.

Oil companies have been major investors in coastal tankers to distribute refined products from refineries to coastal depots, but in recent years have tended to turn to chartering. Under various trading names, Shell has been a major operator of these ships: this is the motor tanker *Shell Technician* of 1982, later renamed *Arianta*. *(Author)*

Coaster builders

Building an iron- or steel-hulled coaster required different skills and equipment from those needed for constructing its predecessor, the wooden sailing ship. The latter was typically built by a handful of journeymen shipwrights in small yards with little more fixed plant than a sawpit, steam chest, timber store and wooden building ways. Working in iron required new skills to cut, bend and rivet plates, to fabricate frames, plus additional blacksmith work. As the iron shipbuilding industry developed, plant for these operations became essential and mechanical handling methods desirable to move heavy items around the yard. Only the larger, better capitalised yards and those with dynamic management made the transition from wood to iron shipbuilding. The majority of yards that built iron, and from the 1880s steel, coasters were newly set up for the purpose.

The construction of a coaster needs less space and deep water than an ocean-going ship. Nevertheless, with a few exceptions coaster builders have clustered in areas where there are other iron ship yards, notably in the United Kingdom on the west and east coasts of Scotland and on the rivers Tyne, Wear and Tees in England. These areas tend to be close to the producers of iron and also have the necessary skills available in the industrial community. The notable exceptions are a few yards in non-industrial areas such as East Anglia and the South West Peninsula, where long traditions of wooden shipbuilding were translated into limited, and often rather short-lived, iron and steel shipbuilding. A more enduring exception are the coaster-builders of the north Netherlands, who prospered by providing local owners in Groningen and Delfzijl with economical motor coasters.

A large yard can readily build a coaster, and some certainly have done during the periods of depression which are a fact of life in shipbuilding. However, the majority of the smaller and simpler bulk-carrying coasters are built in yards specialising in small craft, which also build tugs, yachts, lighters and harbour vessels. These yards often have a portfolio of designs for prospective owners, who

Following her launch by Cochrane & Sons Ltd, Selby, in April 1924, finishing touches are made to *Blue Galleon* as she waits to have her triple-expansion engines installed by Amos & Smith Ltd of Hull. She was completed in June for Heslop and Robson's Galleon Shipping Co Ltd of Newcastle-upon-Tyne.

may delegate detailed planning to the yard, usually specifying merely an overall size or desired carrying capacity. Perhaps even more importantly, the small craft yards build economically, without the expensive overheads of the larger and more sophisticated builders, as winning a coaster order is usually a matter of quoting the best price and, to a lesser extent, the earliest delivery date. Some yards and ship owners have forged unofficial alliances, so that a long series of coasters in one fleet may come from the same builder whom the owner trusts to meet his needs and budget.

The better-equipped ships for short-sea liner trades that had some passenger accommodation always required a more sophisticated approach from a builder, and were generally the province of larger yards which had access to the necessary design skills and fitting out trades. The larger colliers were another type of coastal craft that tended to come from specialists, and these yards were among the few coastal craft builders which successfully moved into ocean-going ships. The classic example is Palmers of Jarrow, which began with coastal colliers and progressed to battleships. More recently, Austin & Pickersgill of Sunderland made the more modest transition from coastal colliers to ocean-going bulk carriers. With even small ships becoming more complex, partly as a result of tightening international regulation of matters concerning pollution and ballast water segregation, building a product tanker or even a dry bulk cargo carrier is a much more specialist operation, and today's coaster building yards are just as sophisticated as those building much bigger ships.

For the coaster yard, repair work is often as important as building. In the rough and tumble of the coasting trade, ships are continually suffering damage, perhaps through minor groundings or collisions in busy locks and harbours. Making good such damage, along with preparing ships for their periodic surveys, is more regular and dependable than building work, which is notoriously cyclical. Indeed, some yards used to lay down a coaster for their own account, allocating labour to its construction only when repair work was slack. It could be several years on the stocks before it was completed.

In contrast to larger shipyards which may have their own engine building facilities, coaster builders tend to concentrate on the hull and to buy in engines from specialist engineering companies. One of the major exceptions was the Ailsa Shipbuilding Co Ltd of Troon, which from about 1906 had the facility to supply steam engines from its own foundry. In the diesel era, engine building became even more of a specialist undertaking, and one on which coaster builders turned their backs.

Coaster crews

Up to a point, the crew of a coaster has similar experiences to that of a deep-sea ship. They are away from their families for extended periods, during which they are part of a closed community, albeit one which has frequent contact with those ashore. They face an equally hazardous environment, although one in which the proximity of the land is a bigger danger than the wrath of the sea itself. For their safety they are largely reliant on the experience, ability and watchfulness of one another.

Differences largely arise from the much smaller size of a coaster's crew, the looser requirement for certification (at least until the 1970s), and the working patterns that entail brief coastal or short-sea voyages and often even shorter stays in port.

Although the crew of a nineteenth-century steam coaster could number well more than a dozen – as large as a modern-day ocean bulk carrier – over the years the complement has always been barely one third or one quarter the size of that of a contemporary deep-sea ship. Today it could easily be just four. A smaller community often means less rigid distinctions between officers and crew and between the seamen and those in the engine room, although in British coasters until recent years separate messing for officers and crew was the norm. Another factor in making the hierarchy in coasters less rigid is that the social backgrounds of the master and mate were often the same as those of the other hands. At one time, neither master nor mate needed be certificated, and had often worked their way up from ordinary seaman. To denote his status, a master or mate might have worn a token uniform jacket or cap, but today there is little in the way of dress code. Naturally, the atmosphere on board depends on the personalities of those in charge. On coastal and short-sea cargo liners – often regarded as good berths because of their regularity and 'clean' cargoes – a martinet of a skipper may have tried to run his ship as if it was a passenger liner, but such a tyrant is now as extinct as the type of ship he commanded.

In some companies, and especially so on regular traders, it was once not uncommon for the entire ship's crew to come from the same coastal town or village, and some remote, rural communities depended heavily on coasters to provide employment. For instance, Richard Hughes' Liverpool-based fleet of steam coasters were often referred to as the 'Welsh Navy' through taking most of its crews from a few villages in Anglesey. As recruitment was often a matter of following in family footsteps, such a crew might include several members of one family, a recipe for making the loss of a ship and its crew particularly tragic. However, on regular runs from, say the Tyne or Wear to the Thames, it was considered desirable to have one non-local who would stay on board in port while the others enjoyed an occasional but regular night at home. The frequency of visits to a home port is an important consideration for some men, and not a few who started their careers going deep-sea have later opted for the less prestigious (in their shipmates' view) berth on a coaster, in which they can expect to see more of their families. In contrast to going deep sea, a coasting man usually has the option of signing off at the next port and going home, after giving the statutory forty-eight hours notice.

Whereas a deep-sea man can expect to settle into a routine on a long voyage, this is much less likely on a coaster, for which a voyage may average only a day or so, arriving in port on one tide and out again on the next. With a small crew the men may work one watch on, one off at sea, and do not always get respite when in port. The need to shift the ship or otherwise to meet the requirements of those involved in discharge or loading can disturb much-needed sleep. The master or mate will usually be on hand during cargo working, and in smaller ships and ports the crew may even have to turn to themselves to work the cargo. Coaster men from all ages complain of long hours, lack of sleep and constant tiredness. A period weatherbound, or finding themselves in port for a weekend where no work is being done, is welcomed as a time for catching up on sleep.

The lack of certification did not mean that the old coaster man lacked skill, despite how his ocean-going counterpart might look down on him. The jibe 'Don't you coaster men get terrified when you are out of sight of land?' is classically countered with 'Yes, but don't you deep-sea men get terrified when you can *see* land?' Long years working on the coast leads to an almost unerring knowledge of the land and sea. At least until the 1920s, charts were often regarded as unnecessary as even in fog the skipper or mate could often tell to within a few miles the position of his ship. Charts, both paper and electronic, are now taken much more seriously, and at least one coastal ship owner has been fined for not providing the appropriate sheets. Foundering and stranding has finished the career of many a coaster, but these vessels pass serious hazards many times on each voyage, and their average life expectancy is similar to that of deep-sea ships. The situation only becomes serious when there is a major misjudgement, an engine breakdown, a stowage error or really atrocious weather. Collisions during fog in crowded coastal waters were, until the widespread use of radar, almost as big a hazard as reefs and sandbanks.

Minor knocks and damage, however, are very frequent. They result from frequent encounters with locks, harbour entrances and quay walls, and from taking the ground at tidal berths and, occasionally, when trying to cross a river bar before the water is deep enough. Damage from unloading equipment, especially grabs, is also frequent. Costs of repairs are often only just behind those of crewing and bunkering in the accounts of coaster owners.

With coastal ships making frequent calls in ports, pilotage is often a major cost (although in some ports it was not compulsory for small ships) and the master might well hold pilotage certificates for a port frequently visited. Holding or gaining such a certificate was once a common condition of being hired, and in times of recession was of paramount importance in finding a man a berth as master or mate. Qualifying for such a certificate would involve voyages to the port in question, memorising courses, buoyage and depths from the local pilot's handbook, a short examination by the local pilot master and – often a nightmare for owners or managers – maintaining this knowledge through continued visits.

At one time, the tradition in coastal shipping of promoting an able and conscientious man through the ranks of ordinary seaman, able seaman and mate to master offered possibilities for advancement not available on an ocean-going ship. This was certainly so for a man of relatively humble origins whose family circumstances would not allow him to become an apprentice or cadet. This could and did go further. After achieving command, possibly even in his twenties, an ambitious man might think about acquiring his own ship. Advances in technology, especially in the steam era, were slow enough that an old coaster would earn little less than a new coaster but, with allowance for more repairs, cost much less. With hard work, good contacts with shipbrokers, and not a little luck in timing his entry into ship owning on a rising freight market, the captain-owner could prosper and appoint another in command so that he could move ashore and manage his growing fleet from an office.

Before radio was installed in most coasters, the master had the problem of contacting his owners to report his position or receive orders for the next voyage. This could involve an operation as crude as being rowed ashore to find a telephone box. The family of a small British owner recall answering the telephone in their home during an evening or weekend and hearing the distant voice of a ship's master reporting, all too often in winter, that his coaster was windbound or otherwise delayed. Modern coaster crews might complain that it is now *too* easy for the owners to contact them. Indeed telecommunication satellites allow such close monitoring that someone ashore may know as much about the ship's position, the weather it is experiencing or even its mechanical functioning than those on board.

Once the most popular recreation for seamen in port was visiting a pub. The relationship between alcohol and coastal seafaring has changed significantly in recent years, with belated recognition that crew members being under the influence of drink (or other recreational drugs) is not conducive to the safety of several million Euros worth of coaster and its cargo. Today, a responsible ship operator will have a drugs and alcohol policy in place, to the extent that these substances are virtually banned on board, and indulging in either shortly before going to sea is a dismissible offence.

Although a coastal seaman from the nineteenth century would still feel at home on the coast, he would find working on one of today's coastal craft a vastly different experience. He would be dazzled by the technology available, possibly frustrated by the demands made on him by those ashore, and – with the shrinking of crew size and time for recreation ashore – would undoubtedly miss the camaraderie of his shipmates and fellow seamen.

Part of the crew of the steamer *Herbert* were photographed in June 1895 when the little steamer made a visit to the Gweebarra River in Donegal to deliver the steel work for a bridge. *(Ron Jones)*

Acknowledgements

Even before acknowledging those who gave permission for their photos to be used, I must thank Captain Ken Garrett for his help. Not only did he provide constructive criticism after reading several key chapters, but his various books on coastal ship owners listed in the bibliography have proved a mine of information. Next, in terms of helpfulness with the text, come the Registers of Bill Schell and Tony Starke plus the companion Miramar Ship Index, which give an immense amount of data on ships' histories. In the same breath, the publications of Lloyd's Register must also be mentioned as the origin of most of the ownership, building and construction data. Last but not least, I thank my wife Heather for proof reading and indexing.

For help with providing photographs, I thank John Clarkson, Ken Garrett, Peter Newall, Bob Todd, plus Tony Smith and David Whiteside and colleagues at the World Ship Society Photograph Library. Where photographs have no attribution the identity of the photographer is unknown. I apologise if use of these infringes anyone's copyright.

Dimensions

With its 1975–1976 *Register Book*, Lloyd's Register moved from using feet to metric units (where one metre equals 3.281 feet), and hence for ships completed from 1974 onwards overall lengths are quoted in metres. Gross tonnages given are generally those recorded when the ship was new, recently converted, or when it assumed the name carried in the photograph: these figures may alter when a ship is surveyed or changes flags, and were dramatically altered when the 1969 International Tonnage Convention came into force.

CHAPTER

1

Coastal Cargo Liners of the Nineteenth Century

Operating services on the Clyde, Henry Bell's *Comet* of 1812 established the credibility of the steamship. The years following saw further pioneering voyages under steam, first down estuaries, then along coasts and eventually across exposed waters, and between 1819 and 1825 several regular steamer services were established. However, the marine steam engine remained an extremely inefficient prime mover and it was only on short routes and with coal readily available that steam vessels could operate economically. They catered for passengers, who would pay a high price for dependability and speed, for small quantities of high-value goods such as mails, and for perishable cargoes such as livestock. Indeed, while paddle wheels were the only option for transmitting the engine's power, the cargo-carrying capacity of coastal vessels remained small. Paddle wheels need to be immersed to an optimal depth in the water for efficiency, and do not take kindly to the considerable differences in the draught of a cargo ship in its ballasted and fully laden states. The viability of the screw steamer was established with *Archimedes* of 1838, but it fell to Brunel's *Great Britain* of 1843 to convince ship owners that the screw and the iron hull were the way forward, at least for cargo vessels.

On the busiest and shortest routes, passenger and cargo carrying were often separated. Passenger steamers were faster and could be turned round more quickly when the protracted business of loading and discharging cargo could be avoided. On such services cargo-only steamers ran in parallel with the passenger ships. On longer and less well trafficked routes, cargo and passenger carrying continued to be combined. The pure cargo and the cargo-passenger steamer therefore developed in parallel.

Ships in the liner trade had usually to cater for relatively small packages of cargo, and for loading or discharging at intermediate ports on its route. Access to the cargo holds had to be simple and fast, and the practice developed of working an intermediate deck into the structure, a 'tween deck or a shelter deck. Cargo-handling gear needed to be extensive and multiple derricks were fitted or, increasingly, steam-powered deck cranes. The water ballast that became such an important factor in the success of the screw collier was not imperative for the vessel on a regular route, which would rarely sail on any leg of its route with no cargo at all. Hence ballast tanks were often smaller, and detracted less from available stowage space, than in the pure bulk-carrying coaster.

This chapter takes in part a regional approach and also compares steamers from different areas which had similar roles.

An asterisk in a caption indicates the vessel shown in the photograph.

Irish Sea cargo liners

As with virtually any ship type, the wide variations in the size, design and appearance of coastal cargo liners reflected the differences in the trades from region to region and, especially, the facilities of the ports they were intended to serve and the nature and size of cargoes they were expected to carry. On Irish Sea trades, livestock carrying was particularly important.

*Lara** of 1868 was an early example of placing the engines aft with a raised bridge amidships. She was unusual in having her forecastle extended far aft, well beyond the bridge. In this aerial view in the Avon Gorge, note the well forward, which opens to a cattle deck. There is also a well ahead of the engines, with a crew member about to cross it by the gangway. Another feature of her time was the use of rails rather than bulwarks at the edge of her decks.

Lara was built for their own account by Malcolmson Brothers of Waterford for their services to Bristol and Liverpool. Malcolmson had been pioneers of Irish Sea steamer services, but by the 1860s were in decline with financial problems and family disagreements, and routes were sold or discontinued. In 1877, *Lara* passed to the newly formed Waterford Steamship Co Ltd, which restricted itself to services from Waterford to Bristol, South Wales and Liverpool. Her original simple engines were replaced by triple-expansion machinery in 1887, and these lasted *Lara* until she was broken up at Widnes on the Mersey in 1910. The iron steamer's tonnage was 917 gross and her registered length 239 ft.
(Nautical Photo Agency)

In the smaller *Sunlight**, also built in 1868, the bridge and engines were placed three-quarters aft, with a small hold worked into the poop. This view illustrates the typical stern treatment of steamers of this period, fuller and less elegant than the classic counter stern that was to evolve. The whaleback treatment, usually confined to just the forecastle, has been extended to her combined bridge deck and poop. An interesting small detail is how the funnel for what is presumably her donkey boiler, ahead of the main funnel, echoes the markings of her owner John Bacon of Liverpool.

Bacon is first listed as a steamer owner in the mid-1860s, trading from his home port of Liverpool and from Preston to Wexford and to Bristol Channel ports. His services partly duplicated those of F H Powell & Co, and this company gained control of Bacon's fleet in 1912, which was preliminary to a bigger amalgamation that in September 1913 produced Powell, Bacon & Hough Lines Ltd, later to become Coast Lines Ltd.

Sunlight was built and given a two-cylinder simple steam engine by Lawrence Hill & Co, Port Glasgow, but within two years of completion was lengthened from 162 ft to 184 ft, giving her a new gross tonnage of 388. Compound engines were fitted in 1883. She just failed to make it into the fleet of Powell, Bacon & Hough Lines because she was sold in February 1913 to France. Now given the splendidly solid name *Menhir*, which suited her antediluvian appearance, she gravitated to the Mediterranean and was owned in Marseille when she was wrecked on a voyage from Mersina to Piræus during January 1920.

By 1892, triple-expansion engines were the undisputed choice for a coastal cargo liner. In the case of *Dungeness** both engines and her somewhat anachronistic iron hull were built by Gourlay Brothers & Co Ltd of Dundee. Owners were Clyde Shipping Company, established as early as 1815 and for many years the world's oldest steam ship company. By the time of the delivery of *Dungeness*, each day of the week except Sunday would see at least one of the company's steamers leave Glasgow, with calls at ports on the east coast of Ireland and the south coast of England between Plymouth to London. As well as coastal liners, Clyde Shipping operated a large fleet of tugs on the Clyde and dabbled in the ocean-going tramp trades.

Dungeness had saloon and probably cabin accommodation amidships for a modest number of passengers and carried an appropriate number of boats. But her major role was cargo carrying, and she was equipped with deck cranes to speed loading and discharge. There were elegant gaffs on both masts, perhaps partly intended to carry fore and aft sails, although by the time she was photographed only a jib remained. Only two years previous to the completion of *Dungeness*, Clyde Shipping had built the steamer *Aranmore*, which still crossed yards on its foremast.

Of 1201 grt and 246 ft registered length, *Dungeness* ran for Clyde Shipping until 1926. She then followed many superannuated coastal steamers into the Mediterranean when bought by the Turkish government and renamed *Inebolou*. She foundered near Izmir in November 1935 while on voyage from Mersin with passengers and cargo.

Scotland to Ireland

The steamer services from Glasgow to the North of Ireland were particularly busy, given the family, religious, sporting and industrial connections between Scotland and Ulster. Dominating the routes were the steamers of two companies that were to merge in the twentieth century: Laird Line, which named its steamers after plants, and G & J Burns, which used animal names. The route was busy enough to have fast paddle and later screw steamers devoted to passengers, but shown here are examples from each company of a small cargo-passenger vessel built for a minor route and of a pure cargo carrier.

Laird Line was among the pioneers of cross-channel steam services, tracing its origins to 1814 when Lewis MacLellan, an associate of Henry Bell of *Comet* fame, began a service on the Clyde. In 1895, *Daisy** was completed for Laird Line's route from the Clyde to Portrush and Coleraine. Blackwood & Gordon of Port Glasgow built her hull and triple-expansion machinery, giving her a unique profile in the Laird fleet with a shelter deck extending almost to her stern. She was of 187 ft registered length and had a gross tonnage of 419. *Daisy* spent her whole twenty-year life running to Portrush and Coleraine, and ended her days near the latter. The River Bann has a notoriously difficult entrance and *Daisy* was unfortunate enough to be caught by a heavy swell and wrecked at Bannmouth when approaching from Glasgow on 23 February 1915. *(Glasgow University Archives)*

Brothers G and J Burns moved into shipping around 1824, while George, the more ambitious brother, was an important backer and investor in Samuel Cunard's North Atlantic ventures. G and J Burns's *Grouse** was built and given a triple-expansion engine by Caird & Co of Greenock in 1891. She had a registered length of 175 ft and a gross tonnage of 410. As her tiny superstructure suggests, she was a pure cargo carrier, it being noted that she could accommodate eighty head of cattle and the rather precise number of eleven horses. She was probably on her regular route between Greenock and Ireland in this view on the Firth of Clyde and appears to be conned from the steering position aft, no bodies being visible behind the canvas dodger, which is all the protection available to those on her bridge.

Grouse was yet another steamer to have an extended career, almost all of it on regular sailings. Soon after the 1922 merger that produced Burns & Laird Lines Ltd she was deemed surplus and sold for just £855 to a company running a service between the Clyde and Preston for which she was renamed *Kelvindale*. When in 1923 this one-ship company was bought by Coast Lines Ltd, Burns & Laird's parent company, *Kelvindale* became *Denbigh Coast*. In 1929, she was transferred to David MacBrayne (1928) Ltd, a company part-owned by Coast Lines, and as *Lochdunvegan* ran mainly between Glasgow and Stornoway. She was broken up in the Gareloch in 1948. *(Glasgow University Archives)*

Coastal packets

Shown like *Sunlight* in the colours of John Bacon Ltd, *Tivyside** was an example of the smallest type of regular trader. She was built in 1869 to run on the Welsh coast, providing her home port of Cardigan with a regular service to Liverpool and Bristol. The rail network of Wales had a predominantly east–west orientation thanks to the principality's geography, and for the whole of the nineteenth century trading links to the main entrepôts of Liverpool and Bristol were provided by small ships. Despite her apparent lack of any accommodation, *Tivyside* would have a small saloon beneath her bridge in which a few passengers could huddle round a coal stove in inclement weather. With tiny ships such as this, the saloon was one of the few structural differences between the regular trader and the coastal tramp.

Tivyside was built by the London & Glasgow Engineering & Iron Shipbuilding Co Ltd at Govan to the order of Thomas Davies of Cardigan, acting on behalf of the recently formed Cardigan Steam Navigation Co Ltd, which took her over in 1885. When this company was wound up in 1888, *Tivyside* moved to an owner in Carmarthen, from whom she was bought in 1895 by John Bacon Ltd. Although she appears tiny in this classic Bristol view, *Tivyside* was originally even smaller, just over 100 ft long, as Bacon had lengthened her to 115 ft in 1896 not long after acquiring her, increasing her gross tonnage to a still modest 125. Under the new ownership she remained on the local service between Carmarthen and Bristol until wrecked on such a voyage, on the Gower in June 1900.

Although running on what could be considered an inland waterway for many years, *Texa** later proved herself quite capable of sea-going employment. She was built as *James Mutter* for a Glasgow owner by Scott & Co, Bowling and when completed in 1884 was just 100 ft long and had a gross tonnage of 186. She was first used on a route to Islay, but after only five years she was bought by David Macbrayne, who decided she was too small and in 1891 had the now-renamed *Texa* sent to Troon to be lengthened by a modest 18 ft by the Ailsa Shipbuilding Company. Her regular employment settled down to a service from Glasgow to Loch Fyne. She would sail from Bridge Wharf, Glasgow on 6.00 am on Tuesday, Thursday and Saturday and after calling at various piers and wharfs on the Firth of Clyde her voyage would terminate at Ardrishaig on Loch Fyne. The next day she would return to Glasgow.

When sold by MacBrayne in 1917, she swapped a sheltered route for service on the boisterous Irish Sea. Now owned by the Douglas Shipping Co Ltd on the Isle of Man, she would spend much of her time bringing coal to the island, often from Preston, where she was photographed in Douglas Shipping colours. After a further sale to a Belfast owner in 1931, the tiny steamer's luck ran out on 30 April 1932 when she was wrecked four miles from Ballyshannon while approaching the port from Preston with a cargo of coal. *(J and M Clarkson)*

Serving islands

Routes to offshore islands were natural early targets for the entrepreneurs who would begin steamer services. Given that inhabitants and visitors had no other way of going to and from the islands, many of the steamers on these routes catered for both passengers and cargo.

*Express** was built of iron in 1869 by Readhead, Softley & Company of South Shields for carrying passengers, mail, livestock and general cargo between the mainland port of Scrabster and Stromness in Orkney. Originally just 103 ft long, she was a tiny steamer for crossing the Pentland Firth, but was lengthened to 138 ft in 1882. Even then, her engines (originally simple but compounded in 1875) and boiler took up about a quarter of her hull, a disproportionate amount of space that could otherwise be devoted to cargo.

Her owner, Captain George Robertson of Kirkwall, took *Express* off regular services across the Pentland Firth in 1877 and employed her tramping or on charter to other local companies, also carrying fish from Stromness to Lossiemouth and Inverness. She was photographed leaving behind Aberdeen and its fleet of fishing vessels in the 1890s. Robertson sold most of his shares in 1896, but *Express* remained in local trades. Perversely, her sale in February 1917 to the North of Scotland, Orkney and Shetland Steam Navigation Co Ltd of Aberdeen saw the steamer move from the north of Scotland, but not for long as in April of that year she sank after a collision off the French coast.

*Fenella** of 1881 illustrates the difficulty of differentiating between coastal cargo and passenger liners. Although virtually no structures are apparent on deck other than the bridge and engine-room casing, she was certificated for a massive 504 passengers. Nevertheless, she was primarily a cargo ship, and the passenger accommodation was there to allow her to work in winter as a relief to the Isle of Man Steam Packet Company's bigger passenger steamers. With voyages from the Isle of Man to ports in England, Scotland and Wales rarely exceeding a few hours, accommodation below decks was considered quite adequate even for this large number of passengers.

As essentially a cargo ship, *Fenella* was something of a thoroughbred. The Barrow Ship Building Co Ltd provided her with two sets of compound engines to drive her twin screws, a total indicated horsepower of 1400, giving her a respectable speed of 14 knots. A chronicler of the Isle of Man Steam Packet fleet, Connery Chappell, claims that she was worked harder than any other Manx ships in her day. Unlike some of the pure passenger ships that were laid up outside the holiday season, *Fenella* took sailings both summer and winter, and with just one other ship maintained sailings between Liverpool and Douglas throughout the First World War. Modernised and fitted with electric lighting in 1894, *Fenella* gave a remarkable forty-eight years of service to her owners before being sold for breaking up at Newport in 1929. Her iron hull measured just 200 ft and her gross tonnage was a modest 557. *(J and M Clarkson)*

It is surprising that, with her anachronistic clipper bow and figurehead, *Claymore** was actually built in 1881, the same year as the much more modern-looking *Fenella*. She was delivered by J & G Thomson, Glasgow, for David MacBrayne's cargo and passenger service from Glasgow to Stornoway on the Isle of Lewis. With stops at Greenock, Oban and Kyle of Lochalsh, *Claymore*'s voyages appear rather leisurely, and after leaving Glasgow at noon on a Thursday she did not arrive at Stornoway until fifty-four hours later. With her good looks and romantic bust of a highlander for a figurehead, she was extremely popular, many regulars treating a round trip on *Claymore* as part of their annual holiday. More direct rail and boat routes to Lewis led to her being laid up in the winter months from 1920, but her appeal endured, and on her sale to breakers in 1931 admirers requested souvenirs and wrote poems about her. *(World Ship Society Ltd)*

Twin funnels were usually the preserve of 'pure' passenger ships, making the cargo-passenger steamer *Lyonesse** of 1889 unusual. Owners were West Cornwall Steamship Co Ltd who since 1871 had been running between Penzance and the Scilly Isles. At 329 grt and 170 ft registered length, *Lyonesse* was reputed to be an enlarged version of the company's *Lady of the Isles* with a triple-expansion engine. Both steamers were built and engined by Harvey & Co of Hayle, Cornwall's largest and most prolific shipbuilders and engineers, although it has to be said that it had little competition in the Duchy. Both steamers had long secondary careers in the salvage business – *Lyonesse* was sold to Queenstown salvage contractor Henry Ensor in 1918. On the evidence of their survival in this notoriously rough business, commentators have suggested that the two west Cornwall steamers were extremely heavily built – presumably to withstand the Atlantic waves met with on their regular route. *Lady of the Isles* served for a remarkable thirty-five years in salvage work, on top of her hardly modest thirty years running to the Scillies. *Lyonesse* did not do quite so well: in 1928 she was sold to breakers, reputedly in the port in which she had been built. *(World Ship Society Ltd)*

North Sea cargo liners

With its ready access by canal to the Yorkshire coalfields and the industrial West Riding, the inland port of Goole was quick to establish steamer services across the North Sea. The title of the Yorkshire Coal & Steamship Co gives a clue to the intentions of one Goole-based operator, and its steamers' German names reveal its intended routes. This was one of three companies operating between Goole and the Continent in the 1870s, and all of which eventually merged.

*Altona** was delivered in March 1877 by W B Thompson & Co, Dundee, which also provided the engines that drove her at 10 knots. A peculiarity of her rig was the gaffs on fore and main masts, not to carry sails (although she has a small jib) but to support the pulleys through which were rigged whips to help get out her frequent cargoes of South Yorkshire coal. At 671 grt and 202 ft registered length, *Altona* was a substantial ship.

In 1895, her owners were taken over by the older Goole Steam Shipping Co Ltd, which itself was bought out by the Lancashire & Yorkshire Railway Company ten years later. The ship's name was not changed until 1914 when, as a result of the xenophobia directed against anything vaguely Germanic, she became *River Crake*. Two more changes of owners but not necessarily of employment were in store for her: in 1922 the owners united with its big rival and took its name, the London & North Western Railway Company, and barely a year later became part of the London, Midland & Scottish Railway Company. *River Crake* was broken up at Sunderland in 1927. *(J and M Clarkson)*

British shipbuilders were so dominant in building steamers in the nineteenth century that it is not surprising to find that a Dutch example of a regular North Sea trader, *Professor Buys** of 1891, was built on Tyneside by William Dobson & Company. Neither is her basic similarity to *Altona* unexpected, although she has the three-island layout wthat was becoming a common alternative to the raised quarterdeck design. Both were single-deck ships, probably because, even for regular traders on the North Sea, cargoes out of British ports often comprised coal. Note the gangways that allowed the crew to walk relatively dryshod between forecastle, bridge and poop. A further measure of progress was her triple-expansion engines, a design that had become standard in larger vessels such as the 780 grt, 205 ft *Professor Buys*. The photograph shows what appears to be her only sail being set.

Professor Buys changed hands quite frequently, but when photographed she was probably running for Hollandsche Scheepvaart Maatschappij, which owned her from 1894 to 1917. The company ran from Amsterdam to London and to south, west and east coast ports in the UK, including Hull. She was probably in the Humber in March 1918 when, in an act of doubtful legality, the British government effectively took her over and registered her as a British ship under management of a Goole company. She was handed back in March 1919 and eventually came into the hands of Wm H Müller & Co NV of Rotterdam. *Professor Buys* was broken up at Ghent in 1933. *(World Ship Society Ltd)*

Traders to Continental Europe

In terms of its route network and fleet size, the 1824-founded General Steam Navigation Company was the doyen of English coastal liner companies. At 1215 grt and 236 ft registered length, the 1879-built *Lapwing** was one of the company's larger steamers, and was used on its longer Continental routes, for instance to Hamburg from the Pool of London in which she was photographed. General Steam was an early exponent of deck cranes, a pair of which is visible beyond the forecastle of *Lapwing*.

Built by a Dundee yard specialising in coastal liners, Gourlay Brothers, the compound-engined *Lapwing* served General Steam until 1911 and then went to Turkey, first as *Sahir* and after 1914 *Antalya*. The latter name was short-lived, because she stranded in the Black Sea in April 1915 while carrying coal from Zonguldak to Istanbul.

Completed in 1876 by John Readhead & Company of South Shields, *India** was an example of a simple design, a single-deck iron steamer with a compound two-cylinder engine by her builders. Of 160 ft registered length and 364 grt, she had a curved casing either side of her bridge and midships house. Well seen in the photograph is the pole compass: the white-painted pole on her bridge carrying the compass well away from the magnetic influence of her iron hull and engines. A seaman would be sent up the ladder to read the bearing when necessary.

India's original owner was John Bennett of Goole, who began as a merchant importing fruit and vegetables from Boulogne but quickly realised that Yorkshire coal would provide a paying return cargo. His service prospered and, as the Red Cross Line, continued until its last ships were lost during the Second World War.

India was photographed at Preston in the first decade of the twentieth century after she had been sold out of the liner trade to James H Bennetts of Penzance. She was probably coming to Preston to load coal, a cargo which she had carried even in the liner trade. This iron ship survived particularly well and, after sale to German owners in 1913, steamed on, first with the less than usual name *Normal* and later as *Klara* and finally *Immenhof*. On 21 November 1928, she sailed from Nordenham for King's Lynn and Great Yarmouth with a cargo of phosphate and disappeared, the only trace found being one of her boats washed ashore at Texel in December. *(J and M Clarkson)*

Australasian coastal liners

The Union Steam Ship Company of New Zealand Ltd was not content with having the largest steamer fleet in New Zealand waters, it also extended its tentacles to Australia: not for nothing was it known as 'the Southern octopus'. William Denny & Brothers of Dumbarton built some of the first steamers that the new company ordered in 1875 and, with other Scottish yards, satisfied its shipbuilding needs for most of its existence. There was considerable variation in appearance from ship to ship, so clearly the builders were told what size of a ship to build and the traffic that it was expected to handle, and were then left to design it themselves.

Denny's *Mahinapua** of 1882 was the first twin-screw vessel built for the Union Company, Denny also being responsible for her two compound engines. She was also an early example of steel used in a hull, because only three years previously Denny had completed for her owners the world's first steel steamer, *Rotomahana*. Of 160 ft registered length and 458 grt, *Mahinapua* was of a size with *India*, but had passenger accommodation in her large poop: its inhabitants can be seen on the forecastle and aft.

Mahinapua was first used on New Zealand's west coast, but in 1898 was transferred to work around Tasmania. Sold in 1909 and subsequently converted to a hulk, her hull lasted until 7 October 1925 when it was scuttled in Port Stephens Bay.

The major short-sea route in Australian waters was that across the Bass Strait between the mainland and Tasmania. Founded in 1853, the Tasmanian Steam Navigation Company was the major operator of services from Hobart to Sydney and Melbourne, and its ships were quite substantial for these lengthy routes, as was the 1758 grt, 290 ft triple-expansion steamer *Oonah**. As with most Australasian operators, all of the company's steamers came from Scotland, *Oonah* being completed by A & J Inglis of Glasgow in February 1888. She had a spar deck, a relatively light upper deck, unsuitable for weight carrying but increasing her capacity but not the tonnage on which harbour dues were calculated, because the openings in this deck meant that the enclosed space did not count towards her net tonnage.

The Tasmanian company was bought by the Union Steam Ship Company of New Zealand Ltd in 1891, but *Oonah* was unaffected. In what must be almost a record innings, she plugged on through a further change of ultimate owner in 1921 when the Tasmanian Steamers Proprietary Ltd was formed to merge the competing interests of Union Steam Ship and Huddart Parker on the Bass Strait. The photograph, which probably shows her approaching Burnie, was taken in this late phase of her career, as evidenced by the funnel colours that were buff base, broad red band and black top. However, she was apparently unaltered and her lines were still those of a mid-Victorian cargo-passenger liner. At the age of forty-seven she was sold to Japan in 1935 and broken up the next year at Osaka. *(Winter's Studio)*

CHAPTER

2

Genesis of the Steam Collier

Although the steamers discussed in the previous chapter were successful in quickly capturing the regular coastal and short-sea carriage of passengers and valuable or time-sensitive goods, the steam ship was much slower to penetrate the bulk trades. Bulk cargoes comprise the majority of commodities moved by sea, and include predominantly coal, grain, various ores, stone, china clay, fertilisers, timber, and semi-processed goods such as bricks, tiles and slate. For these relatively low-value commodities, steam could offer little over the sailing vessel except predictability of delivery, and even this was obtained at considerable extra cost. Bulk commodities did not deteriorate at sea, and – with one important exception – were cheap enough that stockpiles could be held against the inevitable periods when sailing vessels carrying them were weatherbound. Sail continued to move these cargoes well into the twentieth century, although in steadily declining quantities.

At least five unsuccessful or inconclusive experiments with iron-hulled screw colliers are known from the 1840s. *Bedlington* of 1841 and *QED* of 1844 were too difficult to maintain, while *Collier* of 1849, *Conside* of 1847 and *Experiment* of 1845 proved too attractive to liner operators and were immediately diverted to regular services.

In the 1850s, steam colliers succeeded in obtaining a foothold in the important trade in 'sea coal' from Northumberland and Durham to London, but only because of the particular needs of the capital's gas industry. The captions to the photographs in this chapter discuss the reasons for this, and the technological challenges that had to be overcome in providing a practical 'screw collier', as contemporary builders and users referred to them.

Once established in the 1850s and the 1860s, the steam-driven collier blossomed, and quickly began to move beyond coastal trades with the circumstances of the Crimean War demonstrating their long-distance potential. Indeed, it is not stretching credibility to assert that the screw collier of the 1850s, with its adaptations for bulk carrying, was the direct ancestor of the steam tramp and today's diesel bulk carrier, vessels that have brought profound changes not just to shipping but to the modern industrial world in general.

This chapter discusses the initial development phase of the steam collier, a phase almost entirely confined to the UK. The story from 1880 is continued in Chapter 5.

An asterisk in a caption indicates the vessel shown in the photograph.

Early experiments

Best documented of the early bulk carrying steamers, *Collier** of 1849 was evidently conceived as a coal carrier but immediately on completion was placed into regular liner trades, running to the Channel Islands for the London, Brighton & South Coast Railway Company. *Collier* survived for sixty-five years, in the latter part of her life undoubtedly carrying the cargo for which she had been named.

The photograph of *Collier* dates from the early years of the twentieth century, by which time she had been considerably altered. In 1857, she had been lengthened from 95 ft to 128 ft, her tonnage still being little more than 200 gross. She also had a two-cylinder compound engine fitted in place of the simple engine made by Caird & Company of Greenock, which had been installed in 1849 by builder John Reid & Company (at the time his Port Glasgow yard was noted for its construction of successful clipper ships, to which *Collier* provided something of a contrast). After her service on the English Channel, little is known about the adventures of *Collier* for the next twenty years, although rumours of her reaching Australia seem far fetched: if she had gained antipodean shores, surely she would have worked there rather than steam all the way home? From 1877, she was employed on the Bristol Channel, owners alternating between Bristol and Swansea, the best known being Pockett's Bristol Channel Steam Packet Co Ltd. *Collier* was owned by this company when, on 28 January 1914, she was wrecked in fog at Bull Point near Mortehoe in North Devon while on a voyage from Milford to Avonmouth in ballast.

The pioneering *John Bowes*

In the early 1850s, coal owner Charles Mark Palmer bought an existing shipyard at Jarrow on the Tyne with the intention of building screw colliers. His aim was to produce a screw steamer of the greatest possible capacity with engines just sufficiently powerful to ensure regularity of service.

The screw collier had considerable disadvantages when compared with a sailing ship. It cost much more to build, and repairs of its iron hull and machinery needed particular and expensive skills. With its boiler's appetite for fuel and the inefficiency of its low-pressure steam engines it cost much more to run than a sailing craft, and needed firemen and engineers to tend it, in addition to a full deck crew. The steamer's advantages were that it could make voyages of a predictable duration, and significantly more of them in a given time than a sailing collier.

At this time the gas industry in London was expanding rapidly. One if its most pressing needs was receiving regular and reliable shipments of gas-making coal from Northumberland and Durham. Collier brigs and schooners could not guarantee dependability, because in winter especially whole fleets might be held up by gales or contrary winds. If coal supplies to the gas works failed not only were consumers disappointed, but a potentially explosive mixture of air and gas in the mains could rapidly reduce the number of such customers. The gas companies were willing to place massive coal contracts but only if the suppliers could guarantee deliveries all year round. With the rail network still unable to compete with sea transport, Palmer and his coal-owning associates saw that a screw collier was the answer to offering dependable deliveries and attracting large coal contracts.

His pioneering screw collier, *John Bowes** was launched from Palmer's yard on 30 July 1852. Of 149 ft registered length and 485 grt, she had a two-cylinder steam engine built by Robert Stephenson & Company. She had a large hatch to serve her 60 ft hold, a size only possible because her iron hull was much stronger than one built from wood.

For her first voyage, *John Bowes* loaded coal at Sunderland on 29 July 1852 and took just forty-eight hours to reach the Thames, twenty-four hours to discharge, and forty-eight hours to return northwards. Palmer claimed that, by delivering 650 tons of coal in five days, *John Bowes* had done the equivalent of one month's work by two average sailing colliers. The screw collier had arrived.

Unlike other pioneers, *John Bowes* survived to be photographed many times, although there are no photographic images portraying her as she looked according to a model in the Tyne and Wear Museum in which she is rigged as a three-masted topsail schooner. The first of the two photographs may well show her bowsprit being removed (she still has her foresail). Her survival was remarkable, and although sold by Palmer in 1873, she remained in the east coast coal trade (for which she was now rather small) until the 1890s when she was sold to Norway as *Spec*. Owners in Sweden and Spain followed. Only with her third engine and sixth name, *Villa Selgas*, did she succumb to the sea, foundering after springing a leak during a gale while on voyage on the Spanish Atlantic coast in October 1933. *(Newcastle-upon-Tyne City Libraries)*

The ballast problem

Even after *John Bowes* had established the practicability of the screw collier, practices in the coal trade seriously limited its uptake. In the Thames, colliers needed to queue to take on chalk or shingle for the northbound voyage, and on arrival in Tyne or Wear had to wait again to unload it. Standing idle while sailing vessels ahead in the queue laboriously loaded or discharged ballast was death to the steamer with its much higher capital and running costs, and which could be made to pay only by making as many loaded voyages as possible.

The answer was to use water as ballast. After considerable experimentation during the 1850s, a combination of permanent tanks in the hull and water capacity in a double bottom proved successful.

Screw colliers then multiplied very quickly, one of the earliest of which a clear image survive being *J R Hinde**, built by Palmer at Willingdon in 1864. At 694 grt and 199 ft registered length, *J R Hinde* was considerably bigger than *John Bowes*, and the additional length merited a bridge amidships. Although she carried sails on her foremast, *J R Hinde* retained gaffs on both fore and main to help unload her at ports with no mechanical discharging facilities, and whips from near their ends can be seen leading down to her deck. In 1885, *J R Hinde*'s original two-cylinder simple engine was taken into Palmer's shops and converted, and she emerged with triple-expansion machinery, proving just how versatile and capable of development was the inverted design. With her life extended in this way, *J R Hinde* steamed on in the coal trade until sold to breakers at Boulogne in 1910. *(J and M Clarkson)*

The view of *Northumbria** from very much the same angle as *J R Hinde* allows some interesting comparisons. Completed at Palmer's yard at Jarrow in 1869, her yard number 245 gives an idea of just how successful in terms of gaining orders was Palmer's pioneering work on iron steamers, so much so that he opened a second yard at Willingdon. *Northumbria* was a size larger still than *J R Hinde*, at 221 ft overall length and 900 grt. She has a much higher forecastle, the height of the latter being, in any case, partly obscured by her bulwark plating. Very apparent, from the fact of their being painted white, were the substantial rails around her raised poop instead of the bulwarks in *J R Hinde*. It is possible that the *Northumbria* was intended for work beyond the coastal coal trade.

Typical of most early colliers, owners of *Northumbria*'s 64th shares were a mixture of those involved as coal merchants, coal factors and mine owners, including members of the Cory, Joicey and Fenwick families. The photograph was probably taken after 1896 when all sixty-four shares were owned by William Cory & Son Ltd, although it is likely that this company's distinctive funnel, with its black diamond symbolising its coal trade, had been worn for much of her career.

Northumbria's end is a little mysterious. On 23 December 1915 she left Leith Roads for London and was not seen again: a victim of mine or weather. *(J and M Clarkson)*

Early screw colliers were by no means limited to the purely coastal trade, and were quite capable of voyaging to the Baltic, Mediterranean and Black Sea. Indeed, several early collier owners graduated from coastal and near-continental trades to deep-sea tramping. These included the later owners of *Usworth**, seen here at Jersey in a remarkably clear photograph taken between 1878 and 1881.

Usworth was built in 1869 by Charles Mitchell & Company, Low Walker, Newcastle-upon-Tyne, and a rival to Charles Palmer as an early screw collier builder. Her two-cylinder simple engine was built by another long-lived concern, the North Eastern Marine Engineering Co Ltd. At 179 ft registered length and 524 grt, she was more modest in size than *Northumbria* or *J R Hinde*. Her original owner was John Jonassohn, a Tyneside coal owner, who entrusted *Usworth*'s management to William Cory & Son – the outline of the black diamond device can be discerned on the funnel, although painted over.

Features to be noted in the photograph are the flimsy bridge structure perched on an equally minimal boiler casing, and the rag of a sail on the forestay. Her bulwarks look particularly deep, an unfortunate feature of early bulk-carrying steamers, which meant that her decks could fill with water in heavy seas, and required the substantial wash ports visible.

In 1878, *Usworth* was sold to Frederick Gordon of Sunderland, who traded as Gordon & Stamp, in whose colours she is seen. She was one of the smallest vessels in a fleet that included deep-sea cargo vessels. Indeed, *Usworth* was trading to the extent of home-trade limits when she disappeared after leaving Sunderland for Hamburg on 12 October 1881. *(Robert Le Maistre collection)*

In and out of the coal trade

The tendency of owners outside the coal trade to take up steam colliers, apparent with some of the pioneers of the 1840s, was a continuing one. The collier *Fenton** was completed in 1876 for coal interests in London by S P Austin & Hunter, Sunderland, but in the 1900s she began to leave the east coast coal trade and work more widely. It is unclear who owned her at the time of the visit to Bristol depicted here, because from 1902 owners changed quite frequently, but as she is working on the west coast the best guess is a James B Couper of Glasgow. The photograph certainly predates her acquisition by Powell, Bacon & Hough Lines Ltd in 1913, because this company renamed her *Stonehenge*.

Fenton has a more substantial bridge than her predecessors from the 1860s, with accommodation for master and mate below, although this may be a result of a later rebuild. She has a low forecastle like *J R Hinde*, its presence disguised by bulwarks. A feature not seen in the Palmer-built colliers is a 94-ft raised quarterdeck extending aft of her bridge for almost half of her 201-ft length. This became an almost universal feature of colliers and other coasters.

The 784-grt former collier had a remarkably long career after she was renamed *Stonehenge*. Passing through the hands of various London owners that probably used her in the near-continental trades, she was sold to an owner in Catania, Italy, in 1924 and renamed *Adone*. She was wrecked near Pozallo in March 1932, still with the two-cylinder compound engine that George Clark had built for her in Sunderland fifty-six years previously. *(J and M Clarkson)*

Despite, or possibly because of, transfers away from the coal trade, there was a clear demand for further colliers and this resulted in at least one dramatic conversion. The hull of *Allerwash** had been built at Southampton in 1861 as the paddle ferry *American*, probably named in honour of co-owner William H Muntz of Southampton. In view of her other owner's residence in Ventnor, *American* was probably intended to paddle between Southampton and the Isle of Wight. She was so unsuccessful that she was sold in July 1868 and the only use found for her was as a pontoon. But Tyneside shipbuilder Edward Lindsay saw potential in her hull and in 1870 rebuilt her as a collier. Owner was a William Benson, whose residence, Allerwash House, was the inspiration for her new name. At only 131 ft in length, *Allerwash* was small for the east coast coal trade, and in 1875 Benson had Palmers lengthen her to 168 ft giving her a tonnage of 381 gross, and fitting a two-cylinder compound engine. The photograph of her running out of Goole was probably taken just before the First World War when in the ownership of Freear & Dix, whose distinctively upright striped funnel she wears. Vagueness about the date is necessary, because this Sunderland-based collier owner had *Allerwash* under various company titles from 1897 until 1923 when she went for scrap in Germany. A vessel that was initially a failure had survived, at least in part, for sixty-two years. *(J and M Clarkson)*

A Cardiff steam pioneer

Although the image of *Llandaff** portrays her in a precarious position, she was a very significant vessel in demonstrating the practicality of the steam cargo vessel to Cardiff shipping interests.

Llandaff was completed in 1865 by collier builders Schlesinger, Davies & Company of Wallsend on the Tyne for a group of Cardiff merchants that included Charles Stallybrass and Henry Vellacott. Of 411 grt and 153 ft registered length, she was a typical, if small, early steam collier with engines aft and a rudimentary bridge amidships. The photograph shows how on 27 April 1889 she went ashore at Nanjizal Bay, near Land's End, in fog during a ballast voyage from Sheerness to Cardiff. Despite the dramatic setting, this was a relatively sheltered spot, and *Llandaff* was refloated on 5 May and taken to Penzance for repair. Alas, on 2 November 1899 she was in trouble again, driven ashore at Barrel Rock, Bude, during a north-west gale while on a voyage from St Malo to Swansea. Again, *Llandaff* was got off, but this time was declared a constructive total loss and taken to Cardiff to be demolished.

Although not the first bulk-carrying steamer to serve South Wales (which was probably *Augusta* of 1849), *Llandaff* is said to have awoken the interest of Cardiff docksmen in the potential of steam in the coal trade. This they embraced with remarkable energy, building substantial fleets of larger vessels for the export of South Wales coal to the Mediterranean, Black Sea and Baltic ports, and ensuing years saw Cardiff docksmen founding several deep-sea tramping fleets, and rather neglecting the coasting colliers such as *Llandaff*.

Engines amidships

Although most of the early colliers for which images survive had their engines aft, it became the practice in colliers of over 200 ft in length to place the machinery amidships. Such ships were easier to trim on an even keel when light, and there was concern about hull strength that led to the heaviest items of equipment, the engines and boilers, being placed away from the stem. The reasons must have been compelling, as this design has considerable disadvantages, especially in the coal trade. It required a long propeller shaft, which needed supporting at intervals. The long shaft tunnel itself required access for maintenance and detracted from the capacity of after holds. To compensate, engines-amidships colliers often had a raised quarterdeck to increase the depth of the after holds. Another disadvantage was that discharge of coal by grabs easily damaged the plating above the shaft tunnel.

The 944 grt *Medway** was built by Austin & Hunter of Sunderland in 1879. Of her 226 ft registered length, 41 ft was occupied by a bridge deck, with a raised quarterdeck extending 76 ft to her stern. An oddity is the boat mounted on davits alongside her after hold. A shortish but strongly raked funnel gives her rather an anachronistic appearance. *Medway* was the first steamer owned by Francis D Lambert who, trading as Lambert Brothers, became deeply involved in the coal trade, as well as ship and insurance broking, bunkering and agency work. *Medway* worked until 1910, when she was broken up at Boulogne.

The engines amidships arrangement for larger colliers persisted well into the twentieth century, but its disadvantages meant it eventually lost out to the engines-aft layout. *(M Barnard)*

CHAPTER

3

The Ubiquitous Steam Coaster

The screw collier described in the previous chapter proved ideal for the British east coast coal trade, where shipments were relatively large and ports at both ends of the route could take substantial ships. Indeed, colliers proved quite capable of trading as far afield as the Baltic and Black Sea. But for the purely coastal trade of the British Isles, and especially that to the network of smaller but important ports around the Irish Sea, the collier with its optimum size of 190–200 ft was too large. Several important ports or quays where coal was regularly shipped could take nothing larger than 150 ft, for instance the port of Newry and the Grand Canal quays in Dublin. In addition, many smaller merchants could not accept nor afford large shipments of coal.

For steam to break into the west coast bulk trades and displace sail, a smaller, more economic and more versatile coastal vessel was needed. As the cost of building in iron fell and the efficiency of the marine steam engine rose, these goals began to be achieved towards the end of the 1870s, when there was a sudden blossoming of the steam coaster. This term is reserved here for vessels typically smaller than the average screw collier, although with many similarities. Although coal was their most frequent cargo, the steam coasters could carry this turn and turn about with other bulk cargoes. This flexibility proved so useful that these steamers were built in large numbers, ensuring their ubiquity not just in the UK coastal trades, but throughout Europe and well beyond.

The major variable was size, which determined layout, and was dependent on the ports to be served and the cargoes available. Certain national characteristics also became apparent once builders in continental Europe began to produce their own designs. A few specialist vessels were built for niche trades, including carrying slate, stone and timber.

This chapter covers vessels built from 1878 to 1948. This exceptionally long period reflects that, once established, the design of the steam coaster was remarkably durable. In the years after the Second World War, one British owner was still ordering ships which were basically the same as those he had taken delivery of fifty years earlier.

The ships described here have their engines aft: subsequent chapters will deal with the important engines-amidships configurations. The two distinct designs developed by British yards and owners are described first, followed by accounts of how European yards produced their variants of the ubiquitous steam coaster.

An asterisk in a caption indicates the vessel shown in the photograph.

Bridge aft

For the smallest steam coasters, say 90 ft to 130 ft, the bridge was usually placed aft, often on a raised quarterdeck. This deck was an enduring feature of coaster design, and probably arose to accommodate the full height of a vertical marine steam engine. The extra depth of hull aft improved sea-keeping and helped the vessel's trim when loaded, so this feature became almost ubiquitous.

One of the earliest steamers of this layout, and a candidate for the prototype steam coaster, was William Robertson's *Agate*, built in 1878 at Rutherglen. Although from a different builder, John Fullerton & Company of Paisley, Robertson's *Peridot**, completed in February 1890, gives an impression of how *Agate* would have looked. Of 130 ft registered length and 296 grt, *Peridot* had a low forecastle, and – disguised by the bulwarks aft – a short, 7-ft bridge deck, immediately aft of which was a 42-ft raised quarterdeck. The steering position was only modestly raised and had minimal protection from the weather.

In the photograph, *Peridot* carried a jib and sails at both main and mizzen. The position of the mainmast shows she had one small hatch forward and a larger hatch aft of this mast, an arrangement soon abandoned to give larger, uninterrupted hatches.

Peridot's end was singularly tragic, and meant her name was never repeated in Robertson's fleet. On 26 November 1905, she was waiting for the tide off Carnlough, Northern Ireland where she was to load limestone, and from which community came seven of her nine crew. In heavy weather *Peridot* sought shelter in Larne Lough but was wrecked at Skernaghan Point. Her entire crew was lost, a tragedy for Carnlough. *(Glasgow University Archives)*

In terms of size, the 126-ft *Glencona** was typical of the bridge-aft design, with both a forecastle and a quarterdeck, the latter picked out by the white edging to her bulwarks. Cargo gear was enhanced by a second derrick, the choice of a short kingpost rather than a mast at the after end of the hold helping to reduce top weight. She also had the luxury of an enclosed wheelhouse. *Glencona* was built and engined in 1907 by Hepple & Co Ltd, South Shields for a company managed by Matthew Worth of Newcastle-upon-Tyne, a port normally associated with much larger coasters. She found much of her work taking Tyne coal northwards to smaller Scottish ports, although she is seen here on the Ouse, heading to Goole.

During the First World War, *Glencona* was sold to Wilson Brothers Bobbin Co Ltd of Garston. Her owners made bobbins for the textile industry and other wooden items such as soles for clogs. Much of the beech wood that the company preferred was felled around sea lochs in the west of Scotland, and *Glencona* would anchor inshore, often with mooring lines attached to stumps of trees, and use her own gear to load the logs that were floated out from the shore. Both of *Glencona*'s derricks would be required to work in tandem to lift the heaviest logs. Coal out from Garston to an Irish port was a useful return cargo, and *Glencona* succumbed on such a voyage in February 1926. Abandoned by her crew on fire fifteen miles off the Skerries while heading for Dublin, *Glencona* drifted some sixty miles and sank near the Lune Light Vessel.

In the United Kingdom, the building of small steam coasters ended abruptly in the 1920s, because this size of coaster was more economically propelled by an oil engine. Among the last was a group of four built by the Manchester Dry Docks Co Ltd at Ellesmere Port. With the chronic shortage of small ships during the First World War, the British government gave the yard its first two orders for 120-ft coasters. Although these were cancelled at the Armistice in November 1918, work proceeded on the partly built hulls and their compound engines and, encouraged by the high prices being offered for coasters, the yard laid down two more in 1919. Completion of all four was protracted because building proceeded only when the workforce was not engaged on repair work.

The third coaster was launched in March 1924, five years after being laid down, and entered service in April as the 274-grt *Doris Thomas*. In 1938, she was bought by Ramsey Steamship Co Ltd and renamed *Ben Ain**. Three of the Ellesmere Port coasters ended up in the fleet of the Ramsey company, to serve mainly small ports. *Ben Ain* was photographed at a drying-out berth at Douglas in the Isle of Man, showing just a trace of her bilge keel, and demonstrating why coasters needed flat bottoms because taking the ground was essential in some trades. She is unloading coal into the two lorries to the left using her own gear on this sunny day in September 1956. *Ben Ain* still had an open bridge, and retained it when she went to breakers at Cork in 1963. *(World Ship Society Ltd)*

Long-raised-quarterdeck coasters

Most steam coasters of over 125 ft in length had their bridge amidships, at the forward end of a long raised quarterdeck. Extending this deck forward gave an additional depth to the main hold, providing increased freeboard aft and protection from seas sweeping from astern. Steam coasters with this layout appeared almost contemporarily with the short-raised-quarterdeck design described above.

Typical of the earlier and smaller vessels was *Owain Tudur** of just 126 ft in length and 227 grt, launched in October 1882 by Samuel Brothers, Llanelly for a single-ship company managed by one of several Liverpool-Welsh coasting operators, Parry, Jones & Company. Like *Owain Tudur*, many of the earlier long-raised-quarterdeck ships had a forward hold significantly longer than that aft. This was probably to give a relatively large hatch forward for stowing lengthy items of cargo, although later the trend was reversed. *Owain Tudur* is unusual in having bulwarks of wood, beginning just aft of her short bridge deck and extending almost the full length of her raised quarterdeck. Note also the boat on her forward hatch, ready to be slung out of the way to allow her hatch covers to be removed.

In her long life, *Owain Tudur* changed hands six times, and was also transferred on several occasions between companies controlled by the same family. This Bristol photograph was taken between 1908 and 1916 when owned by the Rix family of Hull, although the letter R is missing from the diamond on her funnel. She was renamed just once, becoming *Peggy Grieve* while with Birkenhead owners between 1922 and 1926. Under this name she went to Thomas Ward at Grays, Essex in 1929 to be broken up.

Nugget of 1889 is another example from the William Robertson fleet, which was particularly well photographed while working on the Clyde. Her length of 142 ft was a very popular size, because it allowed use of Ringsend Basin where most of Dublin's coal supplies were delivered. The 396-grt *Nugget** was built by Scott & Company of Bowling and – unlike the compound-engined *Owain Tudur* – had a triple-expansion engine that was almost universal in this design of ship (but see *Oak*, below), in this case made by Muir & Houston of Glasgow.

Nugget was the victim of a U-boat torpedo south of the Scilly Isles in July 1915 while en route to the Dardanelles to work for the Admiralty as a fleet messenger. The submarine, *U 28*, scored a double by also sinking Robertson's *Turquoise* of 1893, which was accompanying *Nugget* on her way to war. *(Glasgow University Archives)*

By 1906, the short after hold was becoming less popular, but not in the fleet of Joseph Fisher & Sons of Newry. The Fullerton-built *Oak** was exactly the same length as *Nugget*, but slightly narrower at 23.6 ft. Unusually for this Paisley yard, which prided itself on elegant-looking ships, her masts and funnels are almost upright, giving her a stumpy appearance. The 346-grt *Oak* lasted until broken up 1952, and in this post-Second World War view she is heading for Garston or Partington on the Manchester Ship Canal to load yet another cargo of coal, probably for Newry. She was fitted with a mizzen mast when built, probably with a long boom like *Nugget* to carry a steadying sail, but lost this in the Second World War when it interfered with the arc of fire of her anti-aircraft guns: in this war coasters such as *Oak* were more at risk from the Luftwaffe than from the Kriegsmarine's U-boat arm. The enclosed wheelhouse was probably fitted at the same time.

Fisher & Sons was notoriously frugal when it came to fitting out its ships, and *Oak* and others had two-cylinder compound engines rather than the more expensive but more efficient triple-expansion machinery. No steam-powered windlass or capstan was provided and, when raising the anchor or warping the ship, the chain or hawser had to be connected to one of the cargo winches. Frugality continued post-Second World War, when Fisher built two steamers, *Balsa* and *Ebony*, to a design barely changed since *Oak*, but with triple-expansion engines. But as will be seen, even these 1947 completions were not the end of steam coaster construction in British yards.

A size larger at 155 ft, and intended for the Scottish east coast trade, *Hove** exemplifies the difficulty in distinguishing between a collier and a coaster. Built in 1913 by the Ardrossan Dry Dock & Shipbuilding Co Ltd for Aberdeen owners as *Collairnie*, she was bought and renamed in 1917 by Stephenson, Clarke & Company, one of London's longest-established coal merchant ship owners. She would then run between coal staithes on the Tyne or Wear and harbours on the south coast of England that could not take, or did not need, the larger specialised colliers. These harbours included Shoreham, the port for the towns of Brighton and Hove.

Hove is seen post-war in the Mersey, running for the Coppack family of Connah's Quay on the River Dee, who bought her in 1935 and without change of name put her back into general coastal tramping, running her mainly on the Irish Sea. A late survivor from the steam coaster era, *Hove* was broken up in Dublin during 1961. *(World Ship Society Ltd)*

Hazelfield has a particular claim to fame as the last steamer built in a British yard for the coastal tramping trades (several specialised steam colliers followed her) when completed and engined by the Lytham Shipbuilding & Engineering Co Ltd in April 1948. As the decision to build to such a traditional design so late suggests, the board of the owning company, the long-established Zillah Shipping & Carrying Co Ltd of Liverpool, consisted of old men. Ordering *Hazelfield* was almost their last independent action, because in 1949 a takeover offer was accepted from Coast Lines Ltd.

The 184-ft length overall, 692-grt *Hazelfield* had some relatively modern features. She was part welded rather than riveted, was oil- not coal-fired, and a cruiser stern in place of the elegant but archaic counter stern. But in the era when the motor ship was dominant, *Hazelfield* was an anachronism. She was too deep-draughted for some of Zillah's important trades, including shipping gravel from Walney to the Mersey, grain to flour mills at Silloth, and china clay from Cornwall to Preston. Nor did she have the bunker capacity for longer voyages and was suitable only for carrying coal across the Irish Sea, a trade that was rapidly declining.

After lay up for much of 1958, the eleven-year-old ship was sold in June 1959 to other Liverpool owners who renamed her *Sprayville*. Within four years she was sold again, this time to Greek owners who fitted an oil engine. Her life was not greatly extended, however, for as *Agios Gerassimos* she foundered in October 1979 west of Naples when carrying a cargo of contraband cigarettes. *(J and M Clarkson)*

Although the ideal point from which to con the ship was a bridge amidships, which also allowed a decent separation of the master's and mate's accommodation from the engines and engineers, this structure could complicate loading of exceptionally long items of cargo such as railway rails and steel bars. The bridge was therefore placed aft in the 200-ft *Ardgryfe**, built in 1918 by the Ardrossan Dockyard & Shipbuilding Co Ltd and owned for most of her long career by P MacCallum & Sons Ltd, steel stockholders of Greenock. So established was the long-raised-quarterdeck design that this featured, even though it must have complicated loading items such as 120-ft steel bars in which MacCallum specialised. Earlier coasters of this size, *Ardgarth*, *Ardglass* and *Ardgour*, built by George Brown & Company of Greenock in 1913 and 1914, had a single long hatch serving their one hold. *Ardgryfe* must have proved a useful ship as the company kept her until 1959 when she was broken up. As well as moving steel from works in South Wales to Glasgow and Belfast, she was used in general coastal tramping.

At 250 ft length and 1600 grt, the 1930-built *Maurice Rose** needed four hatches, served by masts and derricks placed at the centre of the well deck and quarterdeck. Ballast capacity was 532 tons of water in double bottom, fore and aft peak tanks. Owners Richard Hughes & Company specialised in carrying china clay from Fowey in Cornwall to the Mersey, where the ship is seen, and where it would be transferred to narrow boats for delivery to the Staffordshire potteries. The larger ships in the Hughes' fleet were also operated in the east coast coal trade. Her name came from Hughes's son Maurice; contemporaries such as *Moelfre Rose* and *Amlwch Rose* celebrated the Anglesey communities from which many of Hughes' crew members were recruited.

Maurice Rose was delivered by D & W Henderson & Co Ltd, Glasgow, in 1930 at the depth of the worst depression the coastal trade had known. Hughes gambled that, as in earlier recessions, trade would bounce back and ordered an ambitious total of eleven new ships. In fact, the hard times continued right up to the Second World War and, laden with debts from Henderson and from Dutch yards, Hughes was declared bankrupt within a few years. His considerable fleet was taken over by Cardiff shipbroker Thomas Tierney although the founder's name was retained in the company's new title, Richard Hughes & Co (Liverpool) Ltd. Tierney sold some ships and worked the others frugally so that the debts had been settled by when he retired in 1952. *Maurice Rose* was sold in 1947, and as *Richmond Queen* carried coal mainly to Jersey before scrapping in 1957. *(J and M Clarkson)*

Slate steamers

The North Wales slate industry kept a small fleet of specialised steamers employed from 1890 to the 1950s. Slates are heavy but breakable, and an important design requirement for a slate carrier was longitudinal stiffness, which prevented flexing in a seaway, which could have disastrous consequences for the cargo stowed in the hold. Stiffness was achieved by relatively small hatchways with correspondingly larger deck areas. This was the opposite of what was required for steam coasters in the major bulk trades, which needed large hatches for rapid loading and unloading of coal, ore, grain or stone. In the slate trade, small hatchways were not a disadvantage because the slate was loaded and discharged entirely by hand.

The earliest steamers designed for the slate trade were built to serve the Dinorwic Quarries, which had harbour facilities at Port Dinorwic, between Bangor and Caernarfon. *Velinheli** was completed in 1892 by S McKnight & Company of Ayr and at just 95 ft and 126 grt was among the smallest cargo ships working on the coast. She traded locally, from Dinorwic to Preston, Liverpool and other Mersey ports. The small hatches of slate steamers put them at a disadvantage when handling cargoes such as coal or stone, which were increasingly discharged by mechanical means. However, return cargoes to Port Dinorwic were unusual, and the slate traders would usually come home in ballast. *Velinheli* was the exception, often loading coal at the Point of Ayr colliery at the mouth of the River Dee when homeward bound from Liverpool or Runcorn. *Velinheli* was sold in 1941, but did little further work before being broken up at Peterhead in the late 1950s. *(J and M Clarkson)*

The largest Dinorwic ship was the 423-grt, 152-ft *Elidir**, built in 1903 by Ailsa Shipbuilding Co Ltd, Ayr, and at the upper end of the scale of raised-quarterdeck steamers. She had two holds, the smaller one forward usually being left empty with a slate cargo, which was so dense that she was down to her marks with just the main hold filled. The empty forward hold helped her trim by the stern, ensuring she could lift herself clear of heavy seas, avoiding pounding and making steering easier. However, with no bilge keels *Elidir* did roll easily but the crew reduced this tendency by setting the sails. Despite this, Dinorwic steamers were particularly sea-kindly, which was as well because they had a reputation for putting to sea in weather that kept other coasters in harbour.

Elidir regularly ran to ports in the north east of Scotland, including Aberdeen and Kirkcaldy. On these voyages she disdained the Caledonian Canal and braved the stormy waters of the Pentland Firth, where the stiffness that characterised slate steamers came into its own: her cargoes of slate were almost invariably intact no matter what weather she had faced. *Elidir* would sometimes bring building stone back from Scotland, but her small hatches disadvantaged her when she carried coal and iron on the east coast when demand for slate fell after the First World War. After she had been sold to Coppack of Connah's Quay in 1942 and put into general coasting, her hatches were enlarged and her mainmast moved forward to the break of her forecastle. She was broken up at Preston in 1955. *(J and M Clarkson)*

Stone carriers

The dimensions of the tiny harbour at Porthgain in south-west Wales dictated the size of a fleet of five steam coasters built specifically to carry roadstone. The owning company, United Stone Firms Ltd of Bristol, resulted from an amalgamation in 1909 of several quarrying companies working in England, Wales and Ireland. The company's ships that were delivered in 1909 from the yards of Smith's Dock Co Ltd at North Shields and Middlesbrough were just 130 ft long, giving a gross tonnage of just under 300. Like the 297-grt *Liscannor** of 1911, these had a single hold served by derricks on two masts or, in the case of near-sisters *Porthgain* and *Mountcharles*, a foremast and a stumpy derrick post just ahead of the raised quarterdeck. Each day at least one of these ships would leave Porthgain for ports in the Bristol Channel, Newhaven, Cork, Dublin, Belfast or London. The owner's name painted on the hull aft was, for its time, a very rare feature, and much copied in later years.

Overstretched by its aggressive acquisition policy (by no means a twenty-first century problem), United Stone Firms Ltd went into receivership in 1913, and *Liscannor* was sold by her mortgagees to a Newcastle firm that traded her as *Freighter* until broken up in 1934. The quarries at Porthgain and elsewhere continued to work under receivership for some years, although the last of the United Stone quintet was sold in 1919.

The short-raised-quarterdeck design allowed fitting of large hatches to facilitate rapid loading from tips and rapid mechanical discharge. Some of the largest ships of this type were built to carry limestone from quarries in North Wales to an alkali works at Burn Naze near Fleetwood belonging to the United Alkali Co Ltd. This works converted limestone to lime and used the Solvay process to react it with brine to produce sodium hydroxide, widely used in soap making and other industrial processes.

The largest ships in the United Alkali's limestone trade were the 183-ft overall *Calcium**, *Barium* and *Sodium* delivered between 1917 and 1923. The 613-grt *Calcium* came from the yard of George Brown & Co of Greenock, and was unusual in having a tall goal post mast forward and little more than a king post at the after end of a long hold. These coasters mainly shuttled between Llanddulas and Fleetwood, a round voyage taking less than twenty-four hours and with crews paid a bonus if they completed more than twenty-eight voyages in a month. Occasionally, the ships would stray further afield to deliver manufactured products, as with *Calcium* shown in the River Avon. In 1932, United Alkali became a founder constituent of Imperial Chemical Industries Ltd, but its coasters steamed on as before, now with the ICI roundel on their tall funnels. On a ballast voyage to Llanddulas in December 1940, *Calcium* was mined just north of the Little Orme, North Wales with the loss of one member of her nine-man crew. Last of the steamers, *Sodium*, survived until 1959, running alongside a growing fleet of motor ships.

Dutch-built for export

British yards had a head start in building iron and later steel steamers, and it took continental European builders some time to catch up. *Normand** of 1885 was an unusually early example of a steam coaster from a Dutch yard, built and given a compound engine by Maatschappij de Maas at Delfshaven, near Rotterdam. She was built for owners in Le Havre, which explains her name, but in March 1893 she was wrecked. Recovered and rebuilt, in 1894 she came into British ownership with her original name (many owners still considered it unlucky to rename a vessel), and by 1896 was working for Thomas Wilson & Company of Whitehaven, and was still with these owners when photographed in the 1920s. With a short forecastle, even shorter bridge deck and poop, all disguised by high bulwarks, there is little to distinguish her from a contemporary British-built coaster. She had an enclosed wheelhouse, but the cloth-capped seaman steering her towards Preston Dock is still in the open, protected from Irish Sea weather only by a canvas dodger. In 1937, the tiny, 116-ft and 190-grt steamer went to owners in Estonia, and was renamed *Salme*. In 1939 she was renamed *Salmi*. Upon the 1940 annexation of Estonia by the Soviet Union, the vessel was taken over by the state, and in June 1941 became the military transport *VT 588*. She was sunk by war causes in the Gulf of Finland on 28 August 1941. *(J and M Clarkson)*

Yards in the Netherlands were the first overseas builders to make an impact on the British market. With the connivance of British entrepreneur Charles H Pile, who traded as Shipping Investments Ltd, several Dutch-built steamers were sold on the British market in the first decade of the twentieth century. But it was during and just after the First World War that Dutch yards blossomed. In this conflict, losses of coasters were particularly heavy, and the British builders that then dominated the industry could not keep pace because even small yards were directed to building naval vessels. Dutch yards eagerly filled the gap, and found a ready market among British owners that wanted to profit from the inflated freight rates ruling post-war. None were keener recipients of Dutch vessels than Walford Lines of London, which took ten Dutchmen, to supplement two French-built, one Estonian-built and a number of English steamers to build up its coasting fleet for a mix of regular routes and tramping.

Walford's alphabetic sequence began with *Jolly Angela**, delivered in July 1919 by Johs Berg of Delfzijl, who also made her triple-expansion engines. At 160 ft and 537 grt, she was a large vessel to have a long well deck, on which there are two hatches served by three derricks. Dutch-built steamers had a reputation for having lighter scantlings than British craft, and it is significant that none of Walford's Dutch fleet were classed by Lloyd's Register. Several of the ships owned by Walford survived into the 1950s, but *Jolly Angela* was not among these. She was renamed *Rijn* by Walford in 1934 and in the following year went to Contomichalos, Darke & Co (1929) Ltd, London, and was renamed *Sudani*. She met her end in 1941, when, on 15 January, she was wrecked 20 nautical miles west of Mersa Matruh.

Any resemblance between *Charlotte** and a British-built steam coaster is probably not accidental. Indeed, apart from the slightly odd heights of the masts, which become shorter the further aft they are, she could be British, and indeed in 1923 did sail for a few months as *Leckwith* for Cardiff owners. The 187-ft coaster was built in 1921 by Scheeps v/h A Baars & Zonen of Sliedrecht for local owners as *Maria Peulen*. When photographed in the Avon between 1923 and 1926, *Charlotte* was owned by Tramm & Co, Hamburg. After sale in 1926, her name was extended to *Elfriede Charlotte Becker*, an even more cumbersome (to English ears) name coming in 1946 after she was taken by the USSR and registered at Baku on the Caspian Sea as *Syr-dar'ya*. Like many Soviet ships, her fate is unknown.

Dutch yards continued to build similar steam coasters for British owners, Richard Hughes of Liverpool having five built at Hardinxveld in 1930 and 1931. But interestingly, the Dutch did not operate many steam coasters themselves, even those built in the Netherlands. As explored in Chapter 8, the canny Dutch were aware of the potential of the motor coaster as early as 1918. *(Ships in Focus)*

German variants

German shipyards were, like those in the Netherlands, relatively slow to build steam coasters compared with British yards, but produced at least three distinctive variants on the engines-aft theme. Tall, narrow, rather upright funnels were also a feature of German ships.

Like British and Dutch types, the simplest design of coaster had everything aft, with a raised forecastle and poop/quarterdeck. As with the 166-ft, 676-grt *Gerda Kunstmann**, ships of this type were often longer than British examples. Completed in 1911 as *Vulcan* by the 'Vulcan' yard at Stettin, she was also unusual in having a non-compound, twin-cylinder engine, which she appears to have kept until sunk by a Soviet submarine in the Baltic during July 1942, by when she carried her third name, *Anna Katrin Fritzen*.

The long-raised-quarterdeck vessels from German yards came in two forms. That with bridge aft is represented by *Jade**, which has the enhanced cargo gear typical of regular traders when photographed in her home port in July 1932. She had been built for Bugsier-, Reederei- und Bergungs of Hamburg in 1912 by Stettiner Oderwerke, which had also given her a two-cylinder compound engine, when a ship of this size – 165 ft and 536 grt – would normally have a triple-expansion engine. She carried the one name throughout a career, which ended – as it did for many German ships – in May 1945 when a mine or bomb sank her in Fehmarn Sound. *(F W Hawks)*

A distinctively German design for larger coasters had the bridge approximately amidships with the long-raised quarterdeck extending well forward of it, leaving a short well between this and the forecastle. This design necessitated three hatches and at least three derricks to work them, as in the 761-grt *Erna**. Of her 204 ft, a forecastle takes up 27 ft and the long quarterdeck a further 155 ft, leaving a well of just 24 ft. She was built as *Prospero* in 1904 by Schömer & Jensen of Tönning in Schleswig-Holstein, which also provided her triple-expansion engines. When photographed in May 1933, she had recently been renamed *Erna* by her new owners, F Ivers & Co GmbH, Lübeck, and a name with which she survived the war to be broken up at Hamburg in 1954.

German steam coasters would trade largely between German ports in the Baltic and through the Kiel Canal to Hamburg and adjoining areas. Built for a domestic market, and one for which the coastal trade was protected by cabotage laws, it is hard to escape the conclusion that these ships were conservative if not actually anachronistic in their design. German coaster building and ownership was to have a later flowering, and indeed in the motor ship era Germany could be said to have led the world for some years. *(F W Hawks)*

Scandinavian steamers

Denmark, Finland, Norway and Sweden are associated more with smaller motor coasters and with larger, engines-amidships steamers of the so-called 'Baltic' type than the classic steam coaster, and it will fall to later chapters of this book to do justice to builders and owners in these countries. Of the four Scandinavian countries, Sweden had the most developed shipbuilding industry during the heyday of the steam coaster, and produced the most distinctive designs.

Owned by Oscar Emanuelsson, *Elinsborg** voyaged from Swedish waters to Bristol, sometime between 1928 and 1936. The two-cylinder compound-engined steamer had been built as *Gösta* in 1908 by Eriksbergs, Gothenburg, a yard that was to build much larger ships during its lifetime. *Gösta* started small, at only 102 ft, but was lengthened to 126 ft in 1920, giving her a tonnage of 310 gross. Features to note are the flimsy supports for her open bridge, a tall, thin and upright funnel, the gaff on her foremast, and a distinctive style of rounded stem. *Elinsborg* had previously been named *Hamburg* under Swedish ownership, and was to carry four further names after her sale to Finland in 1936. Although seized by the Germans in Norwegian waters in September 1944, she was probably not used by them, and was recovered by her Finnish owners in 1945. As *Savi*, she was broken up at Ostend in 1951.

*Engineer** was actually slightly smaller than *Elinsborg* at just 122 ft, but the stumpiness of her masts disguises her small hull. Lödöse Varv, inland from Gothenburg on the Göta Alv, completed and engined her as *Siri* for Norwegian owners in 1915. Within six years she had carried two other names, *Bols* and *System*, and changed hands four times, reflecting the increased value of coasters because during the First World War both Britain and Germany increasing relied on neutrals to supplement their tonnage. In 1922, a Newcastle owner bought her, retaining her name *System*, and only on transfer to another local owner, 'T' Steam Coasters Ltd managed by Robinson, Brown & Company, was she renamed *Engineer* to match the names of other trades and professions celebrated in his fleet. *Engineer* was broken up in 1936. *(Ships in Focus)*

Survivor

In 1890 the 366grt and 143 ft *Robin* was a typical and largely undistinguished steam coaster. Over 120 years later, however, she is unique: the world's sole surviving representative of the ninetheenth-century cargo ship retaining her original steam machinery.

The only unusual aspect of *Robin* was her place of build. The Thames was for much of the ninetheenth century a major centre of iron shipbuilding, but its output of merchant ships had dwindled to almost nothing by September 1890 when *Robin* was launched by MacKenzie, MacAlpine and Co. at the Orchard House Yard, Blackwall. Indeed, even this builder did not survive to complete her, the work being carried out by a Robert Thomson.

During her ten years under the British flag, *Robin* was owned successively in Newport, Cardiff and Glasgow. In her subsequent seventy-four years under the Spanish flag as *Maria*, she had three owners, all in Bilbao.

In 1974 *Maria* was recognised as the last surviving British steam coaster retaining original triple-expansion engines; older hulls existed, but all had lost their steam machinery. Brought back to Britain, she resumed the name *Robin*, was restored by the Maritime Trust and exhibited in St Katherine's Dock, London. Alas, the expense of maintaining a fleet of preserved ships proved too much for the Maritime Trust, and *Robin* was offered for sale. In July 2011, she returned to London after extensive further conservation work. *Robin* now rests on a pontoon which will also become an exhibition space. Following internal restoration, her owners, the SS Robin Trust, intend that by 2012 she will be opened as a museum and learning centre. *(Ambrose Greenway)*

The Clyde puffer

Despite their name and diminutive size, the steamers that were developed in the waters of central Scotland could and did make substantial coastal and short-sea voyages. They developed contemporarily with the screw collier, the first puffer being identified as the Forth and Clyde Canal lighter *Thomas*, which had a simple steam engine and screw installed in 1856. Puffers multiplied rapidly, and although length was restricted to 66 ft for those that used the Forth and Clyde Canal, and to 88 ft for those navigating the Crinan Canal, these sizes suited the bulk cargoes moving between the two coasts of Scotland and west to its highlands and islands.

Because of the size restrictions, design did not change greatly over a century, the major improvement being the use of compound engines with condensers that meant these steamers no longer puffed. *Kaffir** of 1944 had characteristics of puffers built generations earlier, including the funnel ahead of the steering position, the boat on the deck and crew accommodation in the forecastle. Built and owned by the Hay family of Kirkintilloch, doyen of puffer operators, she was one of sixty-five constructed mainly in English yards during the Second World War, all but two destined for Admiralty service as Victualling Inshore Craft or 'VICs'.

Seen polluting the banks of the Clyde in June 1952, the 66-ft *Kaffir* was in 1962 the last of a handful of Hay puffers converted to diesel propulsion. This allowed the crew's accommodation to be moved aft, but did nothing for her appearance. Conversion prolonged *Kaffir*'s life until September 1974 when she was severely damaged in Ayr Harbour and abandoned. *(World Ship Society Ltd)*

It was somewhat ironic that an English shipyard built the very last steam puffer, indeed the last steam-driven coastal cargo ship built in Britain and possibly anywhere. Ross & Marshall Ltd of Greenock (a rival to Hay, with which it merged in 1968) originally specified a diesel engine, but panicked when a Middle East oil crisis developed, and the 166-grt *Stormlight** was completed in September 1957 with a coal-fired, compound engine. Builders were W J Yarwood & Sons Ltd, not a totally unexpected choice, because this Northwich yard had built small steamers for use on the rivers Weaver and Mersey for over half a century. The new *Stormlight* was photographed off Greenock in October 1957.

In the long term, her machinery proved fatal to *Stormlight*. An 88-ft steamer proved costly and difficult to crew, and she was often laid up for want of stokers. In 1972 her owners, now Glenlight Shipping Ltd, sent her to Scott & Sons (Bowling) Ltd for conversion to a motor vessel. To economise, the owners specified inexpensive diesel engines transmitting their power to the propellor by a hydraulic system. But for reliability this machinery required more tender care than it routinely received, and breakdowns were not uncommon. Some sources blame engine failure for the demise of *Stormlight*, which on 15 December 1973, during a ballast voyage from Campbeltown to Oban, ran on to rocks at Craighouse, Jura and was abandoned. However, other authorities maintain that her rudder jammed during gale-force winds.

Whatever the cause, it was a sad end for a vessel that marked the culmination of 125 years of British steam coaster building. *(Collection of the late Clive Guthrie)*

CHAPTER

4

Steam Engine Amidships

Although the earliest screw colliers and steam coasters had engines aft, it soon became the practice to move the machinery back to the amidships position that is usual in paddle steamers. Reasons given for this include reducing stress on the hull by placing the heavy mass of engines and boilers amidships, and improving trim when in ballast condition. The amidships position had, in fact, many drawbacks, including the need for a long screw shaft and a shaft tunnel that detracted from the capacity of after holds. Other reasons must have motivated designers, builders and owners to sustain this design for so long: was it simply tradition and the sentiment that 'it looked right'?

The smaller steamer with engines amidships could be considered simply as a variant of the steam coasters featured in Chapter 3. But given the extent to which these vessels were built and owned, especially by countries around the Baltic Sea, it is appropriate that they are dealt with more fully and have a chapter to themselves. It could be argued that their inclusion is stretching too far the definition of 'coaster' but, as the introduction explained, this term is of necessity elastic and includes vessels working on short-sea routes, and the so-called 'Baltic' types were ubiquitous in the short-distance timber trade from the Baltic into the North Sea and further south. An arbitrary upper limit of 270 ft has been placed on the size of ships featured in this chapter.

No single nation's builders can claim credit for the designs featured here. Inevitably, British yards built many of the early vessels, simply because these yards were in operation before iron and steel shipbuilding developed to any extent in other industrialised nations. However, yards in Denmark, Germany, the Netherlands, Norway, Sweden and the United States also contributed notably to the fleet. Indeed, a yard in Norway became so closely associated with these vessels that the term 'Fredrikstad-type' was often applied to them. This also means that, for the first time in this book, British yards and owners do not dominate the story.

This chapter, like the previous one, covers the period from the 1870s to the 1950s because, like the vessels in Chapter 3, basic design of these small steamers changed little over these decades.

An asterisk in a caption indicates the vessel shown in the photograph.

Raised quarterdeck, two holds

By far the most common, and probably the oldest, configuration for an engines-amidships steamer was a raised quarterdeck and a forecastle, usually with a short bridge deck and with or without a poop deck. The raised quarterdeck essentially made the after hold or holds deeper, compensating for the capacity lost by the shaft tunnel, and increased the hull's seaworthiness.

A typical example of the smallest coasters of this layout is the British *Helen Craig** of 1891, 175 ft overall length and 417 grt. The very fact of ships in this book surviving to be photographed often testifies to their lengthy life-spans but, even among the long-lived, *Helen Craig* was exceptional in spending her entire career of sixty-eight years with one owner. Hugh Craig & Company of Belfast had her built at the local yard of Workman, Clark & Co Ltd and she served the company all her days. Indeed, she may well have made the distinctly unusual transition from bulk carrier to cargo liner, because in her latter days she ran between Preston and Belfast on a regular service, although coal would have remained a frequent westbound cargo. Her longevity was even more surprising in that she had a two-cylinder compound engine, and she seems to have retained an open bridge until the end. In this post-Second World War photograph of her in the Mersey, note the anchor ball on her forestay. *(K P Lewis)*

*Hailsham** exemplifies a much less common variation on the engines-amidships design. She has no bridge deck, and the after mast is stepped against a poop deck, whose height is disguised by the bulwarks aft. Of 168 ft overall and 516 grt she was built in 1895 by J L Thompson & Sons Ltd, which contracted her triple-expansion engines to John Dickinson, also of Sunderland. As *Skinningrove*, her original owner was Skinningrove Iron Co Ltd, but she is shown here in 1920–2 when she was owned by John Harrison Ltd, London.

Like *Helen Craig*, she was a great survivor. After capture by Spanish nationalists in February 1939 when trying to run the blockade to supply Republican-held ports under the name *Stangrove*, she remained under Spanish ownership until broken up in 1971 at the age of seventy-six.

The 590-grt *Glattesee** seems to have been a case of a Dutch yard, Johs Berg of Delfzijl, imitating a British design. Even to her dimensions of 165 ft length she mimics *Helen Craig*, but has a more substantial accommodation block amidships and (by 1951 at least) an enclosed wheelhouse. Probably built as a speculation, she was completed in 1921 but not until April 1923 was she delivered to Hamburg owners as *Marta Schröder*, taking the name *Glattesee* on sale to W Schuchmann in 1931. After two years with the Norwegian government as a reparations ship under the name *Skarnes*, she returned to Schuchmann ownership until broken up in 1953. The purpose of the short mast mounted on the bridge front is not immediately apparent: it has no derrick but could simply support a radio aerial.

Raised quarterdeck, three holds

When a larger capacity was required an additional hold was worked in forward, with the foremast stepped between the two hatches. Examples of this layout were built in British yards from at least the 1870s. At 250 ft, *Alice Otto* was undoubtedly intended for deep-sea work when built in 1871 by Oswald & Company, Sunderland for owners in North Shields. She moved to short-sea trading only after sale away to the Norwegian flag in 1906. The owner in Christiania who renamed her *Maria** was D/S A/S Maria and she was managed by Weltz & Justad. She was photographed entering Preston some time before October 1910, when she was delivered to breakers in Stavanger.

The photograph serves to illustrate one of the hazards of the Baltic timber trade. Wood being relatively light, the ship would not be down to her marks when her holds were full, so deck cargoes were permitted, although the months when they were allowed varied from flag to flag, with the UK being rather restrictive. Sawn timber especially readily absorbs water, and a storm could result in that portion of the deck cargo on the weather side becoming waterlogged, and causing the ship to take a list, in some cases so severe that a part of the deck cargo might break loose. *(J and M Clarkson)*

Built in the same year as *Maria*, the iron steamer *Pan** was probably in more original condition when photographed: note the plating both sides of her bridge. Built by Denton, Gray & Company, West Hartlepool, as *Seaton*, she was initially owned by Thomas Appleby and others also of West Hartlepool, but was taken over by Appleby's erstwhile partner in 1877 to become an early unit of the Robert Ropner fleet. Of 221 ft and 891 grt, she was again quite capable of deep-sea voyages, but would have been increasingly used for short-sea trading after sale in 1888 to Norwegian owners that had her original compound engines replaced by triple expansion in 1891. A succession of Swedish owners began in 1898 and one of whom, Hviid-Nielsen of Halmstad, renamed her *Pan* in 1919. After sale to an owner in Danzig and returning to the Swedish flag, all without further change of name, *Pan* was broken up, full of years, in 1934.

The three-hold layout became the standard for small cargo carriers in countries bordering the Baltic, and was built in considerable numbers during the first quarter of the twentieth century, particularly in German yards but also in Norway and Denmark. *Manfred** represents the smaller end of the spectrum, at 184 ft length overall and 703 grt, with a very short forward hatch.

She was built by Eiderwerft AG at Tönning in 1909 for German owners as *Liselotte Linneman*, and just a year later became *Bismarck*. The name *Manfred* came in 1915 when she was sold to the Swedish Verkebäcks Ångfartygs A/B. Not long after she was photographed in British waters she was sold in 1952 to Italy, where she was to have several owners and would carry the names *Doride* and *Apulia Primo* before being broken up in Italy during 1964.

German yards and owners persisted with the three-hold design, two late examples coming from the yard of Stettiner Oderwerke in 1925, *Kolberg** and *Heidelberg*, of 195 ft overall length and 693 grt. The former is seen heading for London in May 1953 with distinct signs on her paintwork that she has been navigating through ice in the Baltic Sea or the White Sea. Both ships were sold by Rud Christ Gribel of Lübeck to breakers in 1960, having achieved the feat of retaining their names for their entire thirty-five-year careers.

Raised quarterdeck, four holds

Further extending the size of the quarterdeck steamer involved putting a further hold aft, giving a length of 210 ft to 250 ft, and moving the mainmast to serve both after holds. Ships to this design were built in the same countries as the three-hold ships and over much the same timescale. The profile is well illustrated by the 255 ft overall length *Solhavn**, Norwegian-built by Bergens Mekaniske Verksteder in 1919.

The 1630grt ship spent forty-six years in Norwegian ownership, first as the Sandefjord-owned *Kapland* and from 1927 as *Solhavn*. From 1927 to 1965, she had four owners, but the Norwegian flag painted on her slender funnel in this photograph identifies her as owned by Johan Amundsen & Sønns Rederi A/S, managed by Sverre Amundsen of Haugesund, and the date between 1958 and 1962. Departing the Thames light ship, note how her screw was only partly submerged.

Solhavn left north European waters in 1965 and was successively owned in Greece and Lebanon as *Daidalos* and very briefly Bulgaria as *Bor* before delivery to breakers at La Spezia in 1970.

Danish yards had a variation on the four-hold theme, extending the bridge deck right forward to the fore end of number two hold. Built as *Gulfaxe* by Helsingørs Jernskibs & Maskinbyggeri, Elsinore, for Copenhagen owners, *Vardal** combines this layout with additional derricks at each mast. This suggests she was intended for the liner trade, and this is confirmed as her second owner was Bergen Steamship Co, for which she ran as *Pollux*. By 1948, when she was renamed *Vardal*, she was firmly in the tramping trade for owner Egil Næsheim of Haugesund.

Visible are the wood and wire supports for the deck cargo of timber she has just delivered to a London wharf. The addition of chicken wire made it possible for ships such as this to carry a return cargo of coke from a British gas works to the Baltic. At 263 ft length overall and 1708 grt, *Vardal* was a sizeable ship, quite capable of ocean voyages, and on sale in 1965 went about as far from Norway as possible – sold to owners in Manila. She was broken up in 1981.

*Mina Cantiquin** is a reminder that the raised quarter-deck, engines-amidships steamer was also encountered in trades to the Iberian Peninsula and the Mediterranean. Iron ore from Spain, phosphates or esparto grass from North Africa would be carried to north or west Europe, and often coal or coke on the voyage south.

Mina Cantiquin was built as *Getso* by Compania Euskalduna de Construcciones y Reparacion de Buques in Bilbao during 1905 for owners in this Basque town, Compania Naviera Sota y Aznar. After four renamings and three sales she became *Mina Cantiquin* in 1952 for Naviera del Nalon of Gijon.

Mina Cantiquin is unusual in having a relatively short forward well, with the foremast stepped on the forecastle rather than between the two hatches. Of 1235 grt and 229 ft length overall, she was broken up in her home port in 1972.

The raised-quarterdeck ship was so common that several less frequent variations in disposition of masts turn up. *Halmstadt** had a tall foremast and two rather unequal structures aft of her bridge deck. The 814 grt, 216 ft steamer had but one owner and one name throughout her forty-eight year career. Built by AG 'Neptun' at Rostock for Bissmark Linie GmbH in 1909, she was still carrying the funnel markings of this Hamburg owner when broken up in her home port in 1957.

A whisper of vapour emerges from the steam pipe fronting her funnel as *Halmstadt* heads down the Thames in this view, which also displays evidence of ice damage to her hull paintwork. *(Ships in Focus)*

Two islands

The alternative to the raised quarterdeck layout was to have forecastle and bridge decks. Less popular than quarterdeck ships, except with Swedish owners, these came in three- and four-hold sizes, and with a variety of arrangements of cargo gear.

The three-hold, two-island *Magnhild** exemplifies how a number of former steamers had their lives significantly extended by fitting diesel engines, in her case in conjunction with a major rebuild. She was completed as *La France* in Fevig, Norway, for local owners in 1909, and led a reasonably blameless life until seized by occupying Germans in July 1940 and converted for minelaying. As with so much German-operated tonnage, she became a target for Allied aircraft, and capsized near Skudesnes, western Norway, in December 1944 after a rocket attack. The water was shallow enough for her to be raised but she languished from 1946 until 1950 when rebuilding was completed. As *Magnhild*, she now had a diesel engine by Hamburg Motorenwerke which, judging from its 1943 building date, was probably intended for a U-boat.

The photograph, taken between 1950 and 1955, shows a short, motor ship funnel and a new wheelhouse and chartroom. The deckhouse right aft disguises the fact that the 715grt, 182ft *Magnhild* had no poop deck. Sale to a Greek owner in 1955 began a series of name changes, initially under the flag of Costa Rica which was currently popular as a flag of convenience. As *Pandora*, *Pandokrator* and *Mihalis* she changed hands several times, the last sale recorded by *Lloyd's Register* being in 1972.

Ownership at the eastern end of the Mediterranean was often the fate of superannuated steamers, although operators in Scandinavia and Finland, in particular, often kept seriously aged ships running themselves. The two-island, four-hold steamer *Elpis** was owned by AM Printezis of Piraeus when she was photographed transiting the English Channel some time prior to being broken up in 1962. She had been bought by this gentleman and an associate as far back as 1935. The 1492-grt, 240-ft steamer's origins were in Scotland, with the Dundee Shipbuilding Co Ltd, who completed her in 1919 as *Chaldon*. The most interesting of the four British owners involved with her was Frederick Jones of Cardiff. He bought her when her mortgagees took her over from a failed owner in 1932 and renamed her *Llanthony Abbey*, using her for occasional voyages to the White Sea.

Three islands

The four-hold, three-island design was common, and particularly popular with Swedish owners and builders. Owned by Verkebäcks Ångfartygs A/B, Sweden, *Rosafred** had been built in 1914 at the yard of Kockums MV A/B at Malmo as *Johan Sanne*. She was to spend all her life under the Swedish flag, next as *Oscar* and as *Rosafred* from 1951 until New Years Day 1955 when she went aground in the Gulf of Bothnia whilst nearing the end of a voyage from Amsterdam to Gävle with a cargo of coke. In this photograph on the Thames in the early 1950s, her cargo is probably packages of wood pulp loaded in Sweden for delivery to a paper mill. *Rosafred* measured 233ft overall and her gross tonnage was 1,405.

*Nautik** was owned by J Lauritzen, an Esbjerg owner who has been remarkably successful, having diversified into a number of areas including polar ships and reefers. The Lauritzen business began with importing timber and coal, but by the time *Nautik* was delivered in 1920 the ships were not confined to the Baltic and North Sea trades, but were tramping as far south as the Mediterranean and West Africa. Having sold much of the fleet at a profit during the First World War, Lauritzen then ordered ships in the Netherlands and Germany, *Nautik* coming from Nüsche & Co AG of Stettin. At 224ft and 941gt, she was comparatively large for a three-hold vessel. The ship's name painted in large letters amidships is something of a Lauritzen trademark, and her grey hull was unusual when applied in the late 1920s. *Nautik* was sold to French owners in 1936, and as *Cheik* was torpedoed and sunk by an Italian submarine in the Mediterranean in July 1940. *(World Ship Society Ltd)*

With timber the most frequent cargo for ships working around and out of the Baltic, cargo gear was often placed at the ends of the two wells to give a clear space for the deck cargo. The Norwegian yard of Fredriksstad Mekanisk Verksted became particularly associated with this arrangement, and delivered the 250ft overall *Harald* to Swedish owners in 1915. After a number of changes of name, she was acquired by members of the Påhlsson family in 1929, renamed *P L Påhlsson** and registered at Helsingborg. When photographed having just discharged timber in the Surrey Docks in the 1950s she looks like she has just been repainted. The photograph also shows how bulwarks aft can disguise the fact that she has a poop deck. Like several ageing Baltic ships, she hoisted the Panamanian flag in 1960 as *Peter*. She continued in the Baltic and North Sea trades, managed from Hull, until broken up at Ystad, Sweden in 1967.

As a major exporter of timber, the USSR had several three-island vessels with masts arranged at the end of the wells, favouring the use of kingposts rather than single masts. *Enisei** (also transliterated as *Yenisey*) was bought in 1934 from Dutch owners, for which she had been built in 1916 as *Hillegom* by A F Smulders' wonderfully named Werf 'Gusto' at Schiedam, near Rotterdam. *Enisei* was initially registered in Leningrad for the Baltic timber trades, but moved to Archangel in 1939, which might have contributed to her surviving the Second World War – no mean feat for a Soviet vessel. Secrecy surrounds the fate of many USSR ships, but details are available for *Enisei* because she was sold in 1969 to breakers in Bremen. At 270 ft registered length and 2152 grt, she is the largest vessel in this section, yet can still count as a legitimate short-sea trader. *(Ships in Focus)*

Intermediate in design between the previous two examples is *Britta Christensen*. She is seen in London's Surrey Commercial Docks, unloading timber into lighters using her own gear, which comprised conventional masts at the outer ends of her wells and at the inner ends kingposts that also serve as ventilators. Swedish-built by Oskarshamns Mekaniska Verkstads and owned in Sweden throughout her life, she had been completed in 1915 as *Kalmarsund X* for owners in Kalmar, and was renamed in 1951 upon sale to a company managed by A Th Christensen of Trelleborg. Measuring 235 ft length overall and 1102 grt, *Britta Christensen* was broken up at Gothenburg in 1958.

The North American contribution

In both world wars, North American yards built steamers to the three-island design, and several gravitated to the Baltic trades. Yards on the Great Lakes were particularly involved in both programmes, because the size of canals that connected the Lakes and the Atlantic prohibited construction of ships much longer than 261ft overall.

*Ramsdal** had been completed in April 1919 as *Coperas* by the Manitowoc Shipbuilding Company at the town of that name in Wisconsin. Too late to help the war effort, as were most of her sisters, she was sold by her original owners, United States Shipping Board, in 1926. A variety of names and owners on the Great Lakes followed, but her moment came during the Second World War when the US Navy commissioned her as a transport. War service over, she was bought in 1948 by O/Y Fenno Steamship Co Ltd, Åbo, Finland, which renamed her *Ramsdal*.

With masts and king posts arranged tidily at the end of her well decks, she proved useful for carrying deals, pit props and – far from the Baltic – esparto grass from North Africa to British paper mills. Indeed, a phase of her Finnish career ended when she stranded on the Scottish coast while heading for Granton with a cargo of esparto grass from Arzew in Algeria on 27 May 1964. Although declared a constructive total loss as not economically repairable, other Finnish owners thought otherwise and her forty-six-year-old hull was repaired and she steamed on as *Transdal* until broken up in Helsinki during 1968. Just over 261 ft length overall, her gross tonnage was 2153.

Canada also contributed to the Allied shipbuilding effort during the First World War, in this case with steel and wooden ships ordered by Great Britain to help replace the horrendous losses to U-boats. Again, most were completed too late to be of use during the conflict and, although the wooden ships were soon declared useless, some of the steel-hulled steamers achieved impressive careers.

At 261 ft overall length and 1986 grt, *Eero** was built by the British American Shipbuilding Company at Welland, Ontario. Cargo gear was extensive, and somewhat unusual for the time in incorporating goalpost masts. One advantage of these was that the middle of the deck was not obstructed by mast and masthouses so that large logs or other major articles of deck cargo could be carried. Completed as *War Raccoon* for British account in October 1919, she was quickly sold to French owners as *Shouragallus*, the second of twelve names she was to carry over almost forty years. In the Mediterranean during June 1940, she was in just three years to come under Greek, Vichy French, German, Italian and finally, as the tide of war shifted, Allied control. Helsinki owners Merivienti O/Y acquired her in 1947 and renamed her *Eero* and later *Roine*. Her days ended in June 1958 far from the Baltic, under the name *Mount Adelphi*. Flying the Liberian flag and under ultimate ownership in Greece and managed from London, she hit rocks in heavy weather and sank off Mormugao while on a voyage from Burma to Bahrain with a cargo of timber and rice. *(World Ship Society Ltd)*

A request from Great Britain during the Second World War for ships suitable for use in European coastal waters and a suggestion that the shipbuilding potential of the Great Lakes be better utilised led to the United States Maritime Commission ordering the N3 type of 250-ft steamer to a similar design to ships the United States had built in the First World War. To clear deck cargoes, their gear was stepped high on the three raised decks, but now also included kingposts at the fore end of the bridge deck and at the after end a stump mast, both with pairs of derricks. Practically the last flowering of the three-island steamer, more modern features included cruiser sterns and fittings to burn oil fuel rather than coal – all except the thirty six destined for British use which were coal fired. One of these was the 1791 gt *Bailey Foster*, which was chartered to the British Ministry of War Transport immediately on completion by Walter Butler Shipyards Inc, Superior, Wisconsin in July 1943. The N3 class was closely involved with the D-Day landings, being run ashore on the beaches to unload their cargoes of military supplies.

Once across the North Atlantic *Bailey Foster* remained there after the war, initially with Currie Line Ltd of Leith, for which she ran to Hamburg and Baltic ports at first under her original name and as *Larchland* from 1949. In 1951, she was sold to Erling Mortensen A/S of Oslo, which renamed her *Almora**, as photographed in the Thames Estuary in September 1959. She recrossed the Atlantic in 1964 and after working for Venezuelan owners as *Natividad* was broken up in that country in 1971. *(John G Callis)*

CHAPTER

5

The Collier Develops

Chapter 2 left the specialised steam collier poised on the brink of the 1880s. In terms of designs, much had been worked out, including the engines-aft and engines-amidships variants. With the important exception of the up-river collier, there was to be little innovation in design until the arrival of the motor ship. What did change significantly was, first, the average size of colliers, so that steamers of over 300 feet in length would be used purely on the coast, and eventually colliers were hardly distinguishable from ocean-going bulk carriers.

The move to larger hulls was driven by a number of factors. In the coal trade of the east coast of the UK, where much of the developments chronicled here happened up at least up until the First World War, competition from railways drove owners to build larger ships. Simultaneously, the economies of scale achievable with these bigger colliers encouraged customers in the gas and later the electricity industry to provide facilities for berthing and unloading ever larger examples. British coal exports also grew and large colliers were built that were quite capable of voyages to the Baltic and Mediterranean.

The second major change was in ownership patterns, so that a significant number of colliers were directly owned by the gas and electricity industries rather than by coal merchants or others in the coal trade. The old-established companies did not always lose out from this arrangement, because a new market opened up to manage these ships on behalf of the utility companies. By 1950, for instance, Stephenson Clarke could boast control of a fleet of over one hundred ships.

It needs to be stressed that there is not always a distinction between the collier and other coasters built for the bulk trades. By far the commonest cargo for any steam coaster was coal, and the two types were often interchangeable. On the Irish Sea, for example, standard raised-quarterdeck coasters could spend their entire lives carrying nothing but coal. The colliers illustrated in this chapter were largely owned either by the utility industries or by shipping companies that chose to serve them. Apart from some later developments, such as hopper-shaped holds and the complete omission of cargo gear, ownership and trading patterns were the surest guide to what constituted a collier.

An asterisk in a caption indicates the vessel shown in the photograph.

Engines amidships

Despite the disadvantages of the engines-amidships design discussed in Chapter 2, it remained obstinately popular for larger colliers. Its presumed advantages in terms of stability, trim and strength supported decisions to build to this layout until at least the 1920s.

By the 1890s, the raised-quarterdeck design had crystallised, and was to change little over the next thirty years. *Hurstwood**, owned by Wm Cory & Son Ltd, was an example from 1906, and was relatively small at 1209 grt and 268 ft in length, a size that made her suitable for the coal trade out of Goole on the River Ouse, in which river she was photographed. By 1906, S P Austin & Son Ltd had become one of the major builders of colliers, although not of engines, and it turned to Sunderland engineers George Clark Ltd for triple-expansion machinery that propelled *Hurstwood*. Cargo gear was strictly limited: the foremast carried just one derrick. *Hurstwood* was torpedoed by the German submarine *UB 34* and sank north of Whitby on 5 February 1917. *(C A Hill)*

In contrast to *Hurstwood*, *Eastwood** enjoyed a long life. Built as *Taunton* in 1924, she was part of a massive expansion in the early 1920s of the fleet of H Harrison (Shipping) Ltd, a company related to the J & C Harrison fleet of which had been merged into that of William Cory in 1896. Harrison's resurgence in the coastal and short-sea trade was badly timed given the post-First World War slump in freight rates, and the majority of the company's steamers were soon sold. *Taunton* passed to William France, Fenwick & Co Ltd of London in 1933 for a bargain price of £7300, probably a fifth of her building cost nine years earlier.

A major difference from *Hurstwood* is the raised quarterdeck extended forward, occupying 184 of *Eastwood*'s 254 ft overall length. It is likely that as *Taunton* she had a full set of derricks, because the mountings are in place for these at the foot of her foremast, but all but one had been removed by the time this photograph was taken in the early 1950s. Her radar scanner confirms that this is a post-war photograph. *Eastwood* proudly displays her collier number on her bridge front: this was the number she used to report her arrival at the Tilbury Hailing Station.

Eastwood was sold by France, Fenwick in 1955, but had a few years of life left in her. The London-Greek Tsavliris group ran her briefly as the UK-flagged *Andrew* and the Greek-flagged *Andreas Tsavliris*, before sale to John S Latsis as *Suez*. She was demolished at La Spezia in 1960. *(Ships in Focus)*

The last of the raised-quarterdeck engines-amidships colliers for the coastal trade were Cory's *Corbridge** and *Corminster* of 1928. Externally, the major difference between this 1708-grt, 264-ft pair and the *Hurstwood* was the poop deck built on the after end of the raised quarterdeck to provide accommodation for deckhands and firemen who, in the earlier ships, would be berthed in the forecastle. Builders and engineers were once again S P Austin & Sons Ltd and George Clark Ltd. Both colliers survived the war and found new Greek owners in the 1950s. *Corbridge* went under the Costa Rican flag as *Arion* in 1954, later transferring to the Lebanese flag as *Antonios Ventouris*. She sank in the Aegean in December 1966 while carrying fertiliser from Piræus to Varna.

One of the very few innovations in collier building was the Ayre-Ballard arch-deck design, twenty-seven of which were built, including *Ayton**. The major characteristic of the arch deck vessel was that the upper part of the hull was radiused inwards. The frames stopped where the deck would be placed in a conventional ship, and were joined to the deck beams by arched brackets. The designers claimed that the strength of the radiused plates allowed less steel to be used, saving on cost. However, the ships' real appeal to owners was that freeboard and hence carrying capacity was increased. The ships were also claimed to have particularly good sea-keeping qualities.

Of 2117 grt and 275 ft registered length, *Ayton* was the twenty-fifth arch deck ship built, launched by the Burntisland Shipbuilding Co Ltd as *Carlbeath* in October 1924. As *Ayton*, she is seen in the colours of J B Shipping Co Ltd of Middlesbrough when running in the British East Coast coal trade between 1949 and 1956. Again, she has just one derrick, and is of the two-island design, with no bridge deck. As the Italian-owned, Panama-flagged *Alcyone* she stranded on Crete and was abandoned in August 1958. Refloated and taken to Piræus, she was not broken up until 1961, by which time she was the last surviving arch deck ship.

Engines aft

Compared with the popularity of the engines-amidships collier, the engines-aft version – which was after all in the mould of the original *John Bowes* – took a time to re-establish itself. An early example is the 200-ft, 917-grt *Corbet Woodall** built in 1908 by S P Austin & Son Ltd. She was named to flatter an eminent man in a gas company, among which numbered Stephenson Clarke's major customers.

Corbet Woodall was of the less usual raised-quarterdeck type with two holds forward of the bridge and one aft. This trials shot shows she had a full set of derricks to suit the harbours on the south coast of England, where her owners held contracts to supply gas works and later power stations.

Yet another victim of the First World War, *Corbet Woodall* was bound from the Tyne to Poole with a cargo of coal when mined near the Nab Light Vessel in May 1917.

The more usual arrangement for an engines-aft collier was to have one hold forward and one aft of the bridge. Another Stephenson Clarke collier, *Pulborough** (1) of 1933, has this layout and – unusually – a minimum of masts, with just a pole foremast to display navigation lights. It was clearly expected that she would serve all her days to a harbour such as Shoreham where there was adequate unloading equipment.

Pulborough's days were in fact rather short: in July 1940 she was hit by the Luftwaffe as she passed Dover Pier on passage from the Tyne to Shoreham. Fortunately, her crew was saved. *Pulborough* had an overall length of 205 ft and a tonnage of 960 gross. She had been built in 1933 by the Burntisland Shipbuilding Co Ltd, one of the major rivals to Austin for collier building in the inter-war years. *(World Ship Society Ltd)*

Enlargement of the engines-aft raised quarterdecker invariably produced a four-hold layout, and this became the dominant type in the coal trade out of the UK and elsewhere. The familiar combination of S P Austin and Stephenson Clarke produced *Vaux** of 1920, 1830 grt and 260 ft registered length. Her ownership was nominally in the hands of the Normandy Shipping Co Ltd, a joint venture between Stephenson Clarke and the Powell Duffryn Steam Coal Co Ltd, intended to export coal from South Wales to France. It was short-lived, and the sale of *Vaux* to French owners in 1925 marked the closure of this venture. Named *Nantaise*, the ship fell into German hands in 1940 and was torpedoed and sunk by the Royal Navy submarine HMS *Rorqual* in the Aegean in August 1943.

No excuse is offered for illustrating a second vessel of the four-hold type, *Gripfast*, because the design was almost ubiquitous. So much so, that the wartime construction programme of the British government made provision for this type of collier, William Gray & Co Ltd of West Hartlepool building hulls and machinery for nine during 1940–46. Only four survived the Second World War, and as *Stancliffe* this particular ship was lucky to come through a serious grounding in April 1947. Entering Sharpness Docks from the River Severn with timber from Emden, she stranded and broke her back. When refloated over two months later, underwriters declared her uneconomic to repair, but the Newbigin Steam Shipping Co Ltd of Newcastle thought otherwise, bought the wreck and returned her to service in 1948 as *Gripfast*. By the time she was photographed her derricks had gone, but the supports for her winches remain: even designated as a collier in wartime she would have been expected to carry heavy items as deck cargo and to load and unload these herself. Newbigin sold *Gripfast* in 1960 and in December 1967 under her sixth name as *Pitsa* she sank west of Sri Lanka. Her tonnage when completed as *Empire Brook* was 2852 gross and her overall length 321ft.

Gas industry ownership

The London gas industry's important role in the development of the screw collier in the 1850s was outlined in Chapter 2. Throughout the nineteenth century, the industry preferred to charter its colliers rather than own them, and only in 1902 did the independently minded Commercial Gas Company begin what became a wholesale move towards collier ownership. In the case of Commercial and Wandsworth & Putney District Gas Company, the motivation was to build ships specifically suited to serve their gas works, situated respectively on Bow Creek in east London and at Wandsworth in the west.

Commercial Gas Company's *Stepney** was a relatively conventional collier, completed in 1916 to help deliver coal to works that the company had acquired at Wapping, and she did not require any special features. The almost complete absence of derricks indicates that the Wapping works had more than adequate craneage. Builder was R Williamson & Son, Workington, and dimensions 186 ft registered length and tonnage 808 gross. The gas company sold *Stepney* in 1944 but she stayed on the coast, initially owned in London as *Durhambrook*, then moving to Liverpool-based owners as *Kyleburn*. The new owners progressively upgraded her cargo gear, first fitting a topmast to her stump of a main and later two full height masts both with derricks. *Kyleburn* was broken up at Llanelly in 1957. *(National Maritime Museum P13187)*

For both the mighty Gas, Light & Coke Company and the South Metropolitan Gas Company, acquisition of a fleet of colliers became a necessity early in the First World War. The former company had dipped its toe into the market in 1912 with *Fulgens* from Wood, Skinner & Co Ltd on the Tyne; a big collier of 305 ft registered length and 2512 grt.

Fulgen's loss to a torpedo off Haisboro' in August 1915 rang alarm bells, and to maintain their coal supplies both Gas, Light & Coke Company and the South Metropolitan rushed to buy whatever steamers they could, including old sea-going steamers of considerable vintage. The war convinced both these major gas companies of the wisdom of controlling their own ships, and in the succeeding years the distress purchases were gradually replaced with proper colliers. These were in all respects similar to those they had previously chartered: indeed, *Brockley** was a war-built standard ship, laid down for the British government's Shipping Controller and completed in September 1920 by the Dublin Dockyard Co Ltd for the South Metropolitan Gas Company. She is seen following nationalisation of the gas industry in 1949 when her owners became the South Eastern Gas Board, and as such she was photographed in May 1958. Although still looking smart, *Brockley* was almost at the end of a respectably long career; just four months later, in September, she steamed into the New Waterway heading for Utrecht and the breakers. *(John G Callis)*

The nationalised British utilities carried on building steam colliers right into the 1950s, when most owners had forsaken triple-expansion engines for the more economical diesel. The North Thames Gas Board, as the former Gas, Light and Coke Company had become on nationalisation in 1949, took five gearless, oil-fired colliers of 339 ft in 1954 and 1955. The fourth of these was *John Orwell Phillips** of 339 grt, delivered by William Pickersgill and Sons Ltd, Sunderland.

The gas industry's ships became redundant almost at a stroke in the late sixties as gas came from the North Sea rather than being produced by carbonisation of coal. Nevertheless, the steamers had much life left in them and most had substantial further careers. *John Orwell Phillips* was an exception: as *Agios Fanourios* a collision in dense fog in ther Fehmarn Belt during April 1971 sealed her fate, and she was broken up in Norway later that year.
(Ships in Focus)

Electricity industry ownership

In the 1930s, electricity suppliers followed the lead of the gas companies in ordering colliers. Indeed, the strategy for building power stations was partly predicated on supplying these by water, with London Power Company building its station at Battersea and Fulham Borough Council its own giant power station slightly upriver and on the north bank of the Thames. Both concerns initially ordered up-river colliers, but London Power Company also had a station at Deptford, which could take conventional ships. This was supplied by the 1933-built *Francis Fladgate* and the 1946-built *Oliver Bury**. The latter was a big collier at 326 ft overall length and 2904 grt, built by the Burntisland Shipbuilding Co Ltd. Indeed, ordering the *Oliver Bury* was far-sighted because the Labour government that came to power in Great Britain in 1945 was intent on nationalising the public utility companies, and after less than two years *Oliver Bury* passed to the newly formed British Electricity Authority, in whose colours she appears, deep-laden, inward bound on the Thames. The oil-burning steamer was sold in 1970 and after a few years under the flag of Cyprus as *Alycia* was broken up in Italy in 1973.

A large class of medium-sized colliers came into the nationalised electricity fleet by a circuitous route. In March 1946, the three major competing collier owners – France, Fenwick, Cory and Stephenson Clarke – set up Coastwise Colliers Ltd with the objective of chartering ships long term to the County of London Electricity Supply Co Ltd, a large utility company that had a power station on the Thames at Littlebrook. Coastwise Colliers had wider ambitions, and ordered ten steam colliers from Sunderland to run mainly to power stations in the south west of England with Yorkshire coal loaded at Goole, the locks at this river port restricting their length to 235 feet. Nationalisation of the electricity industry forced a rethink: Coastwise Colliers Ltd was wound up and the ten new colliers (three of which had been delivered) were transferred to the nationalised British Electricity Authority. *Polden**, seen on the River Ouse outward bound from Goole, was delivered by S P Austin & Son Ltd in April 1950, as the eighth of the group. Conversion of many power stations to oil fuel ensured early redundancy for these neat little steamers, but all found new and useful employment, six as cement carriers with the Blue Circle Group. Sold in 1967, *Polden* was one of three that went to Italy and were converted into tankers, the conversion completed in 1969 extending her life by ten years. As *Stintino* she was scrapped at La Spezia in 1979. *(C A Hill)*

The dubious distinction of being the final steam colliers built and the last in regular service goes to a quintet built for the nationalised electricity industry. Almost contemporaries with the gas industry's ultimate ships, they were of similar length and differed largely in having a more rounded design of funnel. The 2947-grt *Charles H Merz** came from the Aberdeen yard of Hall, Russell & Co Ltd in November 1955, five months after the last sister of *John Orwell Phillips*. Because the electricity industry continued to use coal, although in diminishing quantities, these steamers worked on beyond the 1970s. *Charles H Merz* was one of the first to go, in 1976, steaming on as *Eagle I* under the Panamanian flag until French breakers took her in 1980. The very last steamer was the slightly older sister *James Rowan*, not broken up until 1984 and bringing to an end over 130 years of steam collier operation on the east coast of the United Kingdom.

As this book is being compiled in 2011, coal-fired power stations remain in operation, and one or two in southeast England are still served by sea, although coal now comes from continental Europe rather than the Tyne or Wear. The ships that have recently brought the coal are the descendants of the steam collier, bulk carriers which will probably be the last vessels owned by the British electricity industry, which is now – controversially – back in private hands.

Delivered by Govan Shipbuilders, Glasgow in 1985 and 1986, *Lord Citrine**, *Lord Hinton* and *Sir Charles Parsons* have dimensions of 155 metres length overall and 14,201 grt. Essentially, these colliers are medium-sized bulk carriers, not at all surprising since the pioneer screw colliers of the 1850s were the progenitors of this modern ship type, with engines aft, large hatch covers, and water ballast capacity adequate for voyages without cargo.

Of the trio, *Lord Citrine* (photographed from the Eskine Bridge on her delivery voyage) was sold in 2000 to become *Sider Bay* and now runs as the Chinese *Jin Bin*. *Sir Charles Parsons* was sold to Turkish owners during 2010 to become *Barko*. Only *Lord Hinton* remained with the electricity industry in 2011, its owner being E-on UK plc. Quite likely, coal-fired power stations served by water will be phased out during the next decade, ending a connection between shipping and the utility industries that began in the 1850s. *(Jim Prentice)*

Up-river steam and motor colliers

In several cases, gas and electricity concerns built their works on stretches of the Thames which conventional ships were incapable of reaching thanks to low bridges crossing the river. Originally, coal was unloaded from steam colliers to lighters for the last stage of the journey, but the extra handling was costly and reduced the quality of the coal. To serve these facilities was developed the low-air-draught, up-river collier or 'flat iron'. The first were built in 1878 and 1879 by Palmers' Shipbuilding & Iron Co, Newcastle for London owners to serve a gas works at Nine Elms.

No photos are known of these pioneers, but their appearance was probably not unlike *Suntrap**, with minimal superstructure, and masts and funnel that folded on to the deck to clear the bridges. *Suntrap* was built in 1929 to serve Nine Elms Gas Works of the Gas, Light & Coke Company. This concern had its major works down river at Beckton, but also had sites at Nine Elms, taken over from the London Gas Light Company, and at Fulham, for both of which it needed up-river colliers.

Dimensions of *Suntrap* were 225 ft length overall and tonnage 939 gross. Builders were R & W Hawthorn, Leslie & Co Ltd on the Tyne, a yard usually associated with much bigger ships but which would be pleased to receive any orders in the shipbuilding depression of the late 1920s. She survived the Second World War to be sold to Goole owners in 1954, which ran her as *Sunfleet* until she was delivered to breakers in the Netherlands in September 1958. *(J and M Clarkson)*

The gas works of Wandsworth, Wimbledon & Epsom District Gas Company at Wandsworth in south-west London could only be reached by colliers that could pass under no fewer than seventeen Thames bridges. This relatively small gas company was particularly innovative, enjoying a reputation for producing London's lowest priced gas. Its manager, C M Croft, designed up-river colliers with the maximum capacity and with the aim of making its shipping operations as efficient as possible.

Built at Burntisland in 1924, *Woodcote* at 1242 grt and 220 ft registered length could handle 1725 tons of coal, but it was later found possible to bring motor colliers up to 275 ft in length to Wandsworth and these could carry 2875 tons. It was the practice for the colliers to come up river on the ebb tide so they had maximum steerage way for the delicate process of passing under bridges. Unloading was completed in four to five hours, allowing the colliers to get away on the next tide.

In 1934, *Woodcote* was replaced with a larger collier and was sold to Stephenson Clarke and as *Cerne** she worked on for over twenty years. Although chartered to Fulham Borough Council to supply its power station, she was not confined to voyages to the Thames and also worked to the harbours on the south coast of England which the owners served. She was broken up on the Tyne in 1955.

The London Power Co Ltd was formed in the 1920s as an amalgamation of several small electricity suppliers, and planned to build two major power stations at Deptford and at Battersea, the latter becoming the largest in the world. Six up-river colliers were ordered to supply Battersea and began arriving in 1932, the third being *John Hopkinson** from S P Austin & Sons Ltd. At 236 ft overall length and 1314 grt, she was similar in size to contemporary Wandsworth colliers. The photograph was taken in the Pool of London during August 1950 and shows *John Hopkinson* with her gear lowered ready to clear London Bridge. The funnel can just be seen above the starboard boat, bearing the letters BEA for British Electricity Authority, the owners following nationalisation in 1948. *John Hopkinson* lasted until broken up by Thomas Ward at Grays, Essex in 1959, long enough to briefly swap BEA markings for those of the Central Electricity Authority, formed in 1958. *(World Ship Society Ltd)*

The last undertaking to adopt the up-river collier was Fulham Borough Council, which built a power station almost as large as that at Battersea. With no rail connections, supply of the 750 tons of coal the station required each week was to be entirely by coastal collier. Following a request for tenders to supply coal, Fulham decided to buy its own colliers, the first arriving from Burntisland in 1936. The Council was progressive in its outlook and – despite impending nationalisation – ordered the first of the up-river colliers to be given diesel engines, *Fulham VIII** (imaginative names were not the Borough's forte). She was delivered in December 1947 by Burntisland Shipbuilding Co Ltd, which had supplied Fulham's previous seven colliers, and measured 270 ft overall length and 1773 grt. Her engines were built at Stockport in Cheshire by Mirrlees, Bickerton & Day Ltd. The more compact engine room layout possible with a motor ship, which needed neither boilers nor coal bunkers, allowed more space for holds and an improved coal capacity compared with a steamer, which was a major consideration with an up-river collier, for which overall dimensions were strictly limited. In the photograph, an unladen *Fulham VIII* has one anchor down and appears to be using it to turn in the river. Having passed to the nationalised British Electricity Authority within months of delivery, she ran to Fulham Power Station until 1969 when broken up at Antwerp. *(World Ship Society Ltd)*

Motor colliers

Collier operators were slow to adopt the diesel. One reason given was that customers in the coal business would not look kindly on shipping companies that turned their back on coal as fuel. This was a feeble excuse because the major customers for the colliers' services were gas and electricity undertakings that had no interest beyond getting their supplies as cheaply and regularly as possible. A more likely reason was the lack of engineers experienced with diesels, a problem lamented on several times by the owners, which did little to train such men or encourage those with a motor ship ticket to apply.

In 1936, Wm France, Fenwick & Co Ltd took delivery of two relatively small motor colliers from Henry Robb of Leith, *Rookwood* and *Lockwood* of 177 ft registered length, but sold both within three years, and was so unimpressed that they ordered no motor ships for over twenty years. Of the major British owners, the first to build a large motor collier was Stephenson Clarke, with the 225-ft, 1108-grt *Seaford**, completed by S P Austin & Son Ltd in 1947. One of the ships in this fleet with no cargo gear and no provision to add any, her tall funnel makes it hard to distinguish her from a steamer. She was clearly a success, because further ships of this size built for Stephenson Clarke were all motor vessels, although the company clung to steam for two 344-ft colliers, *Borde* and *Arundel*, delivered in 1953 and 1956 respectively. *Seaford* was retained in the fleet until 1971, when she went to the Mediterranean for a succession of Greek owners, and remained there until broken up in 1992. *(World Ship Society Ltd)*

William Cory & Son Ltd watched the development of motor colliers with caution, and did not take delivery of any until 1952 – the 272-ft *Corbrae* from Burntisland, followed in 1953 by the 279ft *Corburn** from the Goole Shipbuilding & Repairing Co Ltd. Again gearless and retaining the familiar raised quarterdeck, these represented another important development in that the bridges were mounted aft and united with the rest of the superstructure. Not only did this give a clear deck space to facilitate the use of mechanised loading and discharge gear, but it also reduced construction costs because services such as water and electricity did not need to be duplicated in bridge and accommodation. While not adopted immediately – Cory reverted to the bridge-amidships layout for bigger colliers such as the 339-ft *Corsea* of 1957 – this layout became the norm.

Judged by her longevity, the 2059-grt *Corburn* was a success. She was sold to Greek owners in 1972 and put under the Cypriot flag as *Aigeorgis*, this being shortened to *Giorgis* on transfer to the Greek flag in 1976. She was broken up at Brindisi in 1979.

Corbrae spent 1971–73 working for Cory's rival collier owners Stephenson Clarke as *Brightling*. Later, under Greek ownership, she traded down to the Mediterranean, and under the name *Verza* stranded in fog on the French coast south of Guernsey in March 1974 when bound from Casablanca to Granville with a cargo of phosphate. *(J and M Clarkson)*

The next logical development was to forget the raised-quarterdeck layout in favour of a two-island design, simplifying construction. As with the last electicity industry colliers, the result was essentially a small bulk carrier strengthened for heavy cargoes. Stephenson Clarke's *Donnington** of 1975 and her sisters *Dallington* of 1975 and *Durrington* of 1981 were by no means confined to the British east coast coal trade, which in any case had now been reduced to a shadow of its former self: these colliers probably loaded coal in Poland as often as in Newcastle. They also broke with tradition by being supplied by a non-UK yard, Verolme Scheepswerf Heusden BV in the Netherlands. At 451 ft overall length and 7788 grt, *Donnington* exemplifies the difficulty of defining a coaster: although intended for coastal trading she is bigger than most ocean-going ships built when the first screw colliers emerged in 1852. She is seen in the Thames Estuary in April 1978, waiting for a berth at Tilbury or Kingsnorth Power Station.

Donnington was sold to Italian owners in 2007 and renamed *Sider Genova*, and as such she now works mainly in the Mediterranean. In 2011 only *Durrington* is still working for Stephenson Clark Shipping Ltd, although this ancient concern – the oldest surviving British shipping company – passed from its previous owners, Powell Duffryn, to the International Maritime Group in 1997. *(Author)*

'Les PLMs'

With the exception of the previous ship, the procession of ships in this chapter has been remorselessly British, which reflects that the British east coast coal trade was not just of pre-eminent importance, but it also stimulated many of the developments in collier building, at least until British yards and owners lost their way in the 1960s.

One of the largest orders to British yards from outside of the UK came from the Compagnie des Chemins de Fer de Paris et à Lyon à la Mediterranée, unsurprisingly known as PLM. The French railway company bought its locomotive coal from British, north French or Dutch ports and shipped it to Port du Bouc near Marseilles, which was a long voyage that can be construed as coastal in that the ships were seldom out of sight of land.

Like certain London gas companies, the railway had been panicked into buying ships to maintain coal supplies during the First World War, but was so convinced of the usefulness of having its own fleet that it invested heavily in colliers after the war. Six 345-ft colliers were ordered from Smith's Dock Co Ltd, Middlesbrough, emerging as *PLM 12* to *PLM 17* in 1920 and 1921. They were relatively conventional four-hatch, three-island, bridge-amidships steamers, propelled by triple-expansion engines made by their hull builder.

Larger and more innovative were *PLM 21* to *PLM 27*, delivered by another Middlesbrough yard, Sir Raylton Dixon & Co Ltd, during 1920–22. Of 414 ft, these were among the first ships fitted with steel hatch covers and with gear to mechanically raise and lower these. They also had quadruple-expansion engines, unheard of in British-owned colliers, and indeed rare in all but large, powerful, ocean-going passenger ships.

The Second World War dealt harshly with both groups, some of which came under Allied control and some German. The 3442-grt *PLM 13** was photographed by the United States Coast Guard at New York in October 1942 after her capture by the Royal Navy in February 1941. She was returned to her French owners after the war and survived until 1961, latterly under Finnish and Greek ownership.

The 5529-grt 'grand PLM' *PLM 22** also came under British control as a result of being in the Tyne to load coal when France fell in June 1940. She was less fortunate in war than *PLM 13*, and was torpedoed south-west of the Canary Islands in June 1941 when carrying ore from Pepel in Sierra Leone to the Tees. *(William Schell; F W Hawks)*

Continental colliers

Even when Continental European owners built their ships elsewhere, designs developed largely by British yards were often followed. 'Polskarob', or to give it its full title, Polsko Skandynawskie Towarzystwo Transportowe SA, was set up in the mid-1920s by a group of collieries in Upper Silesia to export coal to Scandinavia through the newly opened port of Gdynia. Beginnng with a mixed bag of ageing British-built colliers, the company then started its own building programme with orders to Swedish, Dutch and British yards. The two completed by Lindholmen-Motala at Gothenburg in 1930, *Robur IV* and *Robur V*, were 258 ft long, of 1975 grt and might have been built in the UK except that they lacked a raised quarterdeck. *Robur V* is shown in the late 1950s when she was named *Saxonia** and owned in Hamburg: she had already flown the Polish, Panamanian and Belgian flags, and was to go on to be Italian. She was broken up in Yugoslavia in 1968. *(Schiffsfotos Jansen)*

A variation on the raised-quarterdeck theme with very distinctive mast arrangements was built in the Netherlands for NV Scheepvaart en Steenkolen Maatschappij. This Rotterdam company was founded in 1896 and specialised in importing British steam coal into the Netherlands, later expanding into the liner trade with regular services from Rotterdam and Harlingen to ports on the east coasts of England and Scotland. Until 1916, it was contented with owning traditional engines-amidships, raised-quarterdeck colliers built mainly in Dutch yards. In 1915, began a series of five engines-aft steamers with a novel, and probably unique, set of four bipod masts; the attraction being that fewer stays were needed. The middle pair of masts were connected with a bar above the bridge, while the forward and aft bipods had a forestay and backstay respectively.

The example shown is *Foreland**, 1858 grt and 262 ft, built in 1915 by Scheepswerft v/h J Smit at Alblasserdam for an associated company as *Dirksland*, other examples coming from Scheepswerf van Jan Smit Czn at Alblasserdam. *Foreland*, as she was renamed in 1930, was actually owned by a British subsidiary, Shipping & Coal Co Ltd of London until 1937 when sold to another British owner. As *Stanforth* she just survived the Second World War, running ashore on the Swedish coast in August 1945 while on a voyage with timber from Kalix to London. *(Ships in Focus)*

Some examples of a distinctive type of collier were built in Germany, mainly for the Stinnes family and their various ship owning subsidiaries. *Corstream** was built in 1912 as *Helene Hugo Stinnes 14*, the figure after the name being a Stinnes tradition to indicate the order in which the ship entered the fleet. Builder was G Seebeck AG at Geestemünde, tonnage 1735 gross, length 259 ft and propulsion by a triple-expansion engine. After service with the Kaiserliche Marine in the First World War as *Kohlenschiff 15*, she was initially seized by the new state of Latvia, but in 1920 was handed over to the British government, which sold it to Cory Colliers Ltd as *Corstream*, as seen here on an unusual call at Bristol. For a non-standard ship, she did well to clock up thirteen years of work with Cory. Greek owners then took her and, when named *Memas*, she was torpedoed by *U 97* and sank off Haifa during June 1942.

CHAPTER

6

The Coastal Tanker

Coastal tankers have been built to carry a wide range of cargoes. Some of the earliest transported the tar and creosote produced by gas works. Soon, however, these were eclipsed in number by vessels serving the oil industry, carrying refined petroleum products including paraffin and motor spirit, heavy bunker fuel, lubricating oil, bitumen and asphalt. The 1950s saw the development of tankers for liquefied petroleum or other gases, while ships capable of carrying a wide variety of liquid chemicals also multiplied in post-Second World War years. Beginning by loading acids and alkalis, these specialist ships extended their capabilities to accommodate the large range of commodities routinely shipped between petrochemical complexes and manufacturers. Indeed, if it is a liquid and can be practically and economically carried in bulk, a tanker has probably been designed to carry it, as witness the vessels designed to carry water, treated sewage, beer, wine, edible oils, molasses, printing ink and china clay slurry. Basic coastal tankers once carried almost any product available, but regulations have increasingly restricted certain cargoes to ships with specialised features (especially tank coatings), and the same has happened to officers, who require chemical or gas endorsements to their certificates.

The hull of a coastal tanker comprises a series of tanks, usually built in pairs either side of a centre-line bulkhead and with wing tanks in larger vessels, with transverse divisions to reduce surging. Tanks need to be filled almost to capacity to minimise the tendency of the cargo to slop around and potentially cause a serious list. Because liquids expand when heated, many vessels have expansion trunks raised above main deck level, narrow enough so that slopping does not affect trim. Internally, tanks are separated from the engine room and accommodation by void spaces or cofferdams, to contain any leakage of inflammable liquid or gas. Coastal tankers often need to discharge independently of shoreside equipment and have self-contained pump rooms, often located between the tanks and the engine room to provide a further barrier to any escaping gas.

Cleaning between different cargoes is an essential but difficult task, and petroleum products tend to classed as either 'clean' or 'dirty', depending on how much effort is required to prepare the tanks for a more sensitive cargo. Tank washing machines are usually installed and these direct a jet of high-pressure, and sometimes hot, water at the tank sides.

The captions and photographs in this chapter first trace the development of coastal tankers devoted to carrying petroleum products, then look at other more specialised types of vessel.

An asterisk in a caption indicates the vessel shown in the photograph.

Tar and oil

In terms of numbers built, coastal tankers lagged well behind their ocean-going brethren, and multiplied only once the petrochemical industry developed in the years between the world wars. Many of the earliest coastal tankers were built not to carry petroleum and its products but other liquids such as tar, creosote or edible oils. As early as 1883, William Butler & Company of Bristol had the steamer *Clifton Grove* built locally to collect tar produced as a by-product of gas works and deliver it to the company's works.

The tar tanker shown is the 382-grt, 148-ft *Alchymist** of 1895, built by William Dobson & Co at Newcastle-upon-Tyne for timber processors Burt, Boulton & Haywood Ltd to carry creosote to treat railway sleepers. *Alchymist* had a long career, the majority of it spent with the well-known Greenhithe-based dry cargo coaster and tanker owner F T Everard & Sons Ltd, which sold her for scrap 1950 after several months in lay-up. *(Ships in Focus)*

The first major order for small tankers was placed by the British Admiralty, who realised before the First World War that the increasing numbers of warships burning oil would require ships to carry and dispense this fuel. Although not the first of these 'oilers' (this was *Petroleum* bought in 1905), the best known of the smaller Admiralty vessels were a class of fourteen steam and four oil-engined 221-ft *Creosol* class ships launched in 1916–17. These had the bridge structure placed well forward and a tall trunk rose above the well deck. Part of their familiarity stems from ten being sold out of Admiralty service to civilian owners that used them both to distribute refined petroleum products from refineries and to bunker ships in port.

The 1178-grt *Scotol* of 1916 was sold to Hemsley Bell Ltd of Southampton in 1947. Renamed *Hemsley-I**, she was photographed in September 1967 on the Mersey, where bunkering activities and some longer voyages kept her occupied until 1969. In May of that year, she was sold for scrap, but managed to cheat the breakers in spectacular fashion. On her delivery voyage from the Mersey to Antwerp, in fog and with little in the way of navigational aids, she steamed into the Bristol Channel rather than the English Channel and piled up on rocks about six miles from Padstow. There was no chance of salvage and a career of fifty-three years came to a somewhat ignominious end. *(Author)*

One of the first oil companies to own coastal tankers under the British flag was the Standard Oil Company of New Jersey, later known as Esso, which registered its British ships under its subsidiary Anglo-American Oil Co Ltd. Its first coaster was *Osceola**, built by D J Dunlop & Co, Port Glasgow in 1897. With her foresail and derricks, she looks exactly like a contemporary – if rather anachronistic – steam coaster, but in *Lloyd's Register* is described as 'carrying petroleum in bulk'. She was mainly employed distributing to depots round the coast the kerosene that was delivered by ocean-going tankers from the United States to Anglo-American's depot at Purfleet. This 393-grt, 141-ft steamer survived one of the earliest attacks on shipping by an aircraft, in the North Sea on 22 March 1915, but lived on to be scrapped at South Stockton on the River Tees in 1934. She was photographed on the River Humber. *(M Barnard)*

Early oil company motor vessels

The tankers of the National Benzole Co Ltd were, like *Alchymist*, also associated with the gas industry. The owners bought a by-product of gas manufacture, benzole, and sold it to oil companies that blended it with products of petroleum refining to produce motor spirit. National Benzole's first tanker, the Dutch-built *Ialine* of 1913, was bought from Burt, Boulton & Haywood Ltd in 1923 and renamed *Ben Sadler*. Most of the company's further tankers were built for them, eight coming from Rowhedge Ironworks Co Ltd, near Colchester. Orders began with the second *Ben Sadler* of 1931 and kept the yard working during the difficult years between the wars.

The 377-grt *Ben Henshaw** was completed at Rowhedge in 1933 with two Gardner diesels driving her twin screws. Just 142 ft overall length, she had four pairs of tanks, separated from her engine room by the pump room and the oil bunkers. Loading light, inflammable cargoes, a spark arrestor was fitted on her funnel and a flame-proof, electric motor installed to drive the windlass.

Shortly before the National Benzole fleet passed to Shell-Mex & BP Ltd, *Ben Henshaw* was sold in 1956 to a London company that renamed her *Grantez* for conversion to a dry cargo coaster. However, within a few months she passed to a West Country sand and aggregate company and underwent a leisurely conversion into a suction dredger, completed in 1959. She was renamed *Stowmead* and was fitted with replacement oil engines made in 1944. Working out of Padstow in July 1977, *Stowmead* grounded and broke her back. Given her forty-four years, she was not worth repairing and was broken up locally. *(World Ship Society Ltd)*

In the 1920s, oil companies and a few independent ship owners built coastal tankers to move the growing volumes of petroleum products from refineries to waterside depots, from where it would be distributed by rail or, increasingly, by road tankers. Given the oil companies' business, it is not surprising that they often specified diesel machinery for their coastal tankers. Although coaster owners in Britain are rightly criticised for the tardiness with which they adopted the oil engine, those running coastal tankers were a notable exception, with diesel-engined tankers outnumbering diesel dry cargo vessels in British fleets between the wars.

The diesel-driven *British Thrift* was built and engined by Swan, Hunter & Wigham Richardson Ltd in 1928. Her impressively long career involved several owners with famous names in oil shipping. She was ordered by British Tanker Co Ltd and when this company entered a joint marketing operation for the UK with another oil major in 1936 she became *Shelbrit 2*, with managers and later owners Shell-Mex & BP Ltd. This ugly name lasted until 1952, when it was replaced by *Shell Loader**, shortly after which she was re-engined with a Crossley diesel, her new measurements being 707 grt and 194 ft length overall. She was photographed at Swansea, where she was initially registered and where she would frequently load products of British Petroleum's Llandarcy refinery. She remained in British waters until 1961, when she became a very small part of the mighty tanker fleet of Stavros Niarchos. Renamed *Amphitrite* under the Greek flag, she was not broken up until 1985.

Ungainly sounding names were not unusual among oil companies, as exemplified by *Rusoilprod**. This was an acronym of Russian Oil Products Ltd of London, UK, distributors of petroleum products originating in the territories of Soviet Russia. Of 836 grt and 190 ft, she too was a motor ship, given an MAN diesel, although her hull was built in 1930 by Charles Hill & Sons Ltd at Bristol, the port in which she was registered. The funnel positioned well aft, as in *Shell Loader*, was for some years a characteristic of oil-engined coastal tankers, reflecting the position of the engine's exhaust. Despite having an internal-combustion engine for propulsion, her auxiliary machinery was a mix of electrical and steam-driven equipment, reflecting the slowness with which electrical auxiliaries such as windlasses were developed. *Rusoilprod* had three pairs of cargo tanks, the derrick on her single mast showing that she also had a small hold forward for other forms of cargo, which might include specialist oils in drums.

Demonstrating the identity of her real owners, *Rusoilprod* was transferred to the Russian flag in 1936 and was subsequently renamed *Mikhail Gromov*. Her days ended in the Black Sea when she was mined and sunk on 2 June 1942 during a voyage from the oil port of Tuapse to Sevastopol. *(J and M Clarkson)*

Independently-owned tankers

Alongside the company-owned ships, a small number of independents operated coastal tankers for long-term or spot charter to the oil majors. A notably long-standing example was Christopher Rowbotham & Sons, an owner that once specialised in carrying stores for the British Admiralty. When the Admiralty decided in 1925 that it could do this work itself, Rowbotham needed to seek another trade, and bought the twenty-year-old steamer *Lochside*, which had been used to carry barrels of beer from the Tyne to London. Sent to a Tyneside yard to have tanks fitted in her holds, she emerged as *Helmsman* in 1927, but within a few months disappeared during a voyage along the east coast. Undeterred, the company fitted out another, even older, steamer with tanks, and this ship, renamed *Steersman*, was sufficiently successful that Rowbotham went ahead and ordered a small motor tanker from a Dutch yard which was delivered as *Tillerman** in 1931. Her early charterers included Russian Oil Products Ltd and Trinidad Leaseholds Ltd (better known in later years as a constituent of Regent Oil Co Ltd) for which this 115-ft motor ship would traverse the Exeter Ship Canal to serve an oil depot. The 220-grt *Tillerman* gave Rowbotham thirty-two years of service and was the first of over forty mostly diesel-driven tankers built or acquired by the company until it lost its identity when bought by P&O in 1993.

The more conservative British owners preferred steam machinery, initial cost of which was lower than a diesel and which was familiar to engine room personnel. One such was the Bulk Oil Steamship Co Ltd, formed in 1921 as a subsidiary of Thames wharfingers and lightermen James W Cook & Co Ltd. Bulk Oil's first tanker was the 1903-built *Isla*, an Admiralty spirit carrier. Renamed *Pass of Brander* as the pioneer of a delightful naming scheme proposed by one of its executives, Captain Douglas Cable, she also carried funnel markings incorporating a purple band between two white bands, colours inspired by the ribbons of the Military Cross Cable had won during the First World War.

Carrying edible oils between the continent and the Thames, *Pass of Brander* gave the young company the confidence to design its own tanker, built by Blythswood Shipbuilding Co Ltd in 1926 as *Pass of Melfort**, 757 grt and 193 ft overall length, and photographed in July 1952. The owner's confidence was considerable, as few oil companies had yet built depots with water access, and *Pass of Melfort* spent her first years moving edible oils. In this employment her steam machinery was an advantage because steam heating coils were needed in the tanks to ensure that viscous oils could be discharged. *Pass of Melfort* and her successors eventually moved into the oil trades.

Despite her machinery, *Pass of Melfort* had an extended career. Sold in 1959, she spent ten years in Greek ownership as *Theo P G* and *Aghios Nicolaos*, before being broken up at Perama. Bulk Oil itself lost its independence in 1958 on becoming part of the William Cory group. *(World Ship Society Ltd)*

The yard of the Blythswood Shipbuilding Co Ltd at Scotstoun specialised in tanker construction and in 1934 it built a rather more modern-looking steamer than *Pass of Melfort* for the Hadley Shipping Co Ltd. This is a concern never afraid of diversification, which may be why it is still trading when so many British companies have given up ship owning. Hadley's *Bassethound** was comparatively large at 233 ft overall length and 1174 grt. She was delivered at a very difficult time for shipping and spent some time idle and of necessity carried some decidedly unusual cargoes, including a shipment of whale oil loaded in Labrador and delivered across the Atlantic to Copenhagen. Nevertheless, she enjoyed a long life, helped by spending part of the war years in Freetown harbour providing fresh water to ships arriving in convoy. Hadley sold her to a subsidiary of Christopher Rowbotham & Sons in 1956 and as *Pointsman* she worked on charter to Shell, mainly carrying boiler oil from its refinery at Stanlow on the Manchester Ship Canal to the power station at Herculaneum Dock, Liverpool. Despite her outdated triple-expansion engines, she lasted until broken up in Antwerp during 1968.

Continental diesels

For the industrialised countries of western continental Europe with their well-developed network of waterways, distribution of liquids by inland vessels was more important than by coastal tanker. Nevertheless, Germany, the Netherlands and Norway did build up considerable fleets of small seagoing motor tankers.

Originating in 1925, John T Essberger of Hamburg has become a major European operator of both coastal and deep-sea tankers. The motor tanker *Elsa Essberger** was built for subsidiary Atlantic Tank-Rhederi GmbH in 1930 by Deutsche Werft, Hamburg. After just four years, her builders stretched her from 206 ft to 254 ft length overall, increasing her gross tonnage to 1173. She was renamed *Lisa Essberger* in 1938 to free the name for a newbuilding. In 1945, the Allies took her over and she came into British ownership as *Empire Tegenya*, but little use could be found for her, and after a few months laid up she was returned to her German owners and had the name *Lisa Essberger* restored. This aerial view from the 1950s shows her little altered from her pre-war condition. Her amidships bridge is a flimsy affair without the usual accommodation for the deck officers, who are presumably housed in her poop. Sold to other German owners in 1960, she initially worked on inland waterways as *Ölstauer*, and then went to the Mediterranean, where a Greek owner renamed her *Attiki*. A fire in her engine room during 1967 had her declared a constructive total loss, but her owner rebuilt her and returned her to service in 1969 as *Peloponnisos*, and under this name she gave another ten years of service before being broken up. *(Fotoflite/Skyfotos)*

Dutch yards were experts at building small, economical dry cargo coasters and, as in the case of Rowbotham's *Tillerman*, were equally adept at turning out diesel-driven coastal tankers. The 325-grt *Monica** was completed in 1932 at the prolific and innovative 'De Gideon' yard of J Koster at Groningen for NV Tank Kustvaart Maatschappij of Rotterdam.

The Dutch were soon to modernise the appearance of their coasters with raked stems, which helped reduce pitching in a seaway, but that of *Monica* was upright. Possibly this was to ensure the 138-ft long vessel could squeeze into as many small ports and locks as possible. Many owners preferred a straight stem because it was much less vulnerable than a raked version when the vessel was snubbing on a quay wall. Part of *Monica's* wheelhouse and accommodation was built forward from the poop, over her pump room. The single derrick on her mainmast sufficed for loading stores and handling hoses and the small boat stowed just ahead of her superstructure.

Reversing the original trend for dry cargo ships to become tankers, in 1965 *Monica* went in the opposite direction and after conversion was sold to owners in Bahrain, which renamed her *Bab al Bahrain*. In the absence of information about her survival, she was deleted from *Lloyd's Register* in 1997. *(Real Photographs)*

*Redefield** was an example of a Norwegian-built motor tanker that saw service for a British operator, Hunting & Son Ltd, which was better known for its fleet of ocean-going vessels. With her strong sheer, heavily flared bows and cruiser stern, she was an early part of a design trend that flowered fully after the disruptions of the Second World War.

Completed as *Gerdmor* by Sarpsborg MV in September 1940, she was given a two-stroke oil engine made by Atlas Diesel in Stockholm. The 224-ft, 786-grt *Gerdmor* emerged just in time to be requisitioned by the Kriegsmarine, and the Germans used her at Bergen for the duration of the war. In May 1945, she was returned to her Norwegian owner, Rich Jacobsen of Drøback, but in 1949 he ran out of luck, or perhaps ran short of money, and *Gerdmor* was arrested for debt at Glasson Dock in Lancashire.

Doxfield Tankers Ltd, a company managed by Hunting & Son Ltd, bought her from the Admiralty Marshall in May 1950. She was later transferred to another subsidiary, Northern Petroleum Tank Steamship Co Ltd, and she was employed in the British coastal trade until 1958. As *Santa Rita Terza* she passed through the hands of a number of Italian owners until she was broken up in Italy during 1974. *Redefield* was photographed on the Thames in February 1954.

British wartime designs

The combatants in the Second World War were dependent on oil fuel for their motorised and airborne forces. This dependency plus the Allies' need to support huge amphibious invasions, resulted in an unprecedented demand for coastal tankers, and the British wartime shipbuilding effort produced these in large numbers. As a result, so many modern coastal tankers were available post-war that until the 1960s few newbuildings were required and hence the British fleet became relatively antiquated.

Numerically, the largest group built in wartime Britain were the 202-ft overall length *Empire Cadet* type steamers of which twenty-three were delivered by three Scottish yards between December 1941 and 1946. The design was hardly new, being based on the *Pass of Balmaha* built at Blythswood in 1933 for the Bulk Oil Steamship Co Ltd, and herself a development of the *Pass of Melfort* of 1926. The counter stern added to an antique appearance, as did the original narrow funnel, which is retained in the accompanying photograph of the 814-grt *Shelbrit 7**, built in 1943 by A & J Inglis Ltd as *Empire Fay*. Working for the British marketing arm of two oil majors, Shell-Mex & BP Ltd, she was renamed *BP Marketer* in 1952. A very late survivor among a class that was mostly broken up in the late 1960s, and – thanks to her being given the more sedentary role of a bunkering tanker – she lasted until 1983 when demolished at Naples. With its large petrochemical complexes, the Manchester Ship Canal, on which this photograph was taken, was a major haunt of the class, and today the waterway sees many more tankers than dry cargo vessels. *(World Ship Society Ltd)*

Numerically the largest, and aesthetically the least pleasing, class of wartime coastal tankers were the forty-three prefabricated CHANTs, an acronym for 'CHANnel Tanker'. Part of the impeccable planning for Operation Neptune, the seaborne invasion of continental Europe, the 148-ft overall, flat-bottomed tankers were designed to be beached in order to supply water and fuel to the invading armies. Of the planned sixty-nine vessels, twenty-five were completed as dry cargo ships (see Chapter 9). The number originally envisaged was to cover for the possible failure of PLUTO, and when this scheme to supply fuel by a Pipe Line Under The Ocean was felt to be practical, the number of CHANTs was reduced.

Although most of the dry cargo versions stayed under the British flag, the government forbad the post-war disposal of CHANTs to British owners, probably because the bureaucrats felt their limited pumping capacity was not good enough for British ships. Only one UK owner, F T Everard & Sons Ltd, circumvented this ban by buying several from abroad.

The example shown is the blandly named *Tank 1** of 437 grt, completed by the Goole Shipbuilding & Repairing Co Ltd in May 1944 as *Chant 50*. She had been bought in 1947 from the Ministry of Transport by Lysaker Kemiske Fabrik A/S of Norway and was employed carrying chemicals rather than oil. *Tank 1* was sold to Swedish owners in 1956 and carried the names *Tankholm* and *Vingö* until broken up at Ystad, Sweden in 1974. Despite quick assembly with little apparent concern for hydrodynamic niceties, several CHANTs survived for over fifty years in harbour work such as effluent carrying and slops disposal, and as inland barges.

Another distinctive wartime group comprised the coastal tankers designed for service in the Far East. Because of limited availability of building berths, manpower and steel, these vessels were something of an afterthought and only one was completed before the war in the Pacific was concluded, and at least ten were cancelled. Only a few found buyers in the Far East, and instead they became familiar in UK and Mediterranean waters. There were two variants, the diesel (TED, for Tanker, Eastern Diesel) and steam (TES, Tanker, Eastern Steam). Both had a notably large bridge structure well forward to give comfortable accommodation to European officers while the local crews were berthed aft.

No apology is offered for showing an example from the fleet of F T Everard & Sons Ltd of Greenhithe, because this company's tankers were very familiar in northern European waters in the second half of the twentieth century. The 947-grt *Amity** was one of the diesel-driven TEDs, powered by a British Polar four-cylinder two-stroke and completed by Sir James Laing & Sons Ltd at Sunderland in December 1945 as *Empire Tedassa*. Her first civilian owner was Anglo-Saxon Petroleum Co Ltd (more familiarly known as Shell), which named her *Fossarina*, selling her to Everard in February 1950. She worked for that company until 1966, when she was broken up at Great Yarmouth. The type was considered highly suitable for lengthening, and several had an extra hull section installed abaft the bridge, *Arduity*, for example, was extended in 1956 from an initial 201 ft to 234 ft overall.

US wartime coastal tankers

The US Army, like its allies, also needed fuel, and US yards built a series of small motor tankers, titled – if that be the word – with the letter Y followed by a number. Several of those that operated in the European theatre were not taken back across the Atlantic after the war and found owners in continental Europe. *Y-40* was built by the Odenbach Shipbuilding Corporation at Rochester, New York State, in 1943 and given a six-cylinder two-stroke oil engine. Of 630 grt and 183 ft registered length, she had several features typical of US practice, including an upright stem and transom stern, probably for the same reason as the CHANTs had them – to ease construction. Sold to French owners based in Morocco in 1947, she became the wine tanker *Carola*, later becoming *Tamelelt* and *Lisa C*. In 1963, Sarda Bunkers SpA of Cagliari in Sardinia bought her, reconverted her to carry oil, mainly in a bunkering role, and renamed her *Alicudi**. She was photographed in Naples harbour during September 1968. Because of lack of up-to-date information, she was deleted from *Lloyd's Register* in 2010. *(William Schell)*

Operating across the vast Pacific, the huge US Navy was also totally dependent on oil supplies, and a large number of wartime tankers were dedicated to carrying fuel to combat ships. These included all thirty-two of the 1134-grt, 221-ft motor tankers of the T1-M-A2 type, all but four of which were built by East Coast Shipyards Inc at Bayonne, New Jersey. They had twenty-six near sisters of the slightly less powerful T1-M-A1 type, of which twenty-four were loaned to Britain under Lend-Lease arrangements.

Many of both groups gravitated to the Far East after the war. Ships such as these trading in the East have been a challenge to the compilers of register books, who could not always keep up with their changes of name and ownership, and *Vira** photographed at Singapore in 1975 is one such. She is quite recognisable as a T1 type, with its distinctive hull form and a two-deck superstructure carried right to her sides, but there is some doubt about precisely which. A strong possibility is that she originated at Bayonne in 1945 as *Waupaca* of the T1-M-A2 type, the twenty-eight T1s built by East Coast Shipyards Inc. In 1947, *Waupaca* was bought by the Standard-Vacuum Oil Company and worked in the east as *Mei Shan*. Several changes of name and nominal owner followed, and she was reported as possibly broken up at Jurong in 1978 under the name *Leap Deal*. *Vira* was slightly modified from the original design, with the mainmast stepped on the deck rather than the bridge, the wheelhouse rebuilt and the funnel made even smaller. *(R J Kittle)*

Bridge-amidships tankers

Some of the most ungainly tankers in European waters in the 1950s were four vessels built to work out of Lake Maracaibo in Venezuela. The extensive oil fields around the lake could not be accessed by ocean-going tankers because of a shallow bar at the entrance to the 16-mile channel from the sea. The answer was to build a fleet of relatively small, shallow-draught but beamy tankers – the 'mosquito fleet' – which carried the petroleum to a terminal at Aruba in the Dutch Antilles, from where it was reshipped far and wide in larger tankers.

To replace war losses, ten of this type were built in US yards in 1943 and 1945, and in 1956 owners Esso transferred four to the British flag. *Esso Chelsea**, *Esso Fulham*, *Esso Lambeth* and *Esso Wandsworth* were so named because their intended employment was running bunker oil from Fawley to oil-fired power stations on the Thames, although in practice they traded more widely round the British coast. The view of *Esso Chelsea* on the Thames emphasises her broad beam and full hull, and how the bridge and amidships accommodation appear to squat on the lengthy trunk and not reach the sides. At 335 ft in length overall, with a beam of 60 ft and a depth of just 15 ft, she had a tonnage of 4352 gross. Her twin screws were driven by triple-expansion engines. *Esso Chelsea* was built as *Amacuro* by Bethlehem-Sparrows Point Shipyard Inc, Maryland in 1943, and on arriving in the UK was refitted on the Tyne. She worked until June 1965, when sold to breakers in Bruges, being survived for just one year by her sister *Esso Fulham*.

Five tankers of a not dissimilar design to the Maracaibo ships were built between 1949 and 1954 for Shell subsidiaries or, in one case, for charter to Shell. Three of these were steamers, two built specifically to carry bitumen – the British-flagged *Fragum* and the French-flagged *Shellphalte*. As discussed elsewhere, specifying steam machinery simplified the heating of the bitumen cargo. However, there was less reason to cling to triple-expansion engines for the third and last, *Irish Holly** built in 1954 by William Gray & Co Ltd, West Hartlepool, and of 2940 grt and 330 ft in overall length. Owners were Irish Shipping Co Ltd, a company set up during the Second World War to provide desperately needed shipping services to neutral Ireland, and which went on to develop a fleet of dry cargo ships and tankers in post-war years. *Irish Holly* was built for charter to Shell, and initially ran mainly to a depot in Dublin, predominantly bringing diesel oil across the Irish Sea from Heysham.

In June 1957, a consortium of oil companies decided that the domestic demand for petroleum products was sufficient to justify building an oil refinery in Ireland. When Irish Refining Company Ltd completed its refinery at Whitegate, County Cork, *Irish Holly* was the first tanker to call there, on 7 April 1959, and she made many calls thereafter.

Irish Holly was sold in 1967 to an Italian bunkering company and renamed *Etnea*, but in January 1968 she broke moorings in the port of Vibo Valentia and was driven on to rocks. On refloating, she was found to be beyond economical repair and was broken up at La Spezia. *(K Cunnington)*

The trend to place a separate bridge and accommodation block amidships arose as coastal tankers grew larger in the 1940s and the 1950s. It was argued that such a position was better for navigating the ship, although it also helped isolate the deck officers from the noise of the engine room and – some have even suggested – kept them apart from the engineering officers! However, it did mean that those in the midships structure would have to brave the elements when going aft for their meals.

The bridge-amidships trend produced some graceful designs, as shown by a trio of increasingly large motor vessels built by the Goole Shipbuilding & Repairing Co Ltd for F T Everard & Sons Ltd: *Anteriority* of 1954 (266 ft overall), *Assurity* of 1956 (282 ft), and *Grit** of 1958 (310 ft). Features of their external design, including the timber cladding around the wheelhouse, were reminiscent of the attractive motor ships built at Goole and other yards for this owner from about 1949, the 'Yellow Perils' illustrated in Chapter 9.

Grit was the largest of the trio at 2739 grt. She was photographed outward bound on the Manchester Ship Canal in March 1968, by which time her hull had been repainted from grey to black. It is interesting to note that the Ship Canal authorities had insisted that she took tugs. *Grit* was sold just three months later, after a career of just ten years with Everard, but then did various Greek owners proud, giving them a total of eighteen years of service as *Eleni*, *Katerina V* and finally *Alnour*, before being demolished at Eleusis in 1986. *(Author)*

Post-war bridge-aft designs

A universal fashion in cargo ships since the 1960s has been to move the bridge aft, consolidating it with the rest of the superstructure to avoid duplicating pipework for heating, air conditioning, water and other services. There was also a safety concern, in that the midships structure is right above the cargo, and those accommodated there are particularly vulnerable in the event of a gas explosion or fire. Navigators have just had to get used to conning the ship from a position almost aft, and to put up with the proximity of engines and engineers. Although not such a danger in small vessels, a disadvantage is that the officer on watch is remote from the bow and may not be aware of the battering the ship may be receiving in bad weather.

As with all coasters, the variation in size of tankers is a reflection of the physical constraints of the terminals used and the likely volumes of cargo needing to be carried. The smallest size is represented by the Swedish *Margot**, built in 1966 by Bayerische Schiffsbau GmbH at Erlenbach on the River Main, her tonnage of 449 gross and length of 179 ft reflecting her origins at an inland yard. Register books describe her as an 'unspecified tanker', and owners Knut Lundgren & Co A/B of Gothenburg employed her carrying any non-hazardous cargoes, including vegetable oils. *Margot* was proceeding up the Nieuw Waterweg to Rotterdam when photographed on 5 December 1990. More than twenty years later, as the bunkering tanker *Vladimir Nitsulenko*, she is believed to be still afloat with Russian owners that bought her in 2004 and no doubt appreciate her ice-breaking bow. *(Author)*

Development of small tankers in the fifty-five years since the Second World War followed similar lines to that for other coasters: their average size and power increased, as did their complexity, but crew size dramatically declined. Sophistication in coastal tankers extended to systems for monitoring loading and stability and – more controversially – measures to prevent pollution from what was often an environmentally dangerous cargo. The most extreme of these measures – at least in terms of the vehemence of arguments about its efficacy – was the provision of a double hull. The changes were driven as much by legislation embodied in the International Convention for the Prevention of Pollution from Ships (MARPOL) protocols, as by the requirements of the oil majors who progressively disengaged or distanced themselves from tanker owning in favour of more extensive chartering, seemingly wishing to avoid having their name associated with any accident involving a tanker.

*Hummel** is a sophisticated vessel with a double hull, described as an oil/chemical tanker and being capable of carrying non-hazardous commodities such as ethanol as well as petroleum derivatives. Of 7421 grt and 145 metres in length overall, she is by no means exceptionally large for a modern coastal tanker, and has been kept employed exclusively in northern European waters. She was photographed in the summer of 2001 in Kiel Forde, close to where she was built in 1989 by Schiffswerft und Maschinenfabrik Paul Lindenau GmbH for Carl Buttner GmbH & Co of Bremen. This owner sold her in 2008 and as *Vadero Linnea* she is still afloat in 2011, with a Swedish owner. *(Author)*

The growing sophistication of tankers, and especially the requirement for a double hull, has naturally increased their initial cost, and owners have looked for economy by ordering from yards with labour costs lower than in western Europe. A well-known British owner who did so was F T Everard & Sons Ltd who took delivery in 1997 of the 2965-grt, 89-metre products tankers *Asperity** and *Audacity*. Builders were the Singmarine Dockyard & Engineering Private Ltd of Singapore, who fitted the vessels with Norwegian diesel engines. Sadly, these were the last ships built for this well-known coastal operator, which had some years earlier made the decision to concentrate on tankers and dispose of its dry cargo ships. In 2007, Everard's remaining tankers were sold to the Fisher Group of Barrow-in-Furness, making this company the UK's major operator of coastal tankers. *Asperity* was still working for Fisher in 2011, having spent some time laid up in Birkenhead.

Sea-river tankers

Just as the massive network of rivers and canals in the Soviet Union spawned several classes of dry cargo craft at home on both the sea and inland waters (see Chapter 11), so too have tankers been built for this role. Reflecting the dimensions of the Soviet-era waterways, these are often substantial vessels, yet their seagoing service remains largely coastal. *Volgoneft-268** had a gross tonnage of 3475 on a length of 133 metres. She was built in 1979 by Volgogradskiy Sudostroitelnyy Zavod at Volgograd, a town that may be better known by its former name of Stalingrad. Like the majority of Soviet-era sea-river craft, she had machinery built in eastern Europe, her twin screws being driven by two diesel engines made by VEB Schwermaschinenbau 'Karl Liebknecht' (SKL) at Magdeburg, East Germany. These vessels were built in large numbers, and between 1966 and 1989 at least 257 were built, both at Volgograd and at the G Dimitrov yard in Varna, Bulgaria.

The original owner of *Volgoneft-268* on behalf of the USSR was the Joint-Stock Company Volzhski Oil Shipping Company, or 'Volgotanker' for short. Following the dissolution of the USSR and privatisation of many formerly state-owned craft, by 2011 she was owned in St Petersburg by Roschartering CJSC, although retaining her original name, roughly translated as 'Volga petrol 268'.

From new she was registered at Astrakhan, suggesting her usual area of operation was the Caspian Sea and the connecting Volga and Don waterways as well as the Black Sea, from where she was bound when photographed southbound in the Bosphorus during October 2008. *(Martin Wright)*

Larger, more recent and more sophisticated than *Volgoneft-268* is *Caspian Leader**, an ice-strengthened sea-river tanker built in 2000 with a double-hull in anticipation of new MARPOL regulations. Building yard was Sudostroitelnyy Zavod 'Krasnoye Sormovo' at the wonderfully named Nizhniy Novgorod, also known as Gorkiy, a town which is further north than Moscow and some distance inland to be building a 141-metre, 5137grt craft. Machinery comprises two Finnish-built Wärtsilä diesels driving her twin screws, an arrangement to keep draught to a very modest 5.1 metres.

Her original name was the virtually unpronounceable *Sfat-3* for the state-owned Transpetro Volga. In 2001, she became *Trinity* and in 2003 *Caspian Leader*, her owner when she was photographed anchored off Istanbul in October 2008 was Caspian Leader Navigation Co Ltd of Malta, while manager was the Istanbul-based Palmali Shipping Co Ltd as indicated by the website address on her hull. She remained with these owners and managers in 2011. *(Martin Wright)*

Eastern examples

As they are doing with so many types of vessel, yards in the Far East are coming to dominate the building of coastal tankers and offer very competitive prices partly through economies of scale in building long series of identical ships. *Nisyros* was built for Aegean Bunkering Services Inc of Piræus by the Qingdao Hyundai Shipbuilding Co Ltd, an interesting example of a Chinese yard part-owned by one of China's major competitors, Korea. Hyundai supplied her diesel engine. She is one of ten sisters built so far.

Photographed off Gibraltar, *Nisyros* is clearly intended as a bunkering tanker, as shown by the substantial rubber fenders alongside. Bunkering can be an arduous process and tankers in the trade sustain many more knocks than those in normal service: *Nisyros* will not retain her pristine hull paint for long. Note also the crane for handling hoses and stores and the enclosed, free-fall lifeboat aft. It is unusual for a bunkering company – and especially Greek – to order a new vessel for this trade, because bunkering vessels were traditionally superannuated tankers. Clearly, new regulations for tankers aimed at preventing pollution led to the building of *Nisyros*. Delivered in June 2010, the 103-metre, 4599-grt ship was originally registered in Liberia, moving to Gibraltar registration in October 2010 almost contemporarily with this photograph being taken. *(Martin Wright)*

Some owners have regretted the decision to build at yards in, for example, Turkey, Vietnam or Malaysia, experiencing problems of late delivery as inexpert builders have struggled to meet the stringent technical requirements of classification societies and of the oil majors that will usually charter these vessels. However, yards in Japan and South Korea have established an excellent reputation.

Falcon came from the Yongkwang Shipbuilding Co Ltd in Korea and was photographed in October 2008 anchored off Istanbul, her immaculate appearance belying the fact that she had already carried three names since built as *Chang Sung No 3* in 1996. She became *Falcon* in September 2006 (with her Valletta registration she actually became Maltese *Falcon!*) for the rather anonymous Falcon Maritime SA. After working for four years in the eastern Mediterranean in July 2010, she moved on to Indonesian owners as *Griya Flores*. She measures 999 grt and 79 metres.

Evolution has seen cargo lines in coastal tankers evolve from a simple 'spinal' layout with a single line with spurs and valves to each tank, which limited the tanker to carrying one grade or type of product. More flexible is the ring main system, enabling more than one grade or product to be loaded simultaneously. Another refinement to avoid the crew mixing a cocktail of products is to give each tank its own deep well pump. When fitted in a double bottom, these pumps are below the tank bottom and are particularly efficient at removing all but the last few litres of cargo. In most modern coasters the tanks are of the screw displacement type, powered electrically or hydraulically. *(Martin Wright)*

Asphalt and bitumen carriers

Having followed the development of the product carrier, it is the turn of more specialised coastal tankers. A subset has tanks equipped with enhanced steam heating equipment and are dedicated to carrying the heaviest fractions of petroleum, bitumen. This comprises the residue of the refining process that has been blended with other oils for use mainly in road making. Dedication of a ship to this cargo is necessary because the effort of cleaning the tanks to carry a lighter grade of oil is too great to be contemplated routinely.

The 290-ft, 2623-grt *Ebano** was built in 1930 by Harland & Wolff Ltd at Belfast for a company managed by Andrew Weir & Co. Two single-ended boilers provided steam both for her triple-expansion engine and the heating coils necessary to keep her asphalt cargo sufficiently liquid for pumping. An unusual aspect of her design was her portable tanks, and she was intended to run between Lake Maracaibo and the United States with either asphalt or oil. However, within a few years of completion she was working in Europe and her distinctive profile was photographed several times at Preston. Visits to the Lancashire port continued after 1933, when she was moved to a French subsidiary of Standard Oil of New Jersey (Esso) and renamed *Petrophalt*, a name she retained for almost twenty years. At the end of her career she was given a corporate name, *Esso Le Mailleraye*, but carried this only from 1952 until November 1953 when she left Cherbourg under tow for breakers in Aviles, Spain. A near sister, *Stanasfalt*, was built on the Tyne in 1929 for a German subsidiary of Standard Oil. *(J and M Clarkson)*

One of the last steam tankers ever built was designed to carry bitumen or heavy fuel oil, *Esso Preston**, completed by Hall, Russell & Co Ltd in 1956, of 1965 grt and 299 ft overall. The bitumen was pumped aboard at 280–300°F and maintained at this temperature by steam heating coils in the five cargo tanks. The pipework and cargo pumps were steam jacketed and to prevent heat loss through the ship's sides cargo was carried only in the centre tanks, the wing tanks being used for water ballast. Smoke from her oil-fired boilers initially caused problems, not clearing from her after deck and re-entering the engine room via skylights. After wind-tunnel tests, the cage-like structure was added to her funnel and was reported to have solved the problem

Esso Preston mainly ran from the Esso refinery at Fawley on Southampton Water to Preston, Dublin, Purfleet and Grangemouth with bitumen and also carried fuel oil to Belfast, Avonmouth and Manchester. During her final years she worked mainly between Fawley and the power station at Barking on the Thames, now carrying fuel oil for the station's boilers. However, a voyage to the refinery at Whitegate near Cork in January 1975 brought her career to a sudden end. She sustained bottom damage and was laid up at Cardiff. Considered too old for economical repair, she was towed to breakers in Aviles, just like her forerunner *Petrophalt*. *(World Ship Society Ltd)*

Chemical tankers

Chemicals have long been transported by sea in drums, barrels and other containers. However, the growth of the chemical industry in the years after the Second World War, and particularly the development of plastics and other polymers, resulted in ships being built to carry bulk chemicals, some of which are hazardous in nature. Chemical tankers have stainless steel or coated tanks of varying sizes for different chemicals, a facility which leads to them being referred to as parcels tankers.

The quality of chemicals is measured in parts per million, and certain of them can react violently with others. Therefore an abiding principle of chemical tanker design is to avoid contamination of the cargo by each tank having its own dedicated pipe and pumping arrangements. To avoid contamination from a previous cargo, tank-cleaning facilities are sophisticated, and may involve sequential washing with chemicals and water, with the washings retained for discharge ashore.

Photographed in the Mersey in October 1992, the Norwegian-flagged *Stolt Pradera** was owned by a subsidiary of the world's largest parcels and chemical tank operator, the US-Norwegian Stolt-Nielsens Rederi A/S. Built by Batservice Verft A/S of Mandal in 1976, she originally operated under the British flag as *La Pradera*. The 1592-grt, 96-metre vessel had six centre tanks lined with stainless steel permitting her to carry the most hazardous forms of chemicals, with her eight wing tanks suitable for less dangerous liquids. The latter part of her name proved enduring, and sale to Italy in 1995 saw her become simply *Pradera*. A further slight amendment to *Pradera I* lasted for just one voyage to breakers at Alang in December 2007. *(Author)*

Several coastal tankers had subsidiary holds for dry cargo, but *Saint Oran** of 1981 was unique because she could carry general cargo, while having a roll-on, roll-off capability, plus side tanks for chemicals. In this photograph on the Mersey in August 1994, note the addition of a tiny box on the conventional wheelhouse to improve ahead visibility.

Owners J & A Gardner & Co Ltd of Glasgow wanted a flexible vessel for working on the west coast of Scotland, but was also involved in shipping calcium chloride solution, a by-product of the electrolysis of salt solution. It already had a small tanker, *Saint Kearon*, involved in this trade, which originally involved navigating the River Weaver as far as Winnington in Cheshire to load, and *Saint Oran*'s chemical capacity was a useful back up for *Saint Kearon*. A very versatile vessel, *Saint Oran* did much work on Scotland's west coast, loading round timber, delivering equipment for fish farms, and asphalt for road projects. Almost certainly unique was a series of charters in 1985 and 1986 for which *Saint Oran* and another Gardner ship went to Cork to load containers full of racing pigeons for release at a determined time and place at sea. Few ships can have ever carried such a diverse range of cargoes.

Built by J W Cook & Co Ltd of Wivenhoe, *Saint Oran* had this Essex builder's distinctive 'Colne' type hull, which will be visited in Chapter 9. Photographed on the Mersey in July 1994, the 573-gt, 53-metre *Saint Oran* was sold to a Newfoundland owner in 2001 and was still working in Canada in 2011. *(Author)*

Gas tankers

The simplest hydrocarbons associated with crude petroleum, butane and propane, are gases at normal temperature and pressure. In the early days of petroleum extraction and refining, these gases were simply flared off, but this wasted a valuable resource. Methods were devised to liquefy the gas, by pressurising or cooling it, which reduces its volume by about 600 times so that it can be readily transported. The first tanker designed to carry liquefied petroleum gas (LPG) was Shell's *Agnita* of 1931, which shipped the gas from Venezuela to refineries at Rouen and Rotterdam.

As the world's energy needs grew after the Second World War, distribution of LPG became much more important, with coasters rebuilt or constructed to carry the gas. The first vessel designed to carry LPG since the *Agnita* in 1931 was the small tanker *Rasmus Tholstrup**, completed at Marstrand in Denmark in September 1953 for A/S Kosangas, also of Denmark. She was fitted with twelve vertical tanks with a working pressure of around 250 psi and had a total capacity of 600 cubic metres. Originally 165 ft long, *Rasmus Tholstrup* was lengthened to 199 ft in 1959, and her twelve vertical tanks replaced by three spherical tanks. Her twenty-six years with her original owners are an indication both of the standards of care and seamanship required with such hazardous cargoes, and also the non-corrosive nature of LPG compared with other petroleum cargoes. When sold in 1979, she could find other buyers, and as simply *Rasmus*, and later *Don Antonio* and *World Gas No 2*, she soldiered on until broken up in Thailand during 1993, her fortieth year. *(Peter Newall collection)*

Other LPG tankers followed *Rasmus Tholstrup*, most of the coastal vessels of this type carrying gas in pressurised tanks at ambient temperatures, although in larger, ocean-going vessels refrigeration was used to increase capacity. In the case of *Lady Elena**, tanks are cylindrical in shape to achieve strength, and protrude above her weather deck. Of 3465 grt and 100 metres in length, she was built at Anan, Japan in 1998 for a Liberian subsidiary of the Belgian Exmar BV. She was photographed entering the New Waterway en route to a Rotterdam gas terminal on a blustery day in autumn 2004. Following sale to a German owner in 2006, she continueds to sail as *Lady Elena* in 2011 but now under the flag of Antigua and Barbuda.

The volatile and highly inflammable nature of gas cargoes mean that numerous safety features and precautions are essential. Cargo tanks must be protected from damage in case of a grounding or collision. The pipework through which the gas is loaded or unloaded must be allowed to contract and expand with temperature changes. Pressure relief systems are needed for each tank and emergency shut-down systems must operate automatically if power is lost or there is a fire. A feature apparent in the photograph of *Lady Elena* is that all connections to the cargo tanks and hatches protrude above the weather deck so they are accessible to the crew. Precautions like these have ensured that ships carrying LPG have an excellent safety record despite the potentially hazardous nature of their cargo. *(Author)*

As well as carrying LPG, specialised gas tankers can carry other gases used on an industrial scale, including ammonia for fertilisers and butadiene for making synthetic rubber. A few have been built to carry another gas produced and used on an industrial scale, chlorine, a product of the electrolysis of sodium chloride. The extreme toxicity of chlorine, which was used as a weapon during the First World War, means that extreme precautions are needed to protect the crew. In *Northern Star**, 707 grt and 65 metres overall length, built by Moss Værft, Norway, in 1980, the wheelhouse and accommodation were gastight in case a leak did occur from the cargo tank. She was built to work between Warrington on the Manchester Ship Canal and Londonderry on behalf of the chemical company DuPont, owners being DUK Shipping Ltd. On this route, she replaced the Dutch *Marwit*, originally a dry cargo coaster equipped to carry chlorine in tanks installed below deck. Photographed on the Mersey during the short sunlit hours of the winter solstice in 1986, *Northern Star* stood down from this service in 2000 and was converted to a products tanker and renamed *Norvarg*. She was still in service in 2011. *(Author)*

Sludge vessels

In the 1890s, municipal authorities who required a means of disposing of the end-product of sewage treatment turned to tank vessels to take the sludge out to sea for dumping. Among others, London, Manchester, Salford and Glasgow corporations had fleets of sludge vessels built to work between the sewage plant at places such as Beckton on the Thames and Davyhulme on the Manchester Ship Canal and deep water.

Exemplifying the earlier sludge vessels is *Salford City**, a twin-screw steamer built in 1928 for the eponymous municipality by William Beardmore & Co Ltd at Dalmuir, with a gross tonnage of 1170 and overall length of 246 ft. Seen in an industrial Ship Canal setting as built, *Salford City* gained a new lease of life in 1963 when she was rebuilt with twin diesel engines by Manchester Drydocks Ltd and as such she lasted until 1970 when broken up at Fleetwood. Despite modernisation, including a sleek new funnel, her upright bow gave a clue to her real age.

In the 1960s, disposal of effluent from chemical and other works became a significant business, and several ageing coastal tankers and at least one former sludge vessel were bought by commercial operators to carry out this work. However, the municipalities remain unique in building vessels for this work. *(World Ship Society Ltd)*

A more modern sludge vessel is *Dalmarnock**, built for Glasgow Corporation in 1970 by James Lamont & Co Ltd at Port Glasgow. Of 2192 grt and 313 ft overall, she is seen passing beneath the Erskine road bridge on 28 August 1991. The Glasgow sludge vessels numbered among the very few tankers that routinely carried passengers, because they regularly took pensioners for a trip down the scenic waters of the Clyde. As this secondary activity suggests, the sludge vessels were typically kept scrupulously clean, at least above decks, and the holds were thoroughly sealed. Indeed, latterly the sludge consisted essentially of non-toxic waste that could not be digested in the sewage treatment process. Nevertheless, the European Community decided that its disposal at sea was not acceptable, and in 2007 all surviving British sludge vessels were withdrawn and those with life left were sold. *Dalmarnock* had a second career with Northumbrian Water as *Bran Sands*, and in 2007 was sold to Nigerian owners as *Efeomo*. She was still working in 2011. *(Clive Guthrie)*

Beer carriers

In complete contrast to the sludge vessels are tankers whose cargoes are to be consumed by humans. Few ships gave more pleasure to bystanders than those carrying Guinness from the St James Gate Brewery on the River Liffey in Dublin to depots in Liverpool and Manchester. From about 1914, former colliers fitted with refrigeration plant in their holds were used to move the beer in casks, but in 1931 a new steamer was delivered by Ailsa Shipbuilding Co Ltd of Troon, unsurprisingly named *Guinness*, of 1151 grt and 220 ft overall. Not strictly a tanker, because the beer was put into tanks that were loaded on board, *Guinness* was impeccably kept, and with her dark blue hull and a harp trademark displayed on her bridge she was excellent advertisement for her owner's brand. When she arrived at Faslane to be broken up in June 1963, she was one of the few remaining coasters still powered by a triple-expansion steam engine. *Guinness* is seen on the Manchester Ship Canal, her stern showing that, although her cargo was the pride of Dublin, its brewers steadfastly registered their ships in London. *(K Cunnington)*

In 1974, a successor to *Guinness*, *The Lady Patricia*, was experimentally converted to a true a beer tanker, eventually having sixteen cylindrical tanks of 4680 gallons capacity fitted in her holds. The success of this experiment led Guinness to order the world's first purpose-built beer tanker, *Miranda Guinness**, of 1541 grt and 71 metres in length. Her owners are closely associated with records, of course, and *Miranda Guinness* held another, rather melancholy, record: she was the last ship to be built by Charles Hill & Sons Ltd at its Albion Dockyard in Bristol. The bumblers in the local authority's planning department had decreed that this historic but quite viable shipyard had to go, and shipbuilding in Bristol ended after many hundreds of years.

Sadly, the conveyance of Guinness in bulk by sea finished in 1993 when this motor vessel was taken out of service and her stainless steel tanks removed. The porter (technically, Guinness is not 'stout', as generally believed) is now loaded in Dublin as a concentrate in liquid containers and diluted in England. While containerisation has reduced the variety of coastal dry cargo ships, this is a rare example of it making redundant a coastal tanker, a type of ship that seems likely to increase in numbers and diversify so long as an industrial economy survives. *(Author)*

CHAPTER

7

Early British Motor Coasters

There are almost as many claimants to be the first vessel driven by an internal-combustion engine as for the title of first practical steam boat. At least as many nations are involved: Denmark, France, Germany, the Netherlands, Russia, Sweden, Switzerland and the United Kingdom can all make good claims. The earliest record cited by A C Hardy, evangelist for the cause of the marine oil engine, is of the British sailing barge *Spinaway C*. Completed in 1899, she was fitted with a Vosper hot-bulb engine but when she ran up the River Deben in Suffolk, her propeller became so entangled with weed that her captain-owner insisted that the engine be removed. The first sea-going motor vessels were built in 1910; the Italian cargo ship *Romagna* (678 grt) which had two Sulzer oil engines; the Canadian laker *Toiler* (1659 grt) built by Swan, Hunter; and the Dutch tanker *Vulcanus* (1179 grt).

An oil engine could be fitted into an existing sailing coaster relatively easily and cheaply, although usually at the expense of reducing the hold space or the accommodation. Although low powered and capable of giving only five or six knots, such an auxiliary – sometimes dubbed 'an iron topmast' – would be invaluable when becalmed, on a lee shore or working into or out of a difficult harbour or estuary.

Designing a coaster with an oil engine rather than steam machinery was an even more attractive proposition. There could be reductions in manpower, because firemen could be dispensed with, as well as savings on fuel. But most important was the additional carrying capacity for a given size and draught, possible because of the more compact engine room, which did not need boilers or coal bunkers, and oil fuel was readily stored in spaces unsuitable for cargo. Reliability of some early oil engine designs was poor, although their reputation might have been sullied by the unreliability of contemporary engineers. Certainly a major difficulty encountered by early British owners was finding engineers reared on steamships that were capable of maintaining, or perhaps sensitive enough to the needs of, the oil engine.

The Dutch, with a shorter history of steam engineering, proved much more resourceful, and were almost single-handedly responsible for proving the economic value and reliability of the motor coaster. Although it is too simplistic to attribute the eclipse of British coaster owning and building solely to this cause, the decline of the UK's coaster fleet was contemporary with the rise of the Dutch motor coaster.

This chapter focuses on early British attempts to produce a motor coaster.

An asterisk in a caption indicates the vessel shown in the photograph.

The Innis boats

Claims as to the first British motor coaster are hazy. Frank Bevis of Portsmouth had the Bolinders-engined *Ogarita* (95 grt) built at South Shields in 1911, probably for work in the Solent. Described as a motor barge, in her long life she made many coastal voyages. A Scottish candidate is the canal and estuarial trader *Peggy*, reputedly completed at Grangemouth in 1912, but not registered. However, both of these ventures were entirely eclipsed by an order for eighteen coasting motor vessels placed by Glasgow ship owner John M Paton. In partnership with a Peter Hendry, Paton was a substantial operator of puffer- and larger-sized steam coasters. In 1911, he left the partnership, putting money into the Coasting Motor Shipping Co Ltd, which was incorporated in January 1912 to exploit the potential of the oil engine.

Paton ordered ships to several designs, and his eighteen vessels included ten different combinations of hull and machinery. Orders were split between four Scottish shipyards, comprised vessels of five different lengths from 66 ft up to 116 ft, and were fitted with five different types of oil engine. Even those of the same size and from the same yard were not always uniform. Of the four built to 116 ft and 238 grt by William Chalmers & Co Ltd at Rutherglen, *Innisvera** (below, left) and *Innisulva* had wheelhouses mounted on their poops, while *Innistrahull* and *Innisshannon** (below, right) had theirs on the forecastle, although in the latter it was later moved aft.

The Innis boats began emerging in April 1914 with *Innisagra* completed at Kirkintilloch, and problems began almost at once. Although fitted with the well-proven Bolinders hot-bulb engine, *Innisagra* and others suffered from their builders' inexperience of installing such an engine, and fuel tanks, pipes, cooling water and fuel taps all caused problems. The biggest difficulty, however, was finding competent engineers, and their failings of operation and maintenance, ignorance and in some cases laziness combined with the installation problems led to frequent engine failures. Even the smallest Innis vessels were trading widely, up and down both the east and west coasts of Scotland, across to Ireland and down to the Mersey, and out to Scottish and Irish islands and remote lighthouses. Breakdowns could therefore be very hazardous, and indeed three of the fleet were lost within eighteen months of completion with others having narrow escapes.

Paton himself seems to have been over-optimistic about recruiting reliable engineers and his decision to send the new *Innisagra* – which had not yet run trials – on a maiden voyage to Belfast with coal was optimism bordering on foolhardiness. But he seems to have quickly realised that his venture was ailing, and began selling off his fleet, *Innisvera* going to Danish owners in November 1914 when only seven months old. In this Paton was fortunate that the outbreak of the First World War quickly began to inflate prices. In 1915, the Russian government bought four of his fleet and in March 1916 the British Admiralty took six for use as water carriers. Others went to commercial operators, and by December 1919 all had been sold, and the Coasting Motor Shipping Co Ltd was voluntary liquidated.

Several authors have dismissed Paton's bold venture as a failure. However, there was little fundamentally wrong either with the concept or with his vessels, which in several cases survived into old age, and between them served in the waters of four continents. The surviving five of the six sold to the Admiralty found new owners after the war, for example the *Innisinver** (right), one of a 74-ft, 127-grt pair built by A Jeffrey & Co of Alloa and fitted with engines by the Tuxham Engineering Company of Copenhagen. She was with her fifth owner when she sank after striking a submerged object off Portland Bill in September 1930. One hopes that by then those on her bridge had better protection than the canvas dodger seen in the accompanying photograph.

The fate of four is unknown, but the average life of the remainder was over twenty-seven years, and *Innisfree* managed sixty-seven years. In several cases, longevity was helped by new machinery, but the Bolinders engines proved especially long-lived, that in *Inniscroone* being in her when broken up in 1962. Apart from the three early accidents, only one subsequent casualty could be blamed on an engine failure, that in the former *Innisshannon*, when named *Arab Navigator*, which was wrecked in the Red Sea during August 1952 when her original Beardmore engine from 1913 broke down.

However, the perceived failure of Paton's project set back the widespread adoption of the oil engine by British coastal ship owners that were too ready to shake their collective heads at Paton's overambition and return to their beloved steam coasters, with serious long-term consequences for British coastal shipping. With the one or two exceptions detailed below, owners did not readily embrace the motor coaster until the mid-1930s, by when the Dutch motor coaster had ended for good the dominance of the British in European coastal trades.
(Glasgow University Archives)

The British and Bolinders

The Swedish Bolinder hot-bulb engine was a sound and well-tried design, backed by British agents James Pollock & Co Ltd, which had a shipyard at Faversham. Walter Pollock of this company visited the factory of J & C G Bolinders Mekaniska Verksted in Sweden, and by 1910 had become British representatives for the manufacturer. By 1914, Pollock had supplied two- or four-cylinder Bolinders for over 200 craft, the great majority being inland vessels. Pollock did much to market the engine, and even produced designs for small motor vessels for other yards to build. Indeed, Pollock's own yard built few such craft itself and it was not until 1921 that it delivered its first motor coaster, *Admiral Vernon*.

Bolinders engines were fitted in *Ogarita*, in four of the Innis vessels, and – perhaps surprisingly – in a substantial motor coaster of 414 grt and 150 ft purchased on the stocks by the Admiralty and delivered to by the Ardrossan Dry Dock & Shipbuilding Co Ltd in February 1913. Named *Isleford**, she was designated an armament store carrier, and although not a Royal Fleet auxiliary – which are classed as merchant rather than naval ships – *Isleford* was registered. However, her registration documents give no explanation of her rather mysterious sinking off Wick in January 1942. The Admiralty, which was not always noted for innovations in ship design, was easily the largest early users of oil engines for sea-going ships. As well as the numerous motor-driven X-lighters, which, as described later, came into civilian use, they also built four motor tankers as part of the eighteen-strong *Creosol* class, all of which later passed to oil company fleets (see Chapter 6).

Early British motor vessels tended to be much smaller than *Isleford*. Indeed, an important reason for adopting the oil engine was that its compactness gave a motor vessel of a given size a capacity 20 per cent greater than an equivalent steamer. The iron and steel makers John Summers & Sons Ltd had a works on the banks of the River Dee at Shotton and built up a considerable fleet of motor vessels to work on this difficult river, where a shallow draught allowed a vessel to reach Summers' up-river wharf even on relatively low tides. A motor vessel also did not need to maintain steam all the time, as start-up could be effected from cold in twenty minutes.

Summers began acquiring motor vessels in 1913, including two Bolinders-engined craft ordered from local builders I J Abdela & Mitchell Ltd of Queensferry. These emerged as *Carita** and *Fleurita*, a naming scheme which was perpetuated for much of the Summers' fleet which eventually numbered twenty one. At 96 ft and 141 grt, *Carita*'s looks more like a motor barge than a coaster, and is described as such by Pollock, which supplied her engines. Her flush-decked appearance is typical of several small, early motor vessels which regularly made coastal and short sea voyages. The wheelhouse is certainly a later addition: photographs of other Summers' craft show a very open bridge. *Carita* certainly did work off the coast during her long career with Summers, carrying galvanised plates or corrugated iron from Shotton to the Mersey for export. After sale by Summers in 1946, *Carita* was owned successively in Appledore, Bristol and Colchester before being broken up on the River Medway in 1987. *(World Ship Society Ltd)*

Summers' *Fleurita** at 103 ft overall and 171 grt was a more substantial craft than *Carita* and her voyages would take her further afield on the Irish Sea, perhaps to Barrow-in-Furness to load pig iron for the furnaces at Shotton. She would also run to small ports in southern Scotland or in Ireland with basic slag, a by-product of steel making used as a fertiliser. During the Second World War, many of its craft were on government service, and the steelworks came to rely on road or rail transport so that most of Summers' remaining fleet was sold off in 1945 and 1946. Local owners Coppack Brothers of Connah's Quay enjoyed amicable relations with Summers, and were offered first refusal of the craft, but could finance only two, *Fleurita* and the larger *Indorita*.

Seen on the River Mersey, *Fleurita* is in Coppack's colours and has an enclosed bridge and enhanced cargo gear. Coppack worked *Fleurita* hard: Liverpool to Preston with flour; Point of Ayr Colliery to Holyhead, Douglas and Castletown; the North Wales quarries to Liverpool, Preston or Widnes with roadstone; Ayr to Larne or Silloth to Drogheda with coal; and Connah's Quay to a wide variety of Irish and Manx ports with bricks. Gradually, however, she was confined to running between Point of Ayr Colliery and Bromborough with slack, a two-and-a-half hour trip. Sold in 1961, she was put into the sand and gravel trade, a final and often brutal employment for many ageing coasters. It proved too much for *Fleurita*, because in January 1965 she foundered in Barrow Deep after developing a leak during a voyage from Felixstowe to London. *(J and M Clarkson)*

During the First World War, a trio of small motor vessels to Pollock designs were delivered by the Rennie Forrestt Shipbuilding, Engineering & Dry Dock Co Ltd of Wivenhoe, the 89-ft *Cristo* and *Lee Lee**, and the 116-ft *Lutona*, all of which at some point did coastal voyages. *Lee Lee* and *Lutona* were registered in Pollock's name on completion, and both were sold in the mid-1920s. In 1931, *Lee Lee* passed to F T Everard & Sons Ltd of Greenhithe, a company busy expanding from its origins as Thames barge owners and builders into a major owner of dry cargo and tank coasters. Everard fully embraced the diesel engine, to the extent of actually buying its major supplier, Plenty & Sons Ltd, when the Newbury firm was forced into liquidation in 1931. In 1933, *Lee Lee* had an engine installed from this works, known after the take over as Newbury Diesel Co Ltd, and was renamed *Annuity*. Over her long life she was modified further, receiving an enclosed wheelhouse and in 1952 yet another new diesel engine, again made by Newbury Diesel but of a new type. *Annuity* lasted until 1960 when she was broken up at Grays, Essex.

Experiments

Although Bolinders engines predominated in early motor coasters, there were rivals: a Beardmore design was fitted in four of the Innis craft and a few others, and the Dutch Goedkoop and Kromhout engines were occasionally put in British craft.

Overall, British designs of oil engine, with the brilliant exception of larger Doxford units, were not as successful as British steam machinery. One spectacular failure was fitted into a coaster, which, in another context, was an important milestone, the first welded ship built in the United Kingdom and probably the largest welded hull yet built. Interestingly, she was named *Fullagar** to honour her engine's inventor rather than the instigators of her welding, which was to have a much greater impact than her machinery.

Fullagar was completed by Cammell, Laird & Co Ltd in July 1920, and at 398 grt and 150 ft overall she was probably the only coaster this major Birkenhead shipbuilder ever built, whilst owner T & J Brocklebank Ltd of Liverpool specialised in trade from Europe to Calcutta rather than coasting. Neither Brocklebank ownership nor her Fullagar engine lasted long, and after sale in October 1921, she was quickly fitted with a more conventional Beardmore oil engine. After a spell on the United Kingdom coast as *Caria*, she went to British Columbia to work for a cement company as *Shean*, then moved southwards to Mexico to become *Cedros*. She was run down and sunk off Ensenada in August 1937. The photograph of *Fullagar* running trials on the River Mersey on 29 July 1920 illustrates that her all-welded hull was not particularly innovative in design, with its raised quarterdeck, open bridge amidships, and counter stern. *(Williamson Art Gallery)*

Also fitted with an oil engine was another unconventional type of hull, made of ferroconcrete. Shortage of steel and skilled labour during the First World War led the British Admiralty to begin a large programme of building concrete-hulled barges and tugs. As a result of unforeseen difficulties, the hulls were finished neither as quickly nor as economically as had been hoped. In parallel, James Pollock & Sons Ltd, among others, also experimented with concrete hulls about this time, and two, *Molliette** and *Violette*, were completed at Faversham in 1919 Both had two-cylinder Bolinder engines giving a modest seven knots, although these seem to have been intended as auxiliaries, and the ships were rigged as three-masted schooners with a full set of fore-and-aft sails.

Molliette was the only one of the pair accepted by Bernard Oppenheimer who ordered her, and she was restricted to trading between the Thames and Milford Haven, although this allowed her to visit the Channel Isles. Both vessels developed reputations for sluggishness and as difficult to handle under sail, and this may account for their being accident-prone. *Molliette* grounded several times, including once on the Goodwins, and famously damaged herself by striking Tower Bridge. In 1921, *Violette* managed to do such serious damage to Southend Pier that the pier keeper was marooned on the seaward end. Neither vessel had a long trading career, but both hulls were pressed into other uses, *Violette* becoming a refuelling lighter on the Medway and *Molliette* – more exotically – a night club near Clacton.

Conversion

The largest class of early motor vessel employed on British coasts and estuaries comprised conversions from the numerous Admiralty X lighters, designed by James Pollock & Co Ltd and mostly fitted with Bolinders engines. The first were ordered in February 1915 and were delivered up to August 1918 by twenty-eight different contractors, mostly shipbuilders but also engineering companies. They are widely described as designed as landing craft for operations in the Dardanelles, although only a few if any would have been available for the first landings of that frightful campaign in April 1915.

By 1925, many had been sold to commercial operators and shipbuilders that converted them to coasters or river craft. *River Loyne** had been built by J T Eltringham & Co Ltd, Willington Quay-on-Tyne for the Admiralty as *X 214* or *X 215* with a British-built Kromhout engine. She was first registered as *Dyserth* in 1922. Following a rebuild at Connah's Quay in which she was massively lengthened from 98 ft to 188 ft, giving her a tonnage of 153 gross, she worked in the sand and ballast trade of the Mersey as *A H C* until bought in 1925 by Robert Gardner of Lancaster and renamed *River Loyne*. She then carried bulk cargoes such as sand and stone around the Irish Sea, and was photographed in Preston Dock. She eventually acquired a larger funnel, probably when re-engined in 1929, but no wheelhouse. Her end was tragic: on 7 December 1948 she sailed from Penmaenmawr for Liverpool with a cargo of stone and disappeared. Wreckage was later discovered a mile off the north tip of Puffin Island but the crew was never found. *(J and M Clarkson)*

CHAPTER

8

Enter the Dutch Coaster

Although slow to adopt steam in the coasting trade, the Dutch made a quantum leap in the years after the First World War, moving smoothly from pure sailing coasters through auxiliaries so that by the late 1920s they had largely perfected a small motor coaster.

The development process was initially helped by the success of the Dutch in the First World War in trading profitably for both sides of the conflict. Their coastal vessels would work for the British and French, their inland craft based largely on the Rhine for the Germans. Though losses were considerable, profits for neutrals were outstanding. The owners of sailing vessels could afford to install oil engines to make their craft more versatile, but Dutch shipbuilders began to look further ahead. In wartime, diesel engine technology had advanced, partly in order to provide better, more reliable and powerful engines for submarines. After the war, Dutch and German manufacturers were eager to supply diesels and Dutch yards designed small coasters around them. From sailing vessels came a design for a small but seaworthy hull, with forecastle, poop and strong sheer. Inland craft inspired the shallow hulls and low air-draughts, the latter allowing coasters with short funnels, low superstructure and folding masts to trade far up rivers and canals.

The economy of the Dutch motor coaster and its ability to use the smallest harbours began to make itself felt just as the shipping recession that had begun in 1921 turned into a prolonged and deep depression. The Dutch provided the first serious rivalry for British coaster owners who had clung to steam, and who now began to wail about the unfairness of the competition. The trade press rang with complaints that Dutch captain-owners were undercutting 'break even' rates, that manning levels were below those that the British Board of Trade established as a minimum, and that the Dutch and their family crews were prepared to work extended hours. The British owners conveniently forgot that the diesel engine had significant economic advantages over steam reciprocating machinery and that the Dutch captain-owner with a mortgage simply did not have the option of laying up his craft when freight rates fell.

The Dutch coaster went from strength to strength. Not even the devastation wrought on the fleet by the Second World War held the owners back for long, because record numbers of motor coasters were built in the immediate post-war years. Their success was so great, and their influence so widespread, that it is appropriate to devote an entire chapter to the germination, flowering and the eventual partial wilting of the Dutch coaster.

An asterisk in a caption indicates the vessel shown in the photograph.

Sailing ship conversions

Many Dutch owners preferred selling their old ships to converting them, wisely deciding that investing in a more up-to-date design and technology would give them a competitive edge, so conversions from pure sailing ships to motor coasters were relatively uncommon.

*Geziena** was an early conversion, although her appearance had probably altered by the 1950s when this photograph was taken. Builder was W Mulder of Stadskanaal, who completed her as the steel schooner *Velox* in April 1914, just in time for the First World War. In 1918, original owner E Brouwer sold her and a Goedkoop oil engine was fitted, although she retained sailing ship features including a raked bow, exaggerated sheer and a 'chaffcutter' wheel on her forecastle. Renamed *Ella* in 1925 and *Geziena* in 1932, she was re-engined at intervals, although sources vary as to how often and when. Despite this, *Geziena* was still carrying a sail when photographed in the English Channel not long after the Second World War when her owner was P J Schippers of Bloemendaal. Her entry in *Lloyd's Register* indicates that she had a quarterdeck, but she appears to be flush decked, with a large deckhouse topped by a wheelhouse aft. Although tiny at 94 ft and 144 grt, she could still find work, and new owners, right up to 1969 when, carrying her eighth name, *Borssum*, and latterly in German ownership, she was broken up at Bremen.

*Viru** also displays distinct signs of her 1917 sailing ship origins in the snub nose resulting from her bowsprit being cut off. She was built at Franeker by R Brandsma en Zonen as the pure sailing vessel *Helder*, subsequently carrying the names *Margrietha* and *Hinderika*. In 1932 she was bought by a Groningen owner, who had her converted to a motor ship at Zaltbommel, emerging as *Deni*, 213 grt and 108 ft registered length, with a three-cylinder oil engine made by D Goedkoop Jr of Amsterdam.

The photograph shows her as *Viru*, owned by Arnold Nordmann of Tuborg Havn, near Copenhagen, between 1959 and 1965. Apart from her bow, she looks very much the part of a motor coaster. In 1965, she was sold to Greek owners that renamed her *Katerina*, and even considered her worthy of re-engining in 1991, when a Saab-Scania engine – her fifth – was fitted, to give her a modest seven knots. She became *Georgios L* in 1997 and two years later she came full circle, at least as a motor ship, and reverted to *Viru*. She was now under the Honduras flag of convenience but with an owning company registered in Liberia, and probably owned in Greece. Photographs of her as *Viru*, with tourists aboard and a pleasure craft on deck, suggest she is now working as a bijou cruise vessel. She was believed to be still active in 2011, at the age of ninety-three.

Pure motor coasters

By 1924, ships designed and built as pure motor coasters were emerging. *Gideona* of that year was something of a milestone because she had a cruiser stern, a feature that led to her being described as a 'kruiserachterschip' by her builder, J Koster of Groningen, who named his yard Scheepswerf 'Gideon'. *Gideona* was very much a pioneer in this respect, because the cruiser stern was not generally adopted by motor coaster builders until the 1930s, and counters could still be found in vessels built as late as 1936.

One of a number that Koster built to this style was *Express**, completed in 1929 for William H Müller & Co NV of Rotterdam, and seen off St Helier. *Gideona* was just 98 ft in length, with a tonnage of 139 gross, and *Express* was marginally larger at a still-modest 109 ft and 195 grt. A single mast was fitted, splitting the hatchway unevenly, and hinged in a tabernacle to allow it to be lowered to shoot bridges.

Both ships wore well. *Gideona* passed through several hands before sale in 1948 to Germany as *Mars*, a name carried until she was sold for breaking up in 1970. Müller retained *Express* until 1959, and after sale to further Dutch owners and renaming *Aegir*, she continued earning her living until broken up at Hendrik-Ido-Ambacht in 1972. Her diesel by Motorenfabriek 'Deutz' AG drove her until the end. *(World Ship Society Ltd)*

Some characteristics of the sailing vessel survived into the pure motor coaster era, notably the counter stern but also a generous sheer as in the 107-ft, 191-grt *Sirius** of 1927. She was built as *Europa* by NV Noord Nederlandsche Scheepswerven at Groningen, and fitted with an engine by Appingedammer Brons, which served her all her many days.

The name *Sirius* was adopted in 1935 when she was bought by Groningen owner E Sloots, who like many owners of Dutch coasters was probably her master. Such captain-ownership was a Dutch tradition, and financial systems were in place to facilitate it, including ship-mortgage banks, and the willingness of both hull and engine builders to advance loans to prospective owners. Captain-ownership reduced costs because no dedicated office ashore was needed, although some degree of management was supplied, often by semi-cooperative organisations such as 'Carebeka' and 'Gruno'. Often no home ashore was needed either as, in a tradition that probably came from the inland waterways, the ship was regularly the home of the captain's family. But the biggest saving came from use of the captains' (and sometimes the mates') wives and family as crew. The crew was small in any case, and – in contradiction to British wisdom which held that tending oil engines was a singularly skilled occupation – the master, mate or a designated deckhand looked after the machinery.

In 1977, *Sirius* was re-designated as a fishing vessel, offering sport fishing trips to amateurs, a relatively undemanding role in that she would spend much of the day at anchor. Her fate is unknown to the author. *(Ships in Focus)*

Methods of stowing and handling the boat varied considerably. In the case of *Sirius* it was stowed on the poop deckhouse with a simple crane to hoist and lower it. Other vessels had conventional davits, in some cases suspending the boat athwartships above the stern, as with *Frida Blokzijl**. Probably to facilitate launching the boat, the upper strakes of her counter are vertical, not turned inwards like those of *Sirius*, which has a stern reminiscent of a tug. *Frida Blokzijl* has particularly generous sheer, and also protection for those on the bridge which unusually extends right to the vessel's sides. This was probably a late modification, as the typical wheelhouse for a Dutch coaster of the first generation was quite tiny with open bridge wings, as with *Sirius*. *Frida Blokzijl* has a particularly small deckhouse on her poop, with most of her accommodation on the deck below. A size larger than *Gideona* and *Sirius*, she measured 123 ft registered length with a tonnage of 249 gross.

Her name on completion by E J Smit & Zoon at Hoogezand in 1931 was *Mulan*, which she carried until 1956 when she became *Frida Blokzijl*. Somewhat unusually for a Dutch coaster of this period, she was registered in the ownership of a single-ship company, the anonymously named Scheepvaart Maatschappij 'Frida Blokzijl' NV of Vlaardingen, near Rotterdam. Management was undertaken by Muller & Ruitema.

Frida Blokzijl came to grief on 7 March 1962, abandoned by her crew and running aground on Kearney Point, County Down. Refloated and taken to the Clyde, she was broken up at Port Glasgow in 1963. *(Ships in Focus)*

A third treatment of the counter stern is apparent in *Confid*, where there is a rounded tumblehome to the entire poop. Her funnel is hardly worthy of the name, because it is the most basic of uptakes for an exhaust. The paint scheme of *Confid* is more typical of Dutch coasters than *Sirius* or *Frida Blokzijl* in that her hull is grey with black boot topping, rather than the black and red, picked out in both the latter vessels with a white line.

Confid was a survivor. Built in 1928 by NV G J van der Werff's Scheepsbouw at Hoogezand as *Havik*, she was renamed *Wea* in 1932 and as this was requisitioned by the invading Germans after 1940. At the time, many Dutch coasters were away from the Netherlands, but *Wea* was at Dordrecht awaiting machinery repairs, following which she ran between Germany and Norway. A relative of her owner managed the impressive feat of finding her in war-torn Flensburg in August 1945 and, almost undamaged, she motored back to Groningen for reconditioning. Sold again and renamed *Lea** in 1953, she stranded north of Whitby in dense fog on 26 March 1955, the aftermath of which is seen in the photograph. Her cargo of Scottish potatoes was discharged from the cliff top by steel cables, but *Lea* was regarded as a constructive total loss. Nevertheless, ship repairers in Rotterdam bought her from the insurers and returned her to service as *Confid*, a name presumably reflecting belief in their repair work. This was not misplaced as she traded for W Visser of Sliedrecht until 1972, when after a short lay-up she was demolished in Belgium.

Also painted in grey, *Argus** has a feature reminiscent of inland waterways' practice of rounded windows rather than ports in the living quarters in the deckhouse on her poop. Built in 1930 by NV Noord Nederlandsche Scheepswerven as *Aleida*, she was renamed *Enga* in 1937, only to have this changed to *Hanni Lene* when forcibly taken over by Germany in 1941. Restored to *Enga* in 1945, she was initially owned by the Dutch government. She became *Helios* in 1947 and *Argus* in 1955 when acquired by J A Deen and A Dijkema of Delfzijl, who continued to entrust her management to NV 'Carebeka' of Groningen. She was now on her second engine, the original Appingedammer Brons unit being replaced in 1951 by an engine from Klöckner-Humboldt-Deutzmotoren of Cologne.

In what is likely to be a photograph taken relatively late in her career – *Argus* carried the name until sold to France in 1970 – she has had the forward derrick removed. Much to the detriment of their appearance, removal of not just derricks but masts as well bedevilled those Dutch coasters that traded beyond about 1970. As the French *Casam*, the 191-grt coaster was broken up in her home port of Les Sables d'Olonne in 1981.

The photograph of *Suze** demonstrates how the single mast could be lowered on a Dutch coaster, with its two derricks stowed fore and aft. In common with some others, she has a house at the fore end of her poop deck, which was probably a cabin for her deckhands, although in her case daylight is limited to that which enters by three small port holes. *Suze* was built as *Romeja* by Firma J Smit & Zoon at Foxhol in 1928 and fitted with an oil engine by Appingedammer Brons which, apparently, drove her at a modest 7.5 knots for her entire forty-eight-year career.

Away from the Netherlands at the time of the German invasion, *Romeja* came under the control of the Netherlands Shipping & Trading Committee in London, and spent the war working for the Ministry of War Transport, returning to her owner in 1945. The photograph was taken between 1953 and 1961, when she was owned by J Muller of Vreeswijk and took the name *Suze*. Sold in 1961, she was renamed *Alcor W*, and in 1967 was laid up at Zuidbroek. Coasters of her age and modest size – she measured 188 grt and 110 ft overall – were no longer an economic proposition under the Dutch flag. From 1970, subsequent owners put her under the Gibraltar flag or, when she moved to owners in Malta as *Maria Lucia*, that of Panama. On 31 July 1975, soon after adopting the name *Olcet*, she was wrecked on the Libyan coast.

Hull developments in the 1930s

Koster's *Gideona*, described above, was ahead of her time in having a cruiser stern in 1924, because other builders adopted it only slowly so that counter sterns persisted well into the 1930s. The 1931-built *Minerva** from NV Industrieele Maatschappij 'De Noord' at Alblasserdam demonstrated how much fuller was a cruiser stern, increasing the hull's capacity aft. She represented a significant leap in size, with an overall length of 132 ft and a tonnage of 313 gross. Her hull has a forecastle (although the well deck bulwarks disguise this), a short bridge deck and a quarterdeck, although this could also be described as a poop. Engines were by Humboldt-Deutzmotoren AG of Cologne; German diesels such as these were a popular choice among Dutch builders.

Minerva had been built as *Apollinaris VI*, part of a fleet of sail and later motor vessels that shipped branded mineral water down the River Rhine to the United Kingdom and elsewhere. In 1937, she became *Barendsz*, and the photograph of her with her gear lowered on the Thames dates from between 1953 and 1957, when she carried the name *Minerva* in the ownership of Captain J Schuur of Groningen, and management undertaken by Kamp's Scheepvaart & Handelmaatschappij NV. Sale to German owners as *Ingeborg* saw her career close after collision with the Danish motor ship *Manchuria* near Cuxhaven on 7 December 1963. She was raised a few days later and put aground near Pagensand-Nord for emergency repairs, but was later sold to salvage company Ulrich Harms, which broke her up 'in situ' during 1967.

Along with the cruiser stern, the raked stem made an appearance in the 1930s, and began to give the coaster a more modern look, at least to present-day eyes. The raking was rather tentative in the case of *Progres*, built in 1932 by Firma Gebroeder Niestern & Co at Delfzijl. The engine was made by Appingedammer Bronsmotorenfabriek, which was evidently an excellent choice because it did not need to be replaced until 1990.

The 188-grt, 105-ft coaster is shown here as *Fakir**, her second name and which she carried in 1950–52. She was owned at the time by E Smid of Groningen and managed as part of the large fleet of NV Scheepvaartbedrijf 'Gruno' of Amsterdam, one of the largest of the companies which looked after the interests of captain-owners.

On 6 November 1952, *Fakir* stranded off Vaasa in Finland while bound for Nantes with a cargo of timber, and was declared a constructive total loss. Nevertheless, enterprising locals bought the wreck, had it repaired, and returned her to service as *Zenita*. Her later story is complex. Between repeated sales to fresh Finnish owners, she was lengthened by seven metres in 1961, renamed *Jatta* in 1983, and became *Simona* in 1990 after extensive repairs at Helsinki following a lay up on Lake Saimaa. For much of this time she was in the sand trade, and probably remained so until 1 March 2004 when she arrived at Helsinki to be broken up.

Two-mast design

A single mast was an almost universal feature of Dutch motor coasters in the 1920s, but the next decade saw the two-mast design become increasingly popular, although the former style persisted into the 1950s. Koster's 'Gideon' yard may well have led the way again, building the two-masted *Castor** in 1931. She was still of a very modest size, 116 ft registered length and 199 grt, but this arrangement of masts allowed easier stowage when loading a deck cargo such as timber from the Baltic, which was a significant trade for many Dutch owners. The low air-draught facility has not been lost, as both masts are in tabernacles to allow lowering. The whaleback forecastle was also a design feature of some Koster vessels, but one which did not endure.

Castor was another ship to be in British employment during the Second World War, although there was an obvious difficulty in obtaining spares for her engine, built by Klöckner-Humboldt-Deutzmotoren AG at Cologne. It was probably for this reason that she had a fairly sedentary employment as a barrage balloon vessel in the Mersey until she was returned to her former owners, N Mulder of Groningen, in June 1945. Unusually, *Castor* had just one name, one engine and just two further Dutch owners throughout her long career. Acquiring her in June 1970, her third owner had her for barely a month when she foundered in heavy seas off Walton-on-the-Naze on 14 July 1970 while on a voyage from Rotterdam to Ipswich with a cargo of grain. Fortunately, the crew of four was rescued from their life raft by a passing British motor collier.

A further step in evolution of the motor coaster was the addition of a deck to the superstructure, which also gave those navigating the ship a pair of bridge wings. Seen lifting her forefoot in a good Channel swell, *Coen** of 1935 was one of earliest coasters to have this feature, which was to become standard and to endure in new buildings for over thirty years. The twin-mast design has brought with it a cradle between the hatches to accept the ends of the derricks when stowed.

The aerial view of *Coen* shows to advantage the acorn tops to her masts, picked out in a paler colour, a common feature of Dutch coasters and the subject of what is almost certainly a myth. For the captain-owner taking out a loan to finance his ship, it was a moment of joy when he had paid off his mortgage and 'sailed his ship above water'. To celebrate this, it was said he fixed the acorn tops to his mast. Unfortunately for the veracity of this charming tale, examination of photographs of coasters on trial shows that they were universally built with this feature!

Builder of this 290-grt, 125-ft coaster was Scheepswerf Gebroeder Niestern of Delfzijl, which fitted engines made by Appingedammer Brons. Owner at the time of the photograph was C van der Molen of Ymuiden. She was to have a relatively uneventful career, changing her name to *Uranus* in 1953 and three years later to *Uranus-B*, and surviving to be broken up at Krimpen a/d Ijssel in 1972.

Raised quarterdecks

About 1936, the raised-quarterdeck coaster made its appearance in the Dutch fleet, perhaps to improve carrying capacity in the deeper hull aft. However, the suddenness of the design's arrival suggests a change in regulations or an alteration in the way tonnage was measured.

Like their cousins with forecastle and poop, the raised quarterdeckers came in two masting variants. *Meeuw** of 1936, one of the earliest examples found, had the twin-mast arrangement, with light cradles for her derricks at the break of the quarterdeck. She had a poop deck aft: note the height of the deck where the bulwarks beneath the bridge wings give way to rails.

Builder was NV Scheepsbouwwerf v/h de Groot & van Vliet, Slikkerveer, which completed her as *Hasewint*, of 361 grt and 137 ft length, and with an engine made by Klöckner-Humboldt-Deutzmotoren AG of Cologne. *Hasewint* was slow in leaving the Netherlands at the time of the German invasion, and was taken over by the Kriegsmarine as a torpedo transport. Modifications were reportedly made, but this post-war photo of *Meeuw* (she was renamed in 1955) shows no significant differences from a trials shot. Owner at the time was E de Boer of Delfzijl.

In 1963, *Meeuw* was sold and rebuilt, emerging as a flush decker, but without change of name. Another Dutch coaster to have had an extended life in the Baltic, she was sold to Sweden in 1969 and renamed *Sandskar*, and is believed to have moved to Finland and become the suction dredger *Sanna* in 2000. On 1 February 2005 she arrived at Neuss in Germany to be broken up. *(Real Photos)*

Contemporary with the twin-mast ships such as *Hasewint* were similar sized raised-quarterdeck coasters with a single mast. *Cawi** of 1938 belies her age with a raking stem that is positively racy, and a superstructure complete with boat deck and bridge wings. She was completed by NV Scheepswerf 'Vooruitgang' at Foxhol as *Piet Hein*, with engines made by NV Motorenfabriek 'Bolnes'. Once again comparison of a trials shot with this view as *Cawi* between 1957 and 1966 shows little change. The only significant difference is the light mast aft, fitted as a result of regulations that required two navigation lights to be displayed by ships over a certain length: she measured 143 ft and 399 grt.

This was another ship to experience multiple changes of name. The name *Piet Hein* gave way to *Fortschritt* while in German use during 1943–45. This period also saw her fitted with a new engine by Klöckner-Humboldt-Deutzmotoren, her original Dutch unit having been seriously damaged, probably during the German invasion of the Netherlands. Restored in 1945, her original name gave way to *Alice* in 1947, followed by *Marwit* in 1952, *Altho* in 1955, and *Cawi* in 1957, when her major owner was W J Osterveld of Amsterdam. Nineteen sixty-six saw her become *Emerald Trader*, and under this name she was later registered in Panama. She was last reported during 1982 in port damaged and under Italian ownership as *Maria Catania*. Her fate is not known to the author. *(Real Photographs)*

Bridge amidships

A result of the trend to increase hull length was the brief enthusiasm of Scheepswerven Gebroeder van Diepen NV of Waterhuizen for putting the bridge amidships, as British builders had traditionally done. Examples included the raised-quarterdeckers *Alpha* (347 grt, 135 ft length) of 1936 and *Crescendo* (348 grt, 140 ft) of 1938, and the 'flush decked' *Rolf* of 1940 (420 grt, 188 ft). The last-named is seen leaving Eastham locks in August 1968 as *Cito**, when owned by H Paap and W J van Wijk, and is an early example of Dutch owners putting a coaster under the Panamanian flag.

Rolf was completed in April 1940 and, exemplifying the confidence of Dutch owners and masters, her first voyage was to Dakar, where she was lying with a groundnut cargo when Germany invaded the Netherlands. She spent much of the war working for the Allies in African waters, her field of operation being restricted by damage to her Klöckner-Humboldt-Deutzmotoren engines.

The name *Cito* came in 1960 after a spell running as *Westpolder* and was retained until 1969. She subsequently became involved on the sidelines of the peace process in the Middle East. Owned by an Israeli foundation, she was renamed *Peace* and equipped as a radio ship, announcing herself as the 'Voice of Peace'. Broadcasting anti-war messages during the October 1973 Arab-Israeli conflict did not endear her to the Israeli government, which closed down the transmissions. *Peace* then did sporadic work in the eastern Mediterranean for a few years and was scuttled off Ashdod in 1993. *(Author)*

Design maturity

Understandably with their country under occupation, the Dutch built few coasters during 1941–45, while there were losses amounting to about a quarter of the fleet among those working for the British or the Germans. With trade buoyant in the immediate post-war years, the Dutch government was keen to encourage regeneration of its important transport industry. War risk insurance payments for the vessels lost also helped ensure that there was an enormous surge in coaster building, numbers peaking in 1948 with one hundred new coasters. The imperative was to get ships on the water as quickly as possible, and so the two main pre-war variations, the 'flush-decker' and the raised quarterdecker, continued to be built in some numbers, with the twin-masted arrangement slowly eclipsing the older, single-mast design.

The popularity of the raised quarterdecker declined in post-war years, although vessels to this design were still being built well into the 1960s. Up until the late 1950s, examples were still being completed with the single-mast configuration that dated from the 1920s, although in the case of *Walcheren** of 1952, the derricks were no longer offset vertically. Built by Scheepsbouw A Apol of Wirdum, *Walcheren* was relatively small, measuring 149 ft and 400 grt. Interestingly, when in 1963 she was bought by an owner in Dublin, her tonnage rose overnight to 440 gross. Renamed *Glencullen*, she was employed carrying coal to the gas works in Dublin, where locks restricted vessels to under 150 ft in length. Later names, this time under the British flag, were *Lady Sabina* and *Tremont*. A 1976 sale to Dubai saw her renamed *Mumtaz*, but her fate is not known. *(F R Sherlock)*

Post-war changes were as much to style as to design, although size continued to grow. The hull of *Carebeka** of 1957 has an elegantly curved stem, sweeping hances where bulwarks curve up to forecastle and poop, and angled stanchions below the boat deck, but her design is not significantly different from that of the two-masted ships built over twenty years earlier. Although 198 ft long, her tonnage is still a very modest 499 grt. This was something of a magic number: above 500 grt a different manning scale applied, and Dutch builders worked hard to keep coasters below this figure. British owners were aware that, when they bought a former Dutch coaster, Board of Trade surveyors would usually assess its tonnage at a higher figure than the Dutch, which of course would increase harbour and other dues payable.

The coaster's name came from one of the semi-cooperatives that grew up to offer shore-based chartering and management services to captain-owners. After prolonged discussion, this was established in 1939 with the name CApitein-REders-BEvrachting-KAntoor, or CAREBEKA. This organisation was eventually responsible for almost 300 ships and eventually went into ownership itself with *Carebeka*. She was built by Scheepswerf 'Waterhuizen' J Pattje and engined by NV Motorenfabriek 'De Industrie' D & J Boot at Alphen a/d Rijn.

Carebeka was retained in the fleet of NV Carebeka until 1968, when sold and renamed *Alcmaria*. Sale to Greek owners in 1975 saw her become *Lena* and later *Galini* and *Gladiator II*. In 2011 she is believed to be still in existence, registered in Sao Tome.

Landing craft conversions

Such was the demand on building yards immediately after the war that some existing non-coaster hulls were converted. Available in some numbers post-war were landing craft, at least seven of which were turned into Dutch coasters, although such was the extent of the work that it was difficult to guess at the hulls' origins.

*Nigeria** began life in 1945 at the Greenock yard of George Brown & Co (Marine) Ltd as the rocket support landing craft *LCS(R) 12*. Laid up at Leith after the war, in 1948 she was taken to Harlingen and rebuilt as a shelter-deck cargo ship and renamed *Orca* for owners Jan Cremer and Jan Westers. The Second World War had not finished with her, however, because less than two weeks after delivery, in October 1949, she struck a mine off Kiel, although fortunately she did not sink. The original conversion placed her engines amidships but even in her brief two-week career this gave stability problems. During the second rebuild, the mine-damaged ship's original British machinery was replaced by unit from Maschinenfabrik Augsburg-Nürnberg AG (MAN) and moved aft. She was renamed *Nigeria* shortly before work was completed in March 1951, emerging with an overall length of 205 ft and a tonnage of 500 gross. The white-painted bulwarks amidships were probably relics of her brief engines-amidships existence.

Misfortunes continued for *Nigeria*, because in June 1958 she stranded in the Gulf of Kutch, north-west India. On board was a cargo of explosives en route from Lisbon to Karachi, and a few days after stranding the ship caught fire and exploded, putting an end to what had

With her minimal sheer, *Nigeria* looks a little unusual, but there is nothing to show that the converted *Arran** was anything but a standard Dutch coaster. Like that of *Nigeria*, her Glasgow-built hull, *LCT3R* of 1944, was allocated to the Dutch as replacements for some of the war losses they had sustained in British service. Arriving at Harlingen in May 1948, her particularly complete conversion took more than two years, and she emerged in August 1950 as the 499-grt, 179-ft length overall *Arran*, a name possibly reflecting her Scottish origins. She was owned by M Cremer of Groningen and managed by NV Carebeka. *Arran* retained her original engine built by Davey, Paxman & Co Ltd at Colchester until 1955 when replaced with engines by Motorenwerke Mannheim which, rather ironically, were slightly older than the British originals. A slightly odd feature for a Dutch coaster is the derrick platform, enclosed by rails, around the mast. The signal mast aft is a late addition to comply with regulations about displaying navigation lights.

In 1968, *Arran* was the subject of a further conversion into the survey vessel *Vulcan*. Her ageing engine seems to have been her weak spot, because in 1975 she was laid up in Gabon after her crankshaft broke. In April 1976, the abandoned vessel capsized and sank during a particularly violent storm. Salvage costs were beyond the value of her ageing hull, and she was blown up with dynamite that summer.

Shelter-deckers and half shelter-deckers

The shelter-decker when in its 'open' configuration substantially reduces the tonnages on which harbour and other dues are paid, without seriously reducing cargo capacity, and is thus particularly attractive to owners. This additional deck has disadvantages if a heavy, bulk cargo such as coal or ore is loaded but, as such dense cargoes have become less common, the shelter-decker has become more popular, for instance with owners E Wagenborgs Scheepvaart & Expeditiebedrijf NV of Delfzijl, which has long been involved with the Baltic timber trade. Wagenborgs date from 1898 and remain the biggest Dutch owners and managers of coasters and more recently of larger craft.

Oranjeborg was completed in 1954 by Scheepswerf 'Welgelen', C Amels & Zoon at Makkum, and her modest 498 grt does not do justice to the capacity of a ship measuring 212 ft. However, in contemporary Dutch maritime regulations, 500 grt was a point above which manning and other requirements were stricter, so builders became very skilled at completing ships below that figure. It is significant that, when *Oranjeborg* was rebuilt at Alblasserdam in 1969, she emerged with a tonnage of 970 gross, despite the only external change being two new and larger masts and derricks.

In 1974, she was sold to other Dutch owners that renamed her *Frisian*, and soon lost her Dutch registration in favour of Panama and later Singapore. Further names carried were *Coral Venture*, *Patcharin*, *Petch Arat* (under the Thai flag) and *Orient Express 1*. She is apparently no longer in service and her fate is not known to the author. *(World Ship Society Ltd)*

The popularity of shelter-deckers in post-war years is explained, not only by its advantages in reducing apparent tonnage, but also by the desire of owners that were primarily interested in the tramp trades to have a vessel suitable for remunerative charter to a liner company. A peculiarly Dutch variation on the theme, particularly fashionable in the 1960s, was the 'half shelter-decker'. It was almost the mirror image of the raised-quarterdecker, with the forecastle extended well aft, only the forward hold incorporating a shelter deck. Something of a compromise, it meant the after hold was suitable for denser cargoes.

Scheepswerf v/h de Groot & van Vliet at Slikkerveer built *Gerda Priva* to this design for Danish owners in 1967, and she is illustrated here as *Willy Smits** following her sale to Marinus Smits in 1971. She was lengthened by 25 ft in 1973, probably by her builder, because the lettering style of her name was a trademark of the Slikkerveer yard. Once again her open half shelter deck meant that she had a modest measured tonnage, 624 gross, on a length of 215ft. *Willy Smits* was sold in 1982, initially becoming simply *Willy*, and later *Angy*, *Benhill Star*, *Matorma* and *Defi*, under which name she is still listed in *Lloyd's Register*. *(Jim Prentice)*

The gearless coaster

The 1960s saw the last constructions of what can be considered as the 'classic' Dutch coaster, with its single hold, one or two masts, and a tonnage no more than 500 gross. Economics dictated larger vessels, encouraged by changes in manning and other regulations that made the tonnage limit less relevant. .

With the demise of the classic coaster, design went in a number of directions, some apparently conflicting. For owners in the bulk trades, any form of cargo gear was quickly abandoned as it increased maintenance costs. Shoreside gear was now universal in most European ports likely to be served, and it could load and discharge a bulk cargo much more quickly than the ship's own equipment. In newbuildings such as *Kosmos**, masts were sufficient only to carry navigation lights or fly flags.

Kosmos was built in 1969 by NV Bodewes Scheepswerven, Martenshoek as *Apollo II*, a name she retained for just one year. She defies the trends discussed above in showing a diminution in size: she was only 174 ft length overall and 393 grt. Her hull has little sheer to facilitate containers to be carried on her hatch covers, the bridge front slopes inward to lessen problems with reflection on the wheelhouse windows, and the funnel is faired into the back of the bridge as something of her owner's trademark.

Kosmos came into British ownership as Lapthorn's *Hoomoss* during 1979–85, and then became the *Domba* and *Tora*, the latter owned in the Isle of Man. Her final name was *Lady Grace*, and as such she went to the Caribbean. On 12 November 2004, she foundered in heavy weather off St Vincent in the Windward Islands.

There was also a more fundamental social and cultural change affecting the Dutch coaster, the steady decline of captain-ownership. Partly this was because fewer masters and their families were prepared to follow the hard way of life involved in having their home on a ship. The very success of the Dutch coasters in the 1950s also had an effect: a prosperous master could now employ another to command his ship while he came ashore to expand his fleet. The overall result was a move towards company-owned ships, often employing Dutch officers but with crews increasingly from the developing world.

Owner of *Kosmos* was Becks Scheepvaartkantoor, canny and economical minded: seamen reckoned seagulls never followed Becks' ships, because nothing would ever be thrown away. The company dated only from 1957, and had originated with family members who were captain-owners. Its success was impressive, and by the mid-1980s the fleet numbered a dozen, built in various sizes to suit a number of trades. In 1983, Becks took delivery of *Electron** from the Hoogezand yard of the same builders as *Kosmos*, and a family resemblance is apparent. At 1599 grt and 81 metres overall length, she had around four times the capacity as *Kosmos*. Despite her size, *Electron* made do with a crew even smaller than that of *Kosmos*, thanks to developments such as automated engine rooms and also to regulators compliant with owners' wishes who eased further the Netherlands' requirements on crew size. Photographed on the New Waterway in December sunshine during 1990, *Electron* became *Penyez* in 2004, *My Ship 2* in 2006, and in 2008 the Turkish *Yakup Aga*. Under this name she was still in service in the Mediterranean in 2011. *(Author)*

A Dutch solution to intensified competition in shipbuilding was for their small yards to come together in a loose amalgamation known as Conoship BV, which allowed aspects such as design and marketing to be centralised to reduce costs. One result was a class of six coasters ordered in 1973 from six different yards for Frendo London Ltd. To add international complexity, this British-based company was controlled by Fredrik Odfjell, the Norwegian agent for Conoship. The six coasters worked for Associated British Foods, a conglomerate that despite its name was founded by Canadian entrepreneur Garfield Weston. The ships were only chartered to Frendo and, when it had problems paying the hire, the finance company GW Holdings Ltd repossessed them in 1976 and placed them under the management of Mardorf, Peach & Co Ltd, itself part of Associated British Foods along with GW Holdings. The ships were quickly renamed and continued working as before, mainly in the grain trade.

Seen beginning a transit of the Manchester Ship Canal on a sunny 13 February 1982, *Gretchen Weston* had begun life at Scheepswerf Bodewes Gruno BV, Foxhol in 1974 as *Frendo Star*. Her tonnage changed several times, and when renamed *Gretchen Weston* in November 1976 she measured 1582grt on an overall length of 64 metres. A feature of the class was the large cavity beneath the bridge into which the steel hatch covers were folded.

In 1982, she became first simply *Gretchen*, and ran for an Austrian company. A string of sales and renamings followed until as *Arina*, her eighth name, she arrived at Aliaga, Turkey, for demolition in November 2010. *(Author)*

Beyond the classic design

In a diametrically opposite trend to that which saw *Kosmos* and *Electron* built without cargo-handling gear, a growth in size of coasters often saw more of this equipment. An increase in the number and complexity of masts (including bipods) and doubling of the derricks or their substitutions for cranes usually signalled that the vessel was intended for the liner trades. Many Dutch-built vessels with these features were two-deck ships, but some were single-deck ships suitable for the bulk trades.

During 1963–65, NV Scheepswerf 'Waterhuizen' J Pattje built three sisters for Rederij Carebeka, named somewhat prosaically *Carebeka II** to *Carebeka IV*. Masts were placed forward and between the two hatches, allowing three derricks to be rigged. The wheelhouse is a deck higher than in previous practice, and the superstructure below extends to the deck sides. The trio were built to a length of 210 ft overall, but magically their tonnages stayed just below the critical 500 gross. In 1969, however, Niestern's Scheepswerven NV at Groningen began a programme of lengthening and deepening that saw these ships grow to 945 grt and 230 ft. The photograph shows *Carebeka II* in this condition.

In 1975, *Carebeka II* was sold to Greek owners and renamed *Star Ann*. On 7 April 1983 she stranded near Corunna, on her way to Larne in Northern Ireland with blocks of Spanish marble. Refloated and taken to Ferrol, she sank again thanks to major bottom damage. Raised a second time, she was broken up locally.

A Dutch owner that disdains the fashion for pure container ships and remains dedicated to bulk cargo carrying is Wijnne & Barends Cargadoors en Agentuurkantoren BV of Delfzijl. The company originated in 1855 and retains its identity with distinctive orange hulls and use of female names, although since 2003 it has been a subsidiary of Amsterdam-based Spliethoff's Bevrachtingskantoor BV, which itself began owning coasters.

Wijnne & Barends' ships such as *Inger*, seen here emerging from the Kiel Canal at Holtenau in September 1997, also have a distinct style, with particularly tall hatch comings and zero sheer. Something of an innovation in this 1996-built ship is the 20-tonne gantry crane, installed to load timber cargoes in the Baltic: she is ice strengthened for trading to Swedish and Finnish ports. Although non-cellular, containers can be carried – 136 TEUs in the hold and sixty-four more on her hatch covers. Like Wagenborg's *Orangeborg*, she is example of an owner specialised in the timber trade preferring a shelter decker.

The 88-metre, 3323-grt *Inger* was built by Niestern Sander BV in the owner's home port of Delfzijl, a town which along with Groningen helped nurture the Dutch motor coaster and the Baltic timber trade and which, unlike the latter town, is still an active port. A sign of the decline of Dutch marine engineering was the specification of a main engine made by US-based Caterpillar Inc.

Inger was renamed *Lady Inger* during 2009 in a renaming scheme that affected most of the Wijnne & Barends-owned fleet numbering over twenty coasters, which work alongside those managed for other owners. She is still working in 2011 as the Swedish-owned *Listerhav*. *(Author)*

Final flowering

Just before the 'classic' Dutch coaster gave way to gearless small bulk carriers, low-air draught vessels and pure container ships, at least one yard produced a group of ships with more than an echo of the former elegance. *Frisian** was built in 1975 by Barkmeijer Stroobos BV for a company managed by Scheepvaartkantoor Holwerda of Heerenveen in the province of Friesland from whence comes her name.

With its upward sheered forecastle, neat wheelhouse and superstructure arrangements, and two 3-ton derricks, everything is in the right place, and the curving hances help her aesthetic appeal. Updates include a transom stern and a box hold with a hatch covering almost her entire width. The masts are perhaps the feature that most date her to 1975. The foremast has a wide cross tree from which are slung the wires to lift and slew the derrick; the kingposts aft serving the same function. Both masts have metal stays which eliminate the need for wire guys, helping reduce maintenance, if not painting. The grey hull traditional for a Dutch coaster has given way to blue and red. Another sign of the times was that Dutch or German engines which would have been specified a few years earlier have been displaced by a diesel made by the Caterpillar Tractor Company of Peoria, Illinois, giving *Frisian* a decent 11.75 knots service speed.

At 65 metres overall length and 992 grt, *Frisian* and her sister *Spray* were becoming too small to trade economically under the Dutch flag and in 1987 *Frisian* became the Cypriot-registered *Blue Topaz*. In 1997, she became *Caribbean Blue*, under the Cyprus flag and as such was deleted from *Lloyd's Register* in 2004.

Low air-draught

The funnels, superstructure and masts of *Electron* and *Carebeka II* made no concessions to the possibility of low bridges. However, a major trend in European coaster design in the last quarter century has been low-air-draught capability. Often dismissed as 'planks' by enthusiasts, these coasters make a particularly unsatisfactory picture from the waterline, but more detail is apparent in this shot of *Christina** taken from a passing ship on the Kiel Canal in August 1991. Her low, fixed wheelhouse contrasts with the movable facility exemplified by the low air-draught *Short Sea Trader* in Chapter 9 and some container vessels in Chapter 14.

Christina was built in 1985 by Scheepswerf G Bijlsma & Zoon BV at Wartena for the uninformatively titled Motorschip Christina CV of Delfzijl, managed by Amasus BV. She measured 80 metres overall length and 1391 grt, much the same size as *Electron*. The hatches extend almost to the sides, facilitating loading of containers in the single, flush-sided box-hold and on the flat hatch tops: she is credited with a capacity of eighty-six TEUs. Masts are as light as possible consistent with carrying lights and aerials and are readily folded, and her funnel is insignificant. A feature of many recent coasters is that, below a raking bow, her forefoot is upright. In an interesting continuation of pre-Second World War practice, her Dutch builders fitted a diesel engine made by Klöckner-Humboldt-Deutzmotoren in Cologne.

In 1997, *Christina* moved to another Dutch owner and gained the somewhat racy name *Fast Wil*, specified by charterer Fast Lines Belgium BV. By 2011, she was owned in Poland under the same name but registered at Port Vila in far-away Vanuatu. *(Author)*

CHAPTER

9

The British Response

Following the tentative and inconclusive British experiments with motor coasters discussed in Chapter 7, the Dutch picked up the baton and ran with it so successfully that British coaster building never resumed its former dominance. However, through the late 1920s and the 1930s, some British yards and certain coaster owners did try to keep up with their rivals across the North Sea.

Several British motor coaster designs, including those from Goole, were rather blatant copies of Dutch models, in some cases even having acorns atop their masts. Other yards, such as Scott of Bowling and Lewis of Aberdeen, adapted their steam coaster designs, although taking the opportunity presented by the lighter and more compact diesel installation to reduce draught whilst improving cargo capacity. Almost all followed the classic raised-quarterdeck designs, with bridge placed amidships in one variant and aft in another. As crew accommodation was belatedly improved and the officers were no longer isolated from the rest of the crew, the bridge-and-superstructure-aft layout began to predominate, even in larger coasters. With its relatively tall superstructure – before the need was felt for low-air-draught capability – there emerged a distinctively British design of motor coaster, which was not unpleasant aesthetically.

The years from about 1940 to the mid-1960s were particularly productive for British coaster building yards. However, it must be remembered that more coasters built abroad – mainly Dutch but also some German and Danish – were bought by British owners than were ever exported by British yards. From the 1970s, competition from continental European and later Far Eastern yards became more intense, or perhaps British shipbuilders were just losing the will to compete. With the possible exception of the ungainly but economic 'Yorkshire Dry Dock box', the dwindling number of British-built coasters slowly became largely indistinguishable from those made elsewhere in Europe. The obsession with low air-draught was also visited on the declining number of British owners, although one owner confessed that the expensive hydraulic wheelhouse on his ships had never been lowered in the face of a bridge.

In mid-2011, there are only a handful of United Kingdom-based coastal ship owners, and none of the very few surviving British shipyards has built a dry cargo coaster in the twenty-first century. The British had given the world the powered coaster, but after 150 years can no longer build one.

An asterisk in a caption indicates the vessel shown in the photograph.

Early Everards

Greenhithe-based F T Everard & Sons Ltd was an early exponent of motor coasters and for many years was unusually loyal to British hull and engine builders. This nationalism is interesting, because the founder's family came from Germany and changed its name from Eberhardt to Everard in the face of anti-German sentiment during the First World War.

The first dry cargo motor vessels built for Everard – as distinct from those that the company bought or had converted – were *Ability** and *Amenity*, which were delivered by the yard of Fellows & Co Ltd at Great Yarmouth in January and July 1928. They were a modest 115 ft and 262 grt when completed, and during the 1930s were significantly lengthened, *Ability* becoming 137 ft and 293 grt in 1938. The two-stroke, five-cylinder engines were made by Plenty & Son Ltd, Newbury, a company that Everard saved from liquidation in 1932 and which henceforward supplied most of its diesel engines.

By an unhappy coincidence the two coasters were lost through mines within three days of each other in November 1940. *Amenity* was damaged off the Humber on 15 November while on passage from Goole to Margate with coal and was subsequently sunk by gunfire. *Ability* sank off Clacton on 18 November while carrying cement from Everard's home port of Greenhithe to Great Yarmouth. The cargoes they were carrying when lost were typical of Everard's trades up to the Second World War. *(Ships in Focus)*

While continuing to order small motor coasters, after *Ability* and *Amenity* Everard largely standardised on a raised quarterdeck, bridge-amidships design with hull lengths between 130 ft and 170 ft. Between 1930 and 1941, orders were shared between George Brown & Co of Greenock (an impressive seventeen units built) the Fellows yard at Yarmouth (two units) and the Goole Shipbuilding & Repairing Co Ltd (also two units). Cargo gear was invariably one mast and derrick ahead of the fore hatch and one behind the after hatch. *Activity** of 1931 came from Greenock, and was one of the shortest batch, with a hull of 135 ft and 358 grt. Her name was well deserved, as she gave the owners a remarkable thirty-five years of service, punctuated by re-enginings in 1946 and 1962. After being sold out of the fleet in 1966, she sailed on under the Greek flag as *Giankaros* and later *Ioannis K.* Her fate is not known to the author.

The ships of this type were often ordered in pairs, and the detailed design developed almost with each pair. From *Actuosity* of 1933, a cruiser stern replaced the counter seen in *Activity*, the bridge was heightened by an extra deck in the 175 ft *Sincerity* and *Suavity* of 1936–37, and *Summity* of 1939 introduced a raked bow. Four units had a short bridge deck. All had engines by Plenty, known after 1932 as Newbury Diesel Co Ltd. This basic design was successful and continued to be built until the mid-1950s.

Pollock's prototypes

Although James Pollock & Co Ltd was influential in promoting the small motor coaster and the Swedish Bolinders engine as discussed in Chapter 7, this Faversham shipyard built many more lighters, canal craft and tugs than it did coastal cargo vessels. Even some of the motor coasters it built were classified as motor barges, as in the case of four craft completed in 1932 for London-based sailing barge owner E J & W Goldsmith Ltd. The 94-ft *Goldbell*, *Goldcrown*, *Golddrift* and *Goldeve* had twin Bolinders engines. The last of the four is shown as *Leaspray**, following a major rebuild in 1949 that saw her grow very modestly to 97 ft and 199 grt while a Crossley oil engine driving a single screw replaced her original twin Bolinders installation. The modest boom on her solitary mast seems inadequate even for her relatively short hold, and was probably used simply to lift her boat off the hatch covers.

Goldeve took the name *Leaspray* in 1952 when acquired along with her three Goldsmith sisters by Coastal Tankers Ltd, a London company that had recently decided to specialise in dry rather than liquid cargoes. She remained *Leaspray* under subsequent ownerships in London, Cowes and Bridgwater until 1966 when she moved to the Clyde as *Warlight*.

She ended her days working for a civil engineering contractor under the name *Teamwork* and was broken up in 1976. Suitable for relatively short voyages with modest-sized cargoes, *Leaspray* was nevertheless a coaster.

Several characteristics of *Leaspray* are apparent in a larger coaster built by Pollock in 1934, *Camroux I**. She has the same upright bow, single mast (no boom) and full stern, but the wheelhouse is more substantial and, at 137 ft overall and 324 grt, there is room for boats on the poop. *Camroux I* and her sister *Camroux II* were to a standard hull design marketed by Pollock as the 'Landina' type and were by far the largest vessels the Faversham yard had yet built. The launch of *Camroux I* was filmed, and the public invited to inspect her in return for a donation to charity.

The pair was built for the Newcastle Coal & Shipping Co Ltd to work to a coal depot at Rosebank Wharf, Fulham, which required both a low air-draught to negotiate the many Thames bridges and a substantial ballast capacity to ensure they could return down river. Her original four-stroke engines were made by Humboldt-Deutzmotoren AG of Cologne but, when spares became unobtainable during the war, *Camroux I* received a British-made two-stroke engine by H Widdop & Co Ltd, and this was in turn replaced by a British Polar unit in 1945. The latter engine appears to have given particularly long service. Sold by her Newcastle owners in 1960, *Camroux I* became *The Marquis* in the fleet of John Hay & Sons Ltd, Glasgow (by then a subsidiary of F T Everard & Sons Ltd). After a further sale to Greek owners in 1966, she remained in *Lloyd's Register* until 2011, although it had heard nothing of the vessel since 1995, when named *Stamata II*.

Steam coasters updated

In contrast to Pollock, which designed vessels specifically as motor coasters, several British yards simply installed an oil engine in the standard steam coaster hull with bridge amidships and raised quarterdeck. Believed to be the first motor vessels built by the prolific coaster and trawler building yard of John Lewis & Sons Ltd, Aberdeen, were two sisters completed in 1935 for another family which had long owned sailing barges, Horlock of Mistley in Essex. No doubt with a touch of irony, these 131-ft, 351-grt coasters were named *Jolly Nights* and *Jolly Days*. Presumably in an effort to compare designs for future orders, four-cylinder two-stroke engines by different British manufacturers were fitted, that in *Jolly Nights* coming from British Auxiliaries Ltd of Govan and the other from Petters Ltd of Yeovil.

Jolly Nights was sold to Poole owners as *Cranborne* in 1946 and is shown under her final ownership, George Kearon Ltd of Arklow, which renamed her *Seabank** in 1954. Small Irish family owners such as Kearon took ageing motor ships to replace the auxiliary sailing ships to which they had clung for many years. *Seabank* came to grief in March 1963 when she stranded on Mizen Head while on a typical voyage from Dublin to Newport to pick up another coal cargo. Although refloated, she was not worth repairing and was broken up at Troon in 1964.

*Karri** of 1938 was an example of a motor ship for a long-established steam coaster operator, Joseph Fisher & Sons Ltd of Newry. For their first diesel-driven coaster Fisher turned to its regular supplier, Scott & Sons of Bowling, which adapted the design of the 362-grt steamer *Opepe* of 1937. The 354-grt *Karri* had a cruiser stern rather than a counter, and a double bottom to improve ballast capacity, and proved an excellent sea boat. Even more significantly, she offered both a shallower draught and a significantly larger cargo capacity on a 147-ft hull, just inches shorter than her steam predecessor. The shallower draught was a positive advantage in the coastal trade in which tidal harbours were often served. The greater cargo capacity, indicated by her increase in net tonnage to 179 compared with the 131 of *Opepe*, was a direct result of the more compact engine room possible with a diesel.

Despite her advantages, Fisher did not repeat *Karri*. When it ordered new ships post-war, Scott was told to build two coal-fired steamers similar to *Opepe*. Reasons given were the higher cost of a diesel engine, the shortage of reliable diesel engineers, and the cheapness of bunker coal at the usual loading ports.

Unlike her steam successors, *Karri* had a long career. Sold to Leith owners in 1957, ten years later she went to a Greek owner who renamed her *Athanassios I*. During May 1977, she sank in the Mediterranean following engine failure in heavy weather. This unit by British Auxiliaries Ltd was fitted in 1942, when damage from an exploding mine rendered her original Humboldt-Deutzmotoren machinery impossible to repair.

'Goole Proficient' coasters

In the mid-1930s, established British coaster owners belatedly realised that their steamers were becoming obsolete and that the only way to compete with the Dutch was to move into motor coasters. Several owners, including William Robertson of Glasgow and Robert Rix & Sons of Hull, went the whole way and ordered coasters from the Netherlands. A British yard more dynamic than most in moving into motor coaster production was Goole Shipbuilding & Repairing Co Ltd, which marketed its 'Goole Proficient Motor Coaster'.

The yard's output spanned a considerable range of sizes, with five of the largest motor coasters being ordered by T E Evans & Co Ltd of London, a relative newcomer to ship owning, which, after a disappointing speculation in ageing deep-sea tramps in the 1920s, had decided to diversify into motor coasters. Again, a company without a tradition of steam coaster owning had put its trust in the diesel engine.

Evans' *Andoni** of 1937 was a substantial coaster of 187 ft and 678 grt. Despite this considerable length, she had her bridge right aft, although was otherwise of the regular forecastle/raised quarterdeck/poop configuration with masts at the extremes of her two holds. With British engine builders becoming better established, her seven-cylinder, two-stroke came from British Auxiliaries Ltd, Glasgow.

Evans lost two motor coasters in the Second World War and then gradually sold off the others. *Andoni* went to Salvesen of Leith as *Tronda* in 1949 before entering the fleet of Metcalf Motor Coasters Ltd, London, which renamed her *Moira M*. She was broken up at Inverkeithing in 1971.

Despite marketing a standard design, the Goole yard was quite prepared to include modifications requested by prospective owners. Amongst these was Jack Wharton, shipper and shipbroker of Keadby on the River Trent, who ordered his first coaster from Goole in 1936. A simple single-deck ship, *Brendonia* had a raised forecastle and poop, short bridge deck, cruiser stern, teak wheelhouse, two wooden hatches serving one hold, and a Deutz main engine. Dimensions were 150 ft overall length and 360 grt. Similarities to Dutch-built vessels extended to the acorn atop her hinged mast stepped at the break of her quarterdeck.

Brendonia was successful, and Wharton returned for a repeat, *Gladonia**, handed over in July 1939. Her career could have been remarkably short, as the first cargo she was fixed for was fish oil to Hamburg but luckily this was cancelled in time to prevent her being interned on the outbreak of war. Her British career was terminated in January 1962, when she stranded south of the Hook of Holland while carrying china clay to Rotterdam. Following salvage, she was rebuilt and re-engined in Leer, re-entering service for West German owners as *Meike* and later *Walka* before following many aged coasters out to the Caribbean. Renamed *Kimbo* by owners based in the Cayman Islands, she had reverted to *Walka* by the time she foundered off Panama in 1980. *(C A Hill)*

Wartime construction

The Second World War represented a watershed for the British coaster. Until 1939, opinion and investment was divided between steam and diesel power, with the former still dominant for larger vessels, but by 1945 the case for the diesel was proven, despite a small handful of owners persisting in ordering new steamers into the 1950s. Wartime construction of bulk-carrying coasters (as opposed to the larger colliers) was heavily weighted in favour of motor ships, with only the larger vessels of the 'Tudor Queen' type being steam-driven.

With the notable exception of the 'Empire F' type discussed below, the individual classes of ships were numerically quite small. In some cases, all of the ships of one class came from a single yard because government orders allowed individual builders to construct vessels of a size they could accommodate and to an existing design. The smaller yards were also building naval craft and auxiliaries, and coaster orders were fitted in around these. Richards Ironworks Ltd of Lowestoft managed to complete eight coasters of 137 ft during 1941–44. The fifth of these was *Empire Sportsman*, which is seen in the colours of her first commercial owner Robert Rix & Sons, Hull as *Norrix** passing Erith in July 1952. She had a six-cylinder two-stroke oil engine built by Crossley Brothers Ltd of Manchester. Sold to Greek owners in 1961, she lasted under the name *Ionion* until broken up at Perama in 1985.

Examples of wartime coasters built to an existing design include three 193-ft coasters from Vickers Armstrongs Ltd at Barrow-in-Furness and S P Austin & Sons Ltd at Sunderland, *River Fisher*, *Race Fisher** and *Stream Fisher*. The basis of their design was the *Shoal Fisher*, delivered by Vickers to James Fisher & Sons Ltd of Barrow-in-Furness in 1937 as this owner's first motor ship.

The first of the three war-built ships, and the only one from Barrow, *River Fisher* had been ordered by Fisher and had been launched under this name in October 1941, only to be taken over by the Ministry of War Transport and completed as *Empire Jack*. Fisher bought all three sisters in 1946, restoring the name *River Fisher* to the Barrow-built example and naming the Sunderland pair *Race Fisher* and *Stream Fisher*.

The attraction of this design to the British government's planners was its capacity for loading heavy, indivisible items of cargo such as locomotives or complete marine engines. Post-war, Fisher used all three in the heavy-lift capacity, but all eventually lost their cargo gear and were used on pioneering container services across the Irish Sea. The photograph of *Race Fisher* on the Mersey has been chosen to show her retaining her cargo gear. Her layout, with raised quarterdeck and a three-deck superstructure, was almost the prototype for distinctively British motor coaster in post-war years. The 738-grt motor ship was sold to Iranian owners in 1967 as *Fardad* and was deleted by from *Lloyd's Register* in 1995. James Fisher & Sons Ltd also deserted dry cargo shipping, although it is now the major British operator of coastal tankers. *(J and M Clarkson)*

Left until last are the oddest, ugliest, but most numerous war-built type, the twenty-five units of the 148-ft, 410-grt 'Empire F' class. As discussed in Chapter 6, these were planned as CHANT-type coastal tankers for the invasion of Continental Europe, but were completed as dry cargo ships. They were designed to be built from a total of twenty-eight prefabricated units produced by inland factories and delivered by lorry to two shipyards on the Humber that joined the pieces together. An unusual feature was that the aftermost hatch was trunked to the same height as the poop deck. Reflecting the origin of the design as a tanker, freeboard alongside the well deck was low when in loaded condition.

In contrast to the CHANTs, which were all sold abroad after the war, most 'Empire Fs' found British owners, many of which had long service from them, only selling or scrapping them when their twenty-year special survey became due. The first of the class, assembled by Henry Scarr Ltd at Hessle, managed a creditable twenty-eight years' service. Intended to be *Chant 14*, she was then assigned the name *Fabric 14* but was launched in June 1944 as *Empire Fabric*. As *Torridge Lass** she was owned in Bideford from 1952 to 1963 when, like several others of the class, she crossed the Atlantic to work on the St Lawrence, in her case as *Ste Marguerite*. Renamed *Prince Loys*, she was laid up in 1972 with damage to her Ruston & Hornsby engine, but was not broken up until 1977. *(Ships in Focus)*

A distinctively British design

With Dutch and German competition muted in immediate post-war years, British coaster owners enjoyed excellent trading conditions for almost ten years. The diesel engine was by now firmly established as the most economic power-plant for a coaster, and all surviving coaster builders produced examples. As elsewhere, design development was gradual, and most ships were similar in layout to pre-war examples although often with 'styling' which updated their appearance. The bridge-aft, raised quarterdeck layout enjoyed a very strong following. Lacking the Dutch obsession with achieving a minimal air-draught, the superstructure was enlarged so that the wheelhouse was often atop two decks, and generously sized funnels were usually specified to display the owners' colours. The result was a design which was distinctively British even when, in several cases, UK owners ordered them from the Netherlands.

*Beauly Firth** of 1949 exemplifies the type, although with such muted styling of features such as wheelhouse and funnel that she could easily have been mistaken for a vessel built ten years earlier. This view emphasises her graceful sheer line, accentuated by owner Gillie & Blair's insistence on a white line separating red boot topping and black hull. Responsible for this 168-ft, 553-grt coaster was the Greenock yard, which had built extensively for Everard in the 1930s, now known as George Brown (Marine) Ltd. A six-cylinder engine was supplied by the National Gas & Oil Engine Co Ltd of Ashton-under-Lyne. *Beauly Firth* was sold to Canadian owners in 1962 and became *Nelson B*, only to sink after running aground on the coast of Nova Scotia in January 1967. *(Ships in Focus)*

In parallel with the Dutch trend, British owners with experience of sailing barges – which were gradually fitted with auxiliary oil engines – were keener on building fully powered motor coasters than those who owned established steam coaster fleets. Such owners whose ships are featured here are Everard of Greenhithe, Goldsmith of London, Horlock of Mistley and the London & Rochester Trading Co Ltd. The last-named company originated on the River Medway as a wooden barge builder, which was drawn into operating barges for which its customers could not pay. Motor barges came in 1911, gradually becoming more like coasters, and from 1936 true motor coasters followed, beginning with the Goole-built *Crescence*. Her name was inspired by the crescent moon on the London & Rochester flag, and inaugurated a nomenclature applied to over fifty motor ships.

London & Rochester's fourteenth coaster was *Pertinence**, built by Clelands (Successors) Ltd at Wallsend in 1958. She had exactly the same forecastle/quarterdeck/poop-deck layout as *Beauly Firth*, and even has similar cargo gear, albeit she was considerably larger at 206 ft and 868 grt. However, the sweeping curves to the hances where her bulwarks change height and the rounded superstructure and funnel gave her a rather different appearance. The platform around the base of her mainmast on which her winches were mounted was becoming a common feature. *Pertinence* served until 1979, when her Newbury diesel engine needed replacement. She then went to owners in Gibraltar and was put under the Panamanian flag as *Caroline*. She was taken to Annan on the Solway Firth for use as a warehouse, but became derelict and was broken up in 1994.

A Scottish-owned and built example of the bridge-aft, raised quarterdeck design was *Saint Aidan**, completed in 1962 by Charles Connell & Co Ltd at Scotstoun for J & A Gardner & Co Ltd of Glasgow. Her derrick platform is unusually high, and she is in the process of losing her cargo gear: the derrick on the mast immediately ahead of the superstructure has already gone in this photograph. Before becoming steam ship owners in 1876, the Gardners owned slate and granite quarries in the west of Scotland, and stone along with coal and sand continued to be frequent cargoes for their ships. The particular variety of sand found at Lochaline on the West Coast of Scotland was particularly suitable for use in toothpaste, and many sand cargoes were carried along the Manchester Ship Canal to Colgate-Palmolive's Salford factory by Gardner's ships such as the 973-grt *Saint Aidan*. Following her sale in 1983 she went to the Caribbean and was last reported in 2002 as owned in the Dominican Republic as *San Andres*,.

In 1963, Gardner followed *Saint Aidan* with an order to the 'Gideon' yard in Groningen for a very similar ship, *Saint Colman*, which like *Saint Aidan* had an eight-cylinder engine made by the English Electric Co Ltd of Newton-le-Willows in Lancashire. Shorter at 205 ft rather than 211 ft, *Saint Colman* was designed to negotiate another Ship Canal, that to the Irish town of Newry, after whose patron saint she was named. *Saint Colman* worked for Gardner until 1981 when, after a spell in Dutch ownership, she too went to the Caribbean. *(Ships in Focus)*

'Yellow perils'

The desire to place the bridge amidships in larger coasters persisted right into the 1960s, and was responsible for some of the most aesthetically satisfying designs of post-war years. Among these were twelve ships built from 1949 to 1958 for F T Everard & Sons Ltd, exemplified by *Sanguity** of 1956, one of eight members of the class from the Grangemouth Dockyard Co Ltd.

The major change during this building programme was the replacement of the traditional wood and canvas hatch covers with Macgregor steel covers in *Sanguity* and three others. In these ships, the derricks became largely redundant: with wooden hatch covers their main use had been handling the hatch beams. Her steel hatch covers meant that *Sanguity* was one of the last to be sold, leaving the Everard fleet in 1978 and not broken up until 1994.

Of 230 ft in length, *Sanguity* had a gross tonnage of 1577, comfortably under the figure of 1600 grt at which regulations required a larger crew including a radio officer and much more sophisticated radio equipment. The ships were of a suitable size for the locks at Goole, and from there they lifted much Yorkshire coal for South Coast ports, especially Portsmouth. Once discharged, the ships might load road stone for London at Newlyn or Dean Quarry. From the Thames there could be a cargo of cement clinker to Glasgow, Drogheda or Denmark. Other frequent cargoes included grain, while soya beans were often transshipped from ocean-going ships at Rotterdam and brought to Erith on the Thames.

Comben Longstaff contrasts

William Comben Longstaff was a latecomer to coastal shipping, a field he entered only in 1919. However, unlike other late converts, Longstaff's shipping venture, which eventually became Comben Longstaff & Co Ltd, was a devoted user of steam ships. The company ordered two motor coasters from a Dutch yard in 1937 but sold both of these within a few years, buying and then building a long succession of steamers. These culminated in what was almost the last British steamer built for general coasting, *Cardiganbrook*, completed in March 1952. Hedging its bets, the company built an almost identical sister, *Cardiffbrook**, delivered in October 1952 but with a diesel engine made by the shipbuilder, John Lewis & Sons Ltd of Aberdeen. Both vessels adopted the three-hatch layout exemplified by *Sanguity* but were a size larger, *Cardiffbrook* measuring 273 ft overall and 1812 grt. The company's devotion to steam was not surprising because the ships habitually ran in the east coast coal trade, and ship owners worried that their coal industry customers might be upset if the ships in the trade did not themselves burn coal.

The pair remained in the fleet until 1969 when, surprisingly, the motor ship proved more difficult to sell than the steamer, and whereas *Cardiganbrook* went in March, *Cardiffbrook* took until October to find a buyer. Despite this, *Cardiganbrook* was broken up just twelve months later after a brief career under the Panamanian flag as *Maria Than*. In contrast, the diesel-driven *Cardiffbrook* survived until 1983, having had five separate owners and carrying the names *Dimitrios* and *Marietta* under the Greek and Cypriot flags.

After *Cardiganbrook*, Comben Longstaff ordered only motor ships. Initially, Dutch yards built all but one of these, albeit to the distinctively 'British' raised quarterdeck, bridge aft configuration. However, in 1961 the company took delivery of the first five ships to the XL 2400 design of Clelands Shipbuilding Co Ltd, Wallsend. *Cornishbrook* was followed in 1963 by *Chesterbrook*, and in 1964 by *Corkbrook**, *Caernarvonbrook*, and *Clarebrook*. They were readily recognisable with their distinctive stern treatment, a superstructure stopping well short of the stern, and stubby signal mast aft. These measured 265 ft and 1594 grt, just within the 1600 grt size limit. Everard also took several.

The class expanded the company's trading area and, although they carried coal from the Tyne and Goole to southern England, they also ran from South Wales to the Bay of Biscay ports, to the eastern seaboard of Canada and to the Baltic and White seas. They were regularly chartered for liner voyages to North African ports, loading second-hand cars in Hull and returning with Moroccan phosphates or Italian pumice.

The ships were rather flimsily built, with leaking rivets in the ballast tanks and bulwarks which parted company with the deck in heavy seas. In later years, their plating and tank tops suffered badly from corrosion, although contributing factors were the corrosive sulphur and fertiliser cargoes they carried and the salt water used to wash out the holds. All five of the class were sold in 1976, *Corkbrook* following the familiar route into Greek ownership with frequent sales and renamings. When she arrived at an Aliaga scrapyard in September 2001 as *Chios*, she was under her seventh name. *(J and M Clarkson)*

The last conventional coasters

After the XL 2400 designs, Comben Longstaff turned to Cochrane & Sons Ltd for their 1596-grt, 86-metre long S class: *Stirlingbrook*, *Sussexbrook**, *Somersetbrook*, *Surreybrook* and *Solentbrook*. Four were completed at Cochrane's Selby yard in 1970 and 1971, the *Solentbrook* coming in 1972 from the Hull yard of the Drypool Engineering & Dry Dock Co Ltd, which had acquired Cochrane. These were the last ships the company built in a British yard, a contributing factor to the decision to order in the UK being an investment grant from the government.

Although they were used for some coastal voyages, the ships were intended to run to the Mediterranean, the White Sea and the Baltic, and were accordingly fitted with four 3-tonne derricks. The ability to discharge their own cargo earned the ships a premium rate in the packaged timber trade from the White Sea, but as the ships aged the gear became unreliable and needed constant maintenance. A novel feature for the owners was that the engine room was automated for unmanned operation. With a view to loading fruit and vegetable as a back cargo for Mediterranean voyages, the ships' holds were fitted with ventilation fans. Surprisingly, given this fitting, outmoded DC electrical equipment was specified, which continued to hamper the ships' performance. Only the final member of the class, *Solentbrook*, had modern AC equipment. Despite this drawback, and a number of serious incidents, the class was considered very successful, although they were sold in the early 1980s. *Sussexbrook* went in 1982 and then carried no fewer than nine further names. As the Syrian *Mustafa* she arrived at Aliaga to be broken up in May 2010.

Clelands' *Kindrence** of 1976 and sister *Luminence* offer an interesting contrast with the XL 2400 series above. The raised-quarterdeck configuration was now obsolete – not before time, perhaps. Although the amidships section is almost devoid of sheer, the hull has a pleasing appearance thanks to the high, rising forecastle and the generously curved hances that connect the bulwarks alongside the hatches with those on the forecastle and poop. Cargo equipment was eliminated: the gear mounted on a table between the two hatches moved the steel hatch covers. *Kindrence* spent much time on charter to the Central Electricity Generating Board carrying coal for its smaller power stations, a trade in which cargo gear was unnecessary.

Owners were London & Rochester Trading Co Ltd, long devotees of the motor coaster, and at 1596 grt and 91 metres length overall they were the largest ships the former barge operators ever owned. They were also the last of the 'traditional' coasters owned, as subsequent orders were all for low-air-draught vessels. Similar vessels to *Kindrence* but with bipod masts were built at Wallsend and at Goole for other owners, including Everard.

From 1991, the sisters were registered in the Bahamas, a move more to do with employing non-British crews than reducing certification requirements. The owners' title had by now become Crescent Shipping Ltd, reflecting a trading name that had been used for some years.

Kindrence was sold in June 2001 after a very satisfactory twenty-five years of trading for its original owner, no mean feat in the latter part of the twentieth century. New owners in Croatia simply abbreviated her name to *Kindred*. As *Chance* she is still afloat in 2011 under the Tanzanian flag. *(World Ship Society)*

In contrast to *Sussexbrook*, most of the later coasters built in the United Kingdom disdained any sort of cargo gear. *Peacock Venture** was built in 1982 for Peacock Salt Ltd by J W Cook & Co (Wivenhoe) Ltd. At 998 grt and 67 metres overall length, she was the last ship built with the yard's 'Colne' type hull. Introduced with *Moler Venture* of 1972, this was designed with flat shell plating and a multi-chine hull, rather like the dinghies built elsewhere on the River Colne. The aim was to reduce construction and repair costs, and around fifteen hulls of the type were built to various sizes.

Peacock Venture occasionally carried salt for her owner, which was a Glasgow salt merchant, but mainly traded with other bulk cargoes, venturing as far south as Spain. Manager was J & A Gardner & Co Ltd, which already owned several ships with the 'Colne' type hull.

Peacock Venture was sold in 1988 and as *Alila* and later *Alice* had a string of British owners, which managed the unwelcome feat of getting their ship arrested twice in the 1990s in respect of arrears on her mortgage. In 1995, she went to Dutch owners that renamed her *Bluebird*. Retaining this name, she has since moved to a Latvian owner, which, following the lead of many German coaster owners, registered her in St Vincent and the Grenadines. The Wivenhoe yard where she was built was no more fortunate than *Peacock Venture*, going into receivership in May 1986 and closing for good in September, the site later being cleared for housing.

The preponderance at the end of this chapter of ships from the same British fleets is excused on the grounds that they were among the few ordering new coasters from British yards towards the end of the twentieth century. *Selectivity** of 1984 was one of the last dry cargo coasters built for Everard, part of an order for four placed with Cochrane at Selby (three) and Richards Shipbuilders Ltd at Lowestoft (one) for ships measuring 799 grt on an overall length of 79 metres. The photograph shows her in January 1991 carrying desulphurisation equipment for Drax power station in Yorkshire. A temporary wheelhouse has been fitted on her forecastle.

The ships were designed for flexibility, and their tank tops were strengthened for carrying heavy items such as steel coils. Their single box holds had portable steel bulkheads, which could be used to separate different types or grades of cargo. These were also particularly valuable when carrying grain, as they could be arranged so that the grain came high enough up the hold so that stability could be assured without the need to top off the cargo with bagged grain.

Everard originally operated two, *Selectivity* and the Lowestoft-built *Pamela Everard*, with two going to the associated J Wharton (Shipping) Ltd as *Willonia* and *Stevonia*. From 1986, the latter pair was transferred to Everard ownership as *Sanguity* and *Sociality*. In 2001, *Selectivity* found a Cardiff owner, Charles M Willie & Co (Shipping) Ltd, which renamed her *Celtic Pioneer*. After a further sale in 2006, she runs as *Nural Stevns* for Danish owners, under Turkish management and flying the flag of Antigua and Barbuda. *(K S Garrett)*

'YDD boxes'

The story of the British motor coaster began with motor barges, and was to more-or-less end with them. One of the last large series of coaster to be built in the UK was based on an inland waterways craft conceived by the Yorkshire Dry Dock Co Ltd of Hull to carry grain from Liverpool to Manchester. A manager of the shipping company Eggar, Forrester (Holdings) Ltd heard about these twin-screw vessels and believed that they could be modified to make coastal cargo vessels. Three such were eventually ordered from the Hull yard. Delivered from 1976, they were rather basic vessels that, for instance, dispensed with water ballast capacity but which restricted their ability to operate in bad weather conditions. United States-designed Caterpillar diesels were fitted to drive two Aquamaster propellers, although the engines were working so hard that excessive maintenance was required. An attraction for the owner was that the ships could be crewed with just four men; seamen found them less appealing, however. The photograph of the 495-grt *Wilks** in the Ouse in May 1979 helps explain why these, 44-metre vessels from Yorkshire Dry Dock were dubbed 'YDD boxes'.

The Hoo, Kent, family concern R Lapthorn & Co Ltd, managed the three ships, plus three more that were built by A/S Nordsoværftet at Ringkobing. The Danish vessels actually came cheaper than those from Yorkshire, despite being more sophisticated vessels with double bottom ballast tanks and other equipment.

All three of these craft have since been converted to tankers; *Wilks* having the expensive luxury of a double hull, becoming *Teesdale H* in 1986. In 2008, she became *S D Teesdale* and was still afloat three years later. *(L Schofield)*

Although losing the Eggar, Forrester management contract in 1984, Lapthorn's experience of the Yorkshire Dry Dock coasters led it to order a remarkably long series from this builder. The initially box-like hull form was improved through tank testing; habitability and equipment were significantly upgraded, including the fitting of double bottoms. Size also increased: Lapthorn's first five measured 50 metres, no fewer than fourteen were then built to 58 metres, two to 69 metres, and orders concluding with four 78-metre ships, the last of which was delivered in 1992. Cummins engines were later specified in place of the Caterpillar units, still powering Aquamaster units that were modified and improved. Finance was, to say the least, complex. The shipbuilder, its ultimate owner, the shipping company John I Jacobs plc and other companies helped Lapthorn to provide the capital, although all twenty-five eventually gravitated to Lapthorn ownership. Several were converted to bulk aggregate carriers, and with an excavator as part of their deck equipment worked on various civil engineering projects, including some in London's Docklands.

*Hoo Robin** was one of the larger, 58-metre examples, completed at Hull in 1989. Lapthorn gave up ship owning in 2006, and although at least part of its erstwhile fleet continued in British ownership, its story has not been a happy one, and there have been bankruptcies among subsequent owners. *Hoo Robin* went to Coastal Bulk Shipping Ltd, which renamed her *Redwing*, but this company failed and since 2009 she has been owned in Greece as *Danae*, flying the Moldovan flag. However, in 2011 at least eight of this group of ships remained in British ownership, albeit registered in Gibraltar.

Low-air-draught fashion

The last quarter of the twentieth century saw many owners obsessed that their ships needed low-air-draught capability, something the Dutch had specified since they helped perfect the small motor coaster. One solution (as adopted in the YDD boxes) was to keep the height of the wheelhouse very low and make masts as flimsy as possible consistent with carrying navigation lights and allowing them to fold. Such was the approach taken in 1977 and 1979 by J W Cook & Co (Wivenhoe) Ltd when building coasters for Spillers Ltd, *Gainsborough Miller* and *Hull Miller* of 427 grt and 46 metres. Initially, these were owned by Spillers' subsidiary Channel Coasters Ltd, and managed by London & Rochester Trading Co Ltd.

The grain company's decision to build the ships was prompted by high freight rates currently ruling, especially in the trade to their mill at Gainsborough, high up the River Trent. In fact, Spillers had run their own ships in the past, having a not insubstantial fleet of steamers between 1906 and 1953, plus many inland craft. From this they should have realised that freight rates can go down as well as up and, by the time a second, larger pair named *London Miller* and *Birkenhead Miller* had been delivered by Cook in 1979, the boom was over. In 1981 and 1982, the managers acquired the four and renamed them, *Gainsborough Miller* becoming *Westerence**. Sold in 1987, she then had a succession of Irish and French owners as *Eve Rita*, *Mantan*, *Avoca* and *Casam III*. She was delivered to breakers in August 2010, although at the time of writing their whereabouts had not been disclosed. *(J and M Clarkson)*

The ability to clear low bridges whilst providing the navigators with a satisfactory view when at sea was achieved by providing a wheelhouse that could be raised or lowered hydraulically on a pillar. One of the few British yards to build to this design, popular in continental Europe, was Cochrane Shipbuilders Ltd of Selby.

Initial orders came from the Union Transport Group plc of Bromley, which ordered four with an option for a further two. Habitually trading up the Rhine, this owner specified a loaded draught of not more than 4.2 metres and a ballast air-draught of 6.35 metres. A combination of variable-pitch propellor (driven by a Danish diesel), active rudder and bow thrusters made these 100-metre ships particularly manoeuvrable. The first two were delivered as *Union Jupiter* and *Bromley Pearl* in 1990 (the latter subcontracted to a Hull shipyard), but problems that developed with their steel hatch covers seriously restricted their ability to trade, and led to the owners refusing to accept the third and fourth members of the class and to cancel their options on a further pair.

The makers of the hatch covers eventually solved the problems, and buyers were found for the ships still with Cochranes. Three more were completed in 1991 for associates of F T Everard & Sons Ltd, including Short Sea Europe plc, a company formed to benefit from the British government's Business Expansion Scheme: *Superiority*, *Short Sea Trader** and *North Sea Trader*. When in 2001 Everard decided to quit dry cargo shipping, *Short Sea Trader* was sold to Union Transport Group plc as *Union Saturn*, and was still in service in 2011. *(World Ship Society Ltd)*

CHAPTER

10

Other Western European Motor Coasters

The coaster owners and builders of other European countries followed the lead of the Dutch. Their motor coasters evolved partly from local sailing vessels and partly through inspiration from Dutch designs. The countries neighbouring the Netherlands – Germany and Denmark – embraced the Dutch design closest. They developed distinctive designs, initially within the same size and crewing limitations, the Germans later exploiting the liberalisation of these constraints to build ever bigger coasters.

Elsewhere, designs have often reflected the needs of a nation's trade or geographic situation. Countries to the north of the Baltic have specified ice-strengthening of hulls, while their dominant exports of timber and pulp have also influenced designs, in particular popularising the shelter-decker. Norway has a rugged Atlantic/Arctic coast that needs to be served by sea in the absence of direct land links. Many Spanish ships have been designed to carry perishable fruit and vegetables.

It is interesting to consider how and why the fortunes of the coasters of these European nations have waxed and waned. Denmark, in particular, saw a distinct peak in coaster building and ownership in the 1960s, which quickly flattened and then declined, although the country is still an important maritime nation. The most impressive rise, however, has been Germany, reflected in the dominance of its builders in this chapter. Trailing the Dutch until around 1960, Germany's coaster owners and builders have since streaked ahead, its fleet doubling between 1958 and 1984, so that German vessels have become the dominant force in European coastal shipping. Encouraging fiscal and particular taxation regimes have some part to play; but owners, builders and financiers have seized opportunities that have slipped through the fingers of their counterparts elsewhere, most spectacularly those in the United Kingdom. It remains to be seen if German owners and yards can continue to resist economic pressures from eastern Europe and the Far East.

In this chapter, which takes the story of the bulk-carrying motor coaster forward to the present day, general trends over time are apparent, such as increase in capacity of ships and diminution of cargo handling gear. In parallel with the seemingly inexorable growth in size of ships working in short-sea trades, there has been a trend for smaller coasters to become uneconomic in all but very specialised northern European trades. Craft of under 1000 grt have largely gravitated elsewhere for employment, especially towards the Caribbean, while virtually no new ships of this size are being built, helping the survival of a small number of veterans.

An asterisk in a caption indicates the vessel shown in the photograph.

Auxiliary Germans

Nothing demonstrates so graphically the rise of German coastal shipping as the observation that the nation that is today's leading owner of short-sea vessels was still building auxiliary sailing coasters as recently as the late 1930s. In 1928, the steel three-masted schooner *Bishorst* was completed by Werft Nobiskrug GmbH at Rendsburg for a Hamburg owner. Her auxiliary was a modest, two-stroke, hot-bulb engine made by Junkers Motorenbau AG of Dessau. In 1933, this was replaced by a much more powerful diesel engine made by Deutsche Werke AG at Kiel. Sails were not entirely dispensed with, however, as evidenced by this photograph of the auxiliary as *Falkenstein**, a name adopted in 1938 when bought by Otto Fahje of Hamburg.

Although a modest 120 ft registered length and 173 grt, she was quite capable of crossing the North Sea to the River Ouse. As well as ratlines and furled canvas, her auxiliary origins are apparent in her deep sheer, whaleback forecastle, tall masts, wheelhouse placed well aft on the poop and – apparently – the absence of a recognisable funnel.

The little ship survived well into the container era, probably because trading to small German islands in the Baltic and North Sea needs modest-sized vessels, and still does to this day. Following sale by Fahje in 1958, her name was changed to *Mehe* in 1961 and as such she lasted until broken up in 1970. *(C A Hill)*

Caution is needed in interpreting post-Second World War photographs of older German coasters as these vessels were often rebuilt in the 1950s and given modern wheelhouses and cargo gear. However, even if pre-war registers had not listed *Weserland** as an auxiliary when built as late as 1938, her stumpy bowsprit is a giveaway, as are her tall masts and the sheer of her hull. Her engine was a four-cylinder Deutsche Werke diesel delivering 150 bhp, and its power and its retention when she lost her rig suggests that the sails were to help the engine, rather than the other way around.

Builders in 1938 were C Lühring of Kirchhammelwarden and her original name was *Marie Schwinge* for a Herr Schwinge in Brake. A little larger than *Falkenstein*, she measured 147 ft in length and 205 grt. In August 1940, she was drafted into the Kriegsmarine for Operation 'Seelöwe' but, when in one of Herr Hitler's wiser decisions the planned invasion of Britain was cancelled, she was restored to mercantile use early in 1941. The name *Weserland* was bestowed on her by Ernst Otto Bürger in 1957, and it is likely that she retained her distinctive but long-redundant bowsprit as well as her 1938 engine until she was broken up in Hamburg during 1971.

1950s Germans

Dutch influence is apparent in the coaster designs produced when German shipbuilding resumed in the 1950s. Spelling out his protestant work ethic, *Labor et Fides** owner Bernard Tapken of Kiel even gave her a name that could have graced a Dutch coaster, some owners of which were wont to lapse into Latin tags on launch day.

Her builders in 1954 were Büsumer Schiffswerft, length 151 ft and tonnage 299 gross. Features that distinguish her from many Dutch contemporaries are the extra tall masts intended to support the radio aerial stretching from the poop, and generous winch platforms at the foot of each mast.

Labor et Fides was to have a string of further names following sale by her original Kiel-based owner in 1964. As *Jutta Brey* and later *Hubert* she remained in German hands until 1983 when she moved to Gibraltar as *Delta Lady*. The name *Lee Shore* that soon followed appeared to tempt fate. This was succeeded by *Nordica Star* and then *Millsupplier*. Under the latter name she became disabled in the North Sea in December 1990, and was towed into Lowestoft. She was in need of repair, was arrested by the Admiralty Marshall, but found a new 'unlucky' owner that traded her during 1992–93. On 23 February 1993, she sprang a leak off Europoort and was eventually broken up at Amsterdam in 1995.

Owners in one country were quite at liberty to buy from the yards of another, and particularly to purchase second-hand vessels built abroad. The latter was particularly the case in Germany, where coaster owners had to virtually renew their fleets after both world wars. Inevitably, these incoming ships influenced designs from local yards.

Schiffswerft H Rancke of Neuenfelde completed the 165-ft, 387-grt *Bernd-Gunda** for a Hamburg owner in 1957, and again she could have been Dutch apart from her winch platforms. As in *Labor et Fides*, the boat deck continues right aft but is given raking stanchions, a styling feature that was adopted by the Dutch and others. Needing varnishing to maintain it, the wooden wheelhouse is a symbol of the pride of original owner Willi Bartels, whose initials can be discerned on the funnel.

Following her sale in 1974, she became first *Miranda* and in 1981 *Ilwa*. Not long after taking the latter name she was involved in collision with the Nigerian motor vessel *River Mada* while on a voyage from Sölvesborg to Hamburg on 23 December 1981. Fire broke out, which rendered *Ilwa* fit only for scrap and early the next year she was towed to Bremen for demolition. *(F R Sherlock)*

Distinctive Germans

By the 1960s, German coaster builders had gained sufficient confidence to develop their own designs, and some very pleasing and distinctive vessels emerged. The two examples here were photographed in one of the German coaster's natural habitats, the Kiel Canal.

Orion III was built for Jakob Bruhn & Co of Hamburg in 1966 by Husumer Schiffswerft GmbH and was 196 ft long and measured 499 grt. She follows the 1960s trend to provide additional cargo gear, with a mainmast between her two holds. A feature becoming increasingly common was a signal mast above the wheelhouse, in her case pleasingly faired into the funnel. She had a remarkably graceful sheer, with flowing hances where the bulwarks rise to forecastle and poop.

Orion III had numerous German owners, but only in 1984 did her name change, becoming *Lore I*, and later *Södan*. She left German ownership in December 1997, when she was renamed *Malabo*. In 2011, she was believed still afloat. *(F R Sherlock)*

Hans Lehmann II was almost contemporary with *Orion III*, but a size larger. She was completed at the end of 1965 by D W Kremer Sohn at Elmshorn for Lübeck owners, who unsurprisingly had the family name Lehmann. Evidently a larger vessel was really needed, because after less than two years in service she was lengthened from the original 217 ft to 238 ft, growing in the process from 817 to 985 grt. It is likely that at this time any cargo gear that she had at birth was removed, and what remained of her masts sufficed merely to carry navigation lights, to support aerials and to allow flags to be flown. Her hull has the flowing lines of *Orion III*, but the treatment of the wheelhouse was different, with the windows sloping inwards to help avoid reflections.

The *II* was dropped from the name in 1972, but after 1977 renamings came quickly as she changed owners and flags. First she became *Hera* under the Singaporean flag, soon changing to *Perna* and Panama. From 1987 *Hatuey* (Honduras), *Oriente* (Venezuela) and *Genesis* (flag unknown) followed before she was deleted from *Lloyd's Register* in 1992. *(F R Sherlock)*

Shelter-deck Germans

Once Germany was allowed to build ships again after the Second World War and its shipyards had been restored, coaster building became prolific and distinct designs emerged. *Hans Bülow* was completed in 1953 by Orenstein & Koppel at Lübeck for an owner in Kollmar and after sale to the Hauschildt family of Hamburg in late 1964 was renamed *Estedeich**. She was a shelter-decker with a forecastle, sufficient sheer to ensure seaworthiness and a strongly raking bow. As this photograph of her transiting the Kiel Canal shows, hatch covers were still the traditional type of canvas over wooden boards, and her masts had single, conventional derricks. Tonnage was a modest 493 grt on a length of 145 ft. Sale of *Estedeich* in 1975 involved her moving to the Cypriot flag as *Sea Victory*, but was followed in October 1976 by serious damage sustained in collision with another ship near Jeddah, after which she was deliberately sunk in deep water. *(F R Sherlock)*

The layout of *Nautica** of 1963 is similar to that of *Estedeich*, but the intervening eight years has seen ideas on design change. Both the length of typical coasters and the cunningness of naval architects in minimising tonnage have increased significantly, so that this 245-ft shelter-deck coaster measures just 498 grt, despite being one hundred feet longer than *Estedeich*. Conventional derricks have been replaced by 3-ton capacity mast cranes, and her hatches are of steel and capable of carrying containers.

Builders of *Nautica* were J J Sietas Schiffswerft of Hamburg, a yard that was coming to dominate the German market with series construction of coasters, and which will be visited again in Chapter 14. Owner of *Nautica* was the equally prolific and successful Peter Dohle Schiffahrts KG, also of Hamburg. A 1985 sale to local owners saw her name become *Nautila* and in 1993 she passed to Swedish interests who put her under the currently fashionable Belize flag of convenience and restored the name *Nautica*. In 1995, international agreement on how to measure tonnage sensibly saw her measurement increase dramatically to 1196 grt. After renaming *Fatme* briefly in 2003, she became *Lady Aziza* later that year. Reports indicate that she successively flew the flags of North Korea, land-locked Bolivia, and then Moldova, because her Syrian owners sought registers that would tolerate this ageing ship and their crewing practices. She continued to voyage in the Mediterranean in 2011. *(World Ship Society Ltd)*

Functional Germans

Perhaps the politest way to describe the sheerless, gearless, angular modern motor coaster is 'functional', as what they lack in aesthetic appeal they no doubt make up for in economical performance and earning power. *Mühlenberg** of 1986 exemplifies these features, especially with the straight hances to her forecastle and her raked upper stem, the mismatch between which does not help her appearance. She was completed in January 1986 by J J Sietas KG Schiffswerft GmbH & Co, the yard near Hamburg pausing in its frantic series construction of container ships to turn out this bulk carrier of 88 metres and 1957 grt. Her single hold offers a modest container capacity measured at ninety TEU. Motive power is provided by an engine from Klöckner-Humboldt-Deutzmotoren of Cologne.

Owners of *Mühlenberg* were Vega-Reederei Friedrich Dauber GmbH of Hamburg, the letter M on her funnel rather than V for Vega signifying that she is owned by a single-ship part-ownership company, Partenreederei ms 'Muhlenberg'. The part-ownership scheme offers tax concessions to small investors who put their money into ships, and has been a major factor in expanding German coastal shipping in post-war years. Of course, building a ship is one thing, operating it profitably quite another, and German operators such as Vega-Reederei have been eminently successful in this. *Mühlenberg* was sold in 2006 to the Cardiff-based Willie Group, for which she is still in service under the Bahamas flag as *Celtic Mariner*.

Functional also describes the low air-draught craft that have recently become something of an obsession with owners. *Arklow Mill** was built in 1988, fourth of a class of five from Schiffswerft Hugo Peters GmbH, Wewelsfleth, her sisters being *Arklow Manor*, *Arklow Mansion*, *Arklow Marsh* and *Arklow Meadow*. Of 1524 grt and 74 metres overall, their capacity is just thirty-one 20-foot containers, although they are meant for the bulk trades, especially grain. *Arklow Mill* is carrying such a cargo on a wintry 15 December 1997 as she ghosts towards the entrance to the Manchester Ship Canal. Grain carriers were among the last vessels to trade to the upper reaches of this waterway, and she had just passed her fleet mate *Arklow Fame* outward bound from the cereal factory.

The choice of *Arklow Mill* to exemplify this type allows us to celebrate the achievements of Ireland's most successful shipping company, Arklow Shipping Co Ltd. Over the years, its antecedents had moved cautiously from auxiliary sailing vessels to second-hand motor coasters, but in 1966 decided to combine their operations. Arklow Shipping Co Ltd began ship owning in its own right in 1970, and the fleet built up rapidly, with second-hand and later new ships, the 'Ms' representing their first foray into low air-draught vessels. Grain is not their only regular cargo, and other bulk cargoes including scrap, stone, salt and china clay are handled.

Arklow Shipping has a strategy of renewing its fleet regularly, and in 2004 the eight-year old *Arklow Mill* and her sister *Arklow Marsh* were sold to Norway, the former becoming *Falknes* under the Bahamas flag. In 2011, she was still in Norwegian ownership as *Jago*. *(Author)*

Danish single-deck designs

*Fryken** is something of a celebrity, in that she is preserved as a rare European example of a relatively large coaster (1024 grt and 217 ft overall), and is on display in Gothenburg. Builders in 1938 were Aalborg Værft A/S, and so it is interesting that Sweden has chosen to preserve a Danish-built ship. However, she was built to the order of Swedes, the Broström Group, so she embodies some characteristic features typical of Swedish rather than Danish design practice. These include the large, upright funnel, comparatively tall superstructure with its wood-panelled wheelhouse and kingposts rather than a mast forward.

In 1961, her original owners sold *Fryken* to other Swedes and she became *Svanö*. In 1971, she was sold again and placed under the Panamanian flag, although her new name *Isvania* and continued local trading strongly suggested her ultimate new owners were Swedish. She was actually sold to breakers at Skärhamn in 1986, but someone recognised her historical value as a museum exhibit, and she was bought by the Göteborg Maritime Center and returned to Broström colours. Typical of this owner, the letter F on her funnel identifies the actual original owning company, Ångbåts A/B Ferm, while the underlying colours of three red rings on black are those of the parent group.

For a small nation, albeit one with a strong seafaring tradition, Denmark has some remarkable maritime achievements; in marine engineering, in container, reefer and Arctic shipping, and in gas carrying. For a period in post-war years it also challenged the Netherlands and Germany in building and operating small motor coasters, helped significantly by a benign investment and tax regime for ship owners.

Examples from the 1960s often closely imitated the designs of Denmark's neighbours in the Netherlands. *Gittelil**, for example, has the classic Dutch arrangement of two masts and two 2.5-tonne derricks, the latter supported when stowed by a single crutch between the two hatches. Perhaps a small difference is distinguishable in the styling of the wheelhouse and the small funnel perched on it.

Gittelil was built in 1963 by Nordsøværftet of Ringkøbing for A N Svarrer of Esbjerg and measured 164 ft with a tonnage of 400 gross. Sold in 1970, she was renamed *Tinou Bell* for a Copenhagen owner, who was not alone among Danes in not considering her modest size and speed of just 9.5 knots a deterrent to trading further afield. On 31 March 1973, she foundered off Ghana while on voyage from Rotterdam to Cape Town with a cargo of explosives. *(Fotoflite/Skyfotos)*

Danish shelter-deckers

Denmark's motor coasters were readily recognisable although, with several yards building series of ships to their own designs, it is hard to single out characteristics that made them distinctively Danish. Features of *Flemming Scan** found in other Danes include the almost sheerless hull, strongly raked stem, funnel faired into the signal mast and tapering masts. A product of Frederikshavn Værft & Tørdok A/S at Frederikshavn, she was completed in 1969 as *Helle Klint*. She was built with a British engine, made by Lister Blackstone Marine Ltd of Dursley, a rare example of such an engine being exported for fitting in a hull built outside of the United Kingdom. This machinery was replaced with a Danish-built diesel in 1977. A two-deck ice-strengthened ship, she had three derricks of capacity between three and five tonnes, serving her two hatches. Her dimensions were 65 metres overall length and a modest 400 grt.

While owned by Leif A J Hansen of Aarhus from 1974 until 1978, she carried both the names *Flemming Scan* and *Flemming*. Her last owner, based in Jakarta, renamed her *Pulau Seribu* in 1993. In April 2004, she arrived at Chittagong to be broken up. *(Ships in Focus)*

The once prolific Danish yard of A/S Nordsøværftet at Ringkøbing has been met with in other chapters, building single-deck and low air draft coasters. It also built a distinctive class of two-deck ships, of which the 1982-built, 499-grt, 72-metre *Arktis Star** was a part. She was the first of eight delivered to Elite-Shipping A/S of Copenhagen.

She was seen while employed carrying a project cargo, plant for a large engineering contract, and for this she was certificated for worldwide trading. Project cargoes need considerable care because large, indivisible items had to be cautiously lifted on and off, and protected when carried as deck cargo. The *Arktis Star* class had two derricks each capable of a 15-tonne lift, which was very modest when compared with the kit fitted to the dedicated heavy-lift ships considered in Chapter 16.

The substantial Elite-Shipping fleet was financed partly through the tax-efficient K/S scheme once popular in Denmark in which investments in shipping could be deducted from other income. But the fleet disappeared almost as quickly as it was built up. *Arktis Star* was sold in 1995, and since 2007 has been trading under the Indian flag, most recently as *Sakthi*. Interestingly, under the 1969 International Tonnage Convention, her tonnage has more than tripled to 1510 grt.

The Nordsøværftet 72-metre design was available in both 'tween-deck and single-deck form. However, despite selling in good numbers, it did not save the 'North Sea Works', to translate its title, which has since succumbed to East Asian competition. *(Fotoflite/Skyfotos)*

Norwegian wood

*Beco** is unusual: a wooden motor coaster of the twentieth century. During the Second World War, Norway saw an upsurge in wooden shipbuilding, with several varieties built, one around 90 ft and another 120 ft. These last wooden ships built in the country were by South Coast yards that had been active in a wooden shipbuilding boom of the 1870s.

Ten wooden coasters of about 120 ft were built during 1941–46. Six were built by Ancas Treskibsbyggeri near Arendal: *Norfart* in 1942, *Norfisk* in 1942, *Transit* in 1943, *Trollhaug* in 1944, *Randoy* in 1945 and *Peco* in 1946. *Peco* was typical of the design with engine and accommodation aft, one hold and two hatches. Most were employed in the fish trade, and some – including *Peco* – were fitted with refrigeration plants for carrying frozen fish. She was completed in October 1946 as *Peco*, but after the owners went bankrupt in 1955, she was acquired by Kaare Bertnes, Bodø and was renamed *Beco**. In the early 1960s, she was still in the fish trade, with frequent voyages from northern Norway to Grimsby and Hamburg, also from Stornoway to Hamburg and Grimsby to Ventspils.

Beco was sold in January 1966 to North Star Shipping Ltd, Halifax, Nova Scotia for £25,000, and renamed *North Star* under Panama registry. Despite her Canadian ownership, she met her end running aground at Corfu in the Ionian Sea on 8 January 1968, reportedly with a cargo of cigarettes. Although refloated, she was declared a constructive total loss.

Norwegian steel

Norway might have come late to coaster construction, but its yards were successful in winning orders from both domestic and other Scandinavian owners – a notable achievement in a high-wage economy and in a country that does not have a massive industrial base. The yard of Batservice Verft A/S at Mandal was particularly prolific, with a type of two-deck coaster that proved especially popular with Danish owners. The combination of masts, compact superstructure and funnel shape was distinctive, but the hull shape was also readily recognisable in examples with no cargo gear and even in a hull form variant without a forecastle.

A Danish-owned example was *Dumos*, built in 1968 for Albrecht & Boserup of Odense, here seen transiting the Kiel Canal with a deck cargo of timber. Her open shelter deck configuration resulted in a very modest tonnage of 300 grt on an overall length of 180 ft. *Dumos* was sold by her original owners in 1979, and in 2011 was under her sixth name, *Dimitris P*, under the flag of Honduras for an anonymously named but probably Greek-owned company.

This aerial view of *Lysvik* with a well-stowed deck cargo of timber tends to emphasise her beam, yet when completed she was a relatively modest coaster of 67 metres and 499 grt, a rebuild in 1980 increasing these figures to 82 metres and 683 grt. Owners were Simonsen & Slang A/S of Oslo, the logo of which appears on her funnel, and which was proprietor of the Lys Line, which ran between Norway and western European ports for many years. The ice-strengthened, two-deck *Lysvik* was built by Orens at Trondheim in 1974. When masts were fitted at all to coasters of this period, bipods were usually chosen to avoid the need for stays. *Lysvik's* bipods support two 5-tonne derricks. Register entries after her 1980 lengthening mention a side door, reflecting her use in the forest products trade, but omission of such an entry in later registers suggests the door was suppressed when she moved to Mediterranean owners and the facility was no longer needed.

In 1992, *Lysvik* was sold to an owner in Riga when Estonia, no longer part of the USSR, resumed its role as an independent maritime nation. Briefly renamed *Lubana*, she was then chartered by Bremer Reederei Bruno Bischoff & Co GmbH of Bremen, which had her renamed *Bremer Import*. In 1996, came sale to a Greek owner and renaming *Michalis*, under which name she is still in service in the Mediterranean.

Spanish coasters

Spanish builders and owners have concentrated on shelter-deck tonnage, reflecting the importance of their country's fruit and vegetable exports. The country's single-deck coasters are characterised by extensive cargo gear, reflecting the relative lack of equipment at ports served.

The 677-grt, 178-ft *Conde de Figols** came from the Bilbao yard of Astilleros T Ruiz de Velasco in 1957 for Aviles Aznar SA of Barcelona. Her career was cut short on 13 August 1968 when she foundered off the Spanish coast while carrying a cargo of olive oil and cellulose paste from Tenerife to Barcelona.

Long a maritime nation, Spain had a considerable shipping fleet that until the 1950s was composed largely of antiquated steamers. With growing industrialisation, shipyards became an important aspect of the economy, building both for domestic use and, increasingly, for export.

Considerably larger and even more heavily equipped with derricks than *Conde de Figols* was *Puerto de Huelva** at 1520 grt and 266 ft overall. Built in 1959 by Hijos de J Barreras SA at Vigo, she was owned in the iron ore exporting port whose name she bore by Naviera del Odiel SA. She spent her entire life under the Spanish flag, and even helped the national economy when broken up in the port of Cartagena in 1982.

CHAPTER

11

Eastern European Coasters

There are good reasons for considering the products of eastern Europe coaster builders separately from those of the western part of the continent. With their planned post-war economies, the USSR and its satellites could obtain economies of scale by concentrating ship production on several standard types. They did not have to worry over much about adaptations to suit the whims of their clients, who were mostly the shipping industries of their own and other communist countries, which had little choice but to take what they were offered. A growing number of ships were exported, however, particularly from East Germany and Poland where shipbuilding was developed as a means of earning foreign currency, and where very competitive prices could be quoted. For the shipping enthusiast, standardisation gave the interesting challenge of distinguishing the various types by their appearance, one made even more fascinating when the ships were sold and appeared in unfamiliar colours.

The industrialisation of communist countries saw some rather unlikely nations become serious builders of ships. Few were more unlikely than Hungary or Czechoslovakia, which have no sea coast, while Yugoslavia, Romania and Bulgaria also became exporters of ships. These countries make an interesting comparison with their neighbour Greece, which did not develop a significant shipbuilding industry, despite controlling the world's biggest fleet.

A further reason for separating the eastern European coasters is that they do not fall conveniently into the same categories as those built elsewhere. In post-war years Poland, for instance, was building steam coasters in numbers surpassed only by the British. While it has been expedient elsewhere in this book to deal with coasters as intended either for bulk carrying or for the liner trades, this distinction becomes blurred in eastern Europe, where the same ships appear to have been used for both types of operation.

Eastern Europe's coaster builders have had mixed fortunes since the end of communist rule. In some cases, financial involvement of western shipbuilders has helped the yards to modernise, improve quality and compete in the fierce free market for shipbuilding. Romania and Bulgaria, for instance, became involved in ventures with Dutch builders whereby the hulls are constructed cheaply in the east and brought to the Netherlands for fitting out. In several cases, however, the yards have simply closed and their skilled workforce migrated west to find work. It remains to be seen whether the surviving eastern European shipbuilders can fare better than their western counterparts in competition with the still-communist controlled economy of the People's Republic of China.

An asterisk in a caption indicates the vessel shown in the photograph.

Polish standards

For a nation with neither a strong seafaring nor shipbuilding tradition, Poland was fortunate in 'inheriting' shipyards in former German territory at Szczecin and Gdansk. Construction could therefore begin ahead of other countries in eastern Europe, and indeed the shipbuilding industry grew to be the nations's second major exporter. It was surpassed only by the mining industry, and thus it was inevitable that Poland's earliest ships were coal carriers. The collier *Soldek** was Poland's first newbuilding, completed at Zjednoczenie Stoczni Polskich, Gdansk, in October 1949. Machinery was a four-cylinder compound, coal-fired, steam engine built at Katowice, which elsewhere might be regarded as obsolescent, but given the state of Polish industry was all that could be hoped for.

The name of the 284-ft, 2005-grt collier honoured the many Poles who had fought against Nazism in various armies during the Second World War, a somewhat hypocritical gesture given how the regime treated with enormous suspicion those servicemen who did return to Poland.

Soldek and her four sisters of the B30 type were largely employed on the 'coal bridge' between Poland and Denmark, but as the photograph shows they also visited British ports, including London, in this case in January 1954. As befits something of a celebrity, *Soldek* was preserved at Gdansk when withdrawn in 1978 and represents a very rare example of a surviving steam-driven coastal cargo vessel.

In common with their fellow eastern European states with planned economies, Poland aimed to build its ships in long series. The first and eventually one of the largest series of general cargo motor coasters built was the B51 design. *Nysa** was the second of the type, delivered to Polska Zegluga Morska (Polish Steamship Company) in 1951 from the Gdansk yard, now known simply as Stocznia Gdanska. The class was 197 ft long and around 486 grt and underwent various developments over its building lifetime, including substitution of kingposts for the aftermost mast, and superficial changes to make features such as stanchions and funnel appear more 'modern'.

Nysa was singularly unfortunate in foundering in heavy weather weather in the North Sea on 10 January 1965 while carrying steel rails from Leith to Oslo. The voyage demonstrates that Polish ships were not necessarily confined to routes to and from Poland, but ran in cross-trades.

In 1960, the B51 was superseded by the B57 type, which was longer at 216 ft overall. Like the B51s, they had two decks while other differences included the forecastle-only hull configuration, the bipod mast amidships, and a completely remodelled superstructure and wheelhouse. At least a dozen were built for Polish Zegluga Morska, the builders formally and rather ideologically known as Stocznia im Komuny Paryskiej (the Paris Commune Memorial Shipyard), or Stocznia Gdynia for short.

The 1006-grt *Chochlik* of 1960 was given yard number B57/4, suggesting she was the fourth of the series. Her official ownership changed several times: to Polskie Linie Oceaniczne (Polish Ocean Lines) in 1971 and in 1981 to the newly formed Polska Zegluga Baltycka (the Polish Baltic Shipping Company). Once communist rule ended, she was renamed *San* in 1991 under yet another owner. In 1998, the coaster became one of the few ships owned by Albania, which did not bother to rename her. Details of her end are uncertain, as she is reported on two separate occasions to have been sold to breakers at Aliaga, but most likely she was demolished there in 2006. *(Ships in Focus)*

East Germans

On its formation, the new state of East Germany, or the Deutsche Demokratische (*sic*) Republik, had to build a merchant fleet virtually from scratch, such had been the depradations among German ships during and just after the war. Like other Soviet satellites, East Germany soon settled to series production, and two designs dominated its coaster output.

*Insel Reims** was to a basic design dubbed 'Kümo 840' that originated with *Nordstern* of 1957. It had a deadweight tonnage of around 840 tons, with a gross tonnage of 617 and a length of 194 ft. The twin deck cranes suggest they may have been intended for liner services, but were used for general trading as well. A total of twenty-four were built between 1959 and 1962 by VEB Peene-Werft at Wolgast. Later units were taken west to Wismar to be completed, and received dual yard numbers from their builder and from VEB Mathias-Thesen-Werft. Names were initially those of stars, but East German place names were later used, as with *Insel Reims*, which had emerged in 1961 simply as *Reims*, the *Insel* added to her stern in 1965 appearing to be an afterthought.

Insel Reims left the East German fleet in 1981 and began wandering westward, changing owner, name and flag quite frequently. In 1989, she sailed as *Ari* from Lübeck for the Caribbean, and after six further name changes was last heard of there in 2002 as *Watering Bay*, her ninth name. *(F R Sherlock)*

Semlow of 1971 was part of an equally ubiquitous group, 'Standardkümo 299 brt' also known as the 'Boizenburg type', of 189 ft. This emerged in 1970 with *Boltenhagen*, delivered by VEB Vereinigte Elbewerften at Boizenburg, on the river Elbe just inside the border of East Germany. The first nine delivered (two going to Norway) were gearless, but from *Hagenow* of 1971 two slightly offset deck cranes were fitted. *Semlow* worked for VEB Deutsche Seereederei until 1991, when she was sold and went to East Africa, and was reported still in existence in 2011.

After eleven of the 'Standardkümo 299 brt' type had been delivered to VEB Deutsche Seereederei, production at the Boizenburg yard switched to a stretched, gearless version known as 'Containerkümo 499 brt'. The flat deck of the early 299-grt version was, of course, equally container-friendly, and these ships could stow a modest twenty-seven TEUs.

Yards in East Germany frequently built for other members of Comecon, but most of the coasters of the types featured here were destined for the national fleet, VEB Deutsche Seereederei, with a couple of the 'Standardkümo 299 brt' going to the USSR. It would seem East Germany could not build sufficient coasters, because once the foreign currency situation permitted it in the 1960s, a typically Dutch, raised-quarterdeck type with conventional derricks known as 'Kümo 614' was ordered in some numbers from yards in the north of the Netherlands. *(F R Sherlock)*

Budapest-built

Lack of a sea coast did not deter Hungary from developing a modest shipbuilding industry and a small deep-sea fleet. Output of the Angyalfold Shipyard in a suburb of Budapest was limited to ships of a large coaster size by the dimensions of the River Danube which provided its outlet to the sea. Again, distinctive standard types were built, examples going not only to the Hungarian national fleet, but also to the USSR, and – more surprisingly – to Norway.

The first Hungarian type emerging in 1953 had a 230-ft hull with traditional masts mounted between its three holds. In 1960, the hull design was enlarged to 259 ft, and cargo gear modified to give kingposts just ahead of the bridge and a bipod mast between the first and second holds: some authors describe this as the 'Adria' type, although the ship of this name was built in 1965, five years into the building programme. Photographed at Antwerp in May 1985, the USSR-owned *Angyalfold** of 1970 represents a further development, with a hull measuring 78 metres and 1350 grt, and minor stylistic changes to features such as the wheelhouse and funnel casing. Diesel machinery for the class came from various eastern European factories, *Angyalfold* having a license-built Sulzer engine.

Sold in 1996, *Angyalfold* became successively *Gladiator*, *Ikaria*, *Phoenix I* and *Ostria*. The former *Phoenix I* failed to rise again after foundering in the Aegean on 11 September 2004 while on a voyage from Egypt to Albania with an unlikely cargo of marble. Equally unlikely, she was under the flag of Tonga at the time. *(Author)*

Unsurprisingly, the Angyalfold yard on the Danube also built several low air-draught sea-river ships, to rather idiosyncratic designs. One of these, *Builder**, had come a long way from Budapest to be photographed at Singapore in the late 1970s. She had been built in 1962 as *Borsod* for the Hungarian-Danube Sea Navigation Co Ltd or, if you prefer it in Hungarian, Magyar Duna-Tengerhajozasi RT. Evidence from the appearance of later members of this group which were supplied to Czechoslovakia suggests that the bipod masts were late additions: the Czech members of the group built around 1966 had very light masts and deck cranes.

At 269 ft and, in *Borsod*'s case, a modest 1207 grt, these single-deck ships might penetrate well inland, but they were more than capable of lengthy deep-sea voyages. The Czech-owned *Lednice*, for example, was part of the convoy trapped in the Great Bitter Lakes when the Suez Canal was closed from 1967 to 1975.

Borsod was sold to Singapore owners as *Ningpo Lilac* in 1974 and became *Builder* a year later, again with Singapore owners, which by the time of the photograph had become Liu Tong Shipping (Pte) Ltd. Her fate is, like so many ships that gravitate east, uncertain. There is evidence she was renamed *Devi* in 1984, but there are also reports that when broken up in the 1980s she was still named *Builder*. Quite possibly, the name *Devi* had never been formally applied. *(R J Kittle)*

In the early 1970s, a distinctive class of coaster was built at Budapest for a German owner, and it was one of the first to take advantage of highly competitive prices being offered in an eastern European country eager to obtain hard currency. Built for Otto A Muller of Hamburg (although most were soon registered in Singapore), of 1399 grt and 244 ft, they were named in order of completion *Basalt*, *Diabas* (both 1970), *Diorit* (1971), *Gabbro*, *Granit* (1972) and *Dolomit** (1973). Using east European-built engines was something of a risk, because western European buyers of early Hungarian coasters had found that a supply of spares could not be guaranteed. Muller therefore specified West German engines, from Motoren Werke Mannheim AG. This was good policy, because the engines in *Dolomit* gave her at least thirty years of service. Gearless as was the growing trend, the coasters had a distinctive treatment of superstructure and wheelhouse, the sides of the latter being used to display Muller's colours.

Along with her sisters, *Dolomit* was lengthened at Bremerhaven in 1975, in her case when only two years old, emerging with a tonnage of 1510 gross and 81 metres long. Sold in 1983, she first became *Orchid Star*, but then with her sister, the former *Diabas*, she came to the attention of Rochester-based ship owner Thomas Watson (Shipping) Ltd, which bought and renamed the pair *Lady Dorothy* and *Lady Patricia*, placing them under various flags of convenience. After 1994, *Lady Dorothy* traded as *Dana* and *Kris* until on 27 September 2007 she stranded after her anchor dragged in heavy weather off Samandag, Turkey. The wreck was cut up in July 2010. *(Reinhard Nerlich)*

Slovakian ships

The USSR mounted a major challenge to Western maritime supremacy in the post-Second World War years. A large part of this effort involved vessels built by yards in its satellites in eastern Europe and by those in Finland, some of the latter demanded as reparations for the 'Winter War', which Russia itself started in 1939.

It is perhaps surprising to find that a yard at Komarno in what was Czechoslovakia (now Slovakia) has been building ships for well over one hundred years, and that since the 1960s it has turned out hundreds of hulls for the USSR. These have mostly comprised the 'Volgo-Balt' type, which was similar in size and number to the 'Sormovskiys' described below.

The 'Volgo-Balts' were succeeded from Slovenske Lodnice A/S by a series of the twin-funnel 'Amurs'. Representing a small sub-group of this class, *Dnepr–2* is seen chasing a 'Baltiskiy' northbound up the Bosphorus in September 2006. Of 3086 grt and 116 metres overall length, *Dnepr 2* was completed in 1989 and sails for Ukrichflot of Kiev and as can be seen is registered in the Black Sea port of Kherson.

Since the last of the seven sisters of *Dnepr–2* was completed in 1991, the yard on the Danube has continued to turn out smaller sea-river ships but now for western European customers as well as those in the former Soviet Union. Unlike the distinctive 'Amurs', however, there is little to distinguish these low-air-draught coasters from the products of other yards. *(Martin Wright)*

Born in the USSR

Although the USSR ordered many ships from its satellites, its own yards did build many sea-river ships. Their size reflected the length and dimensions of the USSR's extensive navigable river and canal network, half a million miles of them potentially navigable, and a major factor in its transport infrastructure, particularly in its northerly territories and the Volga-Don basin to the east.

The largely Saint Petersburg-based twin-screw 'Baltiskiy' class became the most familiar type of USSR-owned coaster in western European waters. Between 1962 and 1967 'Krasnoye Sormovo' at Gorki and other yards built at least seventy-four of the original type, with a batch of eleven of similar-sized but modernised hull following from the yard of Oy Laivateollisuus at Turku/Åbo in Finland during 1978–80.

With the dissolution of the Soviet Union, the 'Baltiskiys' underwent a sort of diaspora, with several going to the emerging fleets of former Soviet republics, where it has to be said that maintenance was not always a strong point. As well as a good coating of rust, the hull of *Partner-1** shows distinct signs of sagging, a not-uncommon observation as these 96-metre ships aged. The former *Baltiskiy-23* had been built not at Gorki but on the Baltic at Kaliningrad by Pribaltiskiy Sudostroitelnyy Zavod 'Yantar' during 1964. Owners of the 2014-grt rust bucket were the apocryphally named F & F Co Ltd of Riga in Latvia, which put the ship under the flag of the distant St Vincent and the Grenadines, which probably did not inspect it very often. Unsurprisingly, she had gone for scrap within a year of being photographed at a Bosphorus anchorage in October 2008. *(Martin Wright)*

At least twenty-four classes of sea-river ships have been built for or by the USSR. One of the most numerous dry cargo types has been the 'Sormovskiys', with 120 completed between 1967 and 1986, and probably holding the record for the longest construction lifetime of any class of ship. The majority were built by Sudostroitelnyy Zavod 'Krasnoye Sormovo' at Nizhniy Novgorod, with some units from a yard at Rybinsk and a later batch of slightly longer hulls from Viana de Castello in Portugal.

Photographed heading north in the Bosphorus in September 2010, *Front* was completed in 1975 as *Sormovskiy 111*. Sources differ as to her builder; *Lloyd's Register* favouring Sudostroitelnyy Zavod 'Volodarskiy' at Rybinsk, well to the north of Moscow, but with the Nizhniy Novgorod yard also quoted by an authoritative book on sea-river shipping. At 2478 grt and 114 metres overall with four holds, she is a size larger than the 'Baltiskiys', but like these has twin screws to keep her draught to 3.4 metres.

The state-owned Volga Shipping Company sold her in 2003 to owners in the former Soviet republic of Georgia, which registered her at Batumi on the Black Sea as *Aukuba*. The name *Front* came after a further sale in 2005. One of the benefits of an interest in shipping is in enlarging one's geographical knowledge, but in the case of ships such as *Front* this gives way to bewilderment. Trading to and from the Black Sea, she is registered in Phnom Penh in distant Cambodia. So far, not unexpected, but she belongs to the Front Shipping Co Ltd and is both owned and managed in, of all places, Toronto. *(Martin Wright)*

Large Romanians

At 330 ft and 3090 grt, a large class of ships from Santierul Naval Galati on the lower Danube at Galati in Romania are at the upper limit of what were until recently considered coasters. *Galati* of 1960 was the first of at least thirty-seven three-hold shelter-deckers from this yard, seventeen of which went to China with most of the remainder for the Romanian state enterprise, NAVROM of Constanta. Their inclusion partly results from their familiarity in western European waters when operating a liner service to and from Romania. The author has vivid memories of the bright green boot-topping applied to members of the class that ran to Manchester in the 1960s and the 1970s. They were well equipped with derricks and their Sulzer engines gave them a respectable 12.5 knots service speed. *Cluj** was completed in 1962 and served her native country throughout her career, arriving in tow at Aliaga in Turkey on 15 June 1990 to be broken up.

A further type of Romanian shelter-decker built in some numbers from 1974 to 1977 was supplied to the USSR (twenty-four vessels, four of which went to the Soviet Navy), to NAVROM (twelve), to Czechoslovakia and Cuba (two each). Given the numbers several builders were involved, and *Yasha Gordiyenko* was completed for the USSR in 1975 by Santierul Naval Oltenita SA at Oltenita, an inland town on the Danube not far from Bucharest. Dimensions were 89 metres overall with a tonnage of 2163 gross, and one 20-tonne and two 10-tonne derricks served her three holds.

Yasha Gordiyenko was sold by Russian Federation owners in 2000 and became *Sea Wind**, as photographed at Antwerp in August 2001. Her real nationality is, to say the least, obscure. She was registered at Batumi, Georgia; her registered owners had an address (or at least a brass plate) in Main Street, Gibraltar; but her managers – and probably her ultimate owners – were based in Odessa in Ukraine. Voyage patterns give little clue, because she was trading widely, from the Black Sea to Scandinavia. In 2002, *Sea Wind* became *Oka*, and as such was broken up at Chittagong in May 2007. A Romanian-built class of sea-river ships features in Chapter 14. *(Author)*

CHAPTER

12

Coastal Steam Liners in the Twentieth Century

This and the subsequent chapter covers the long story – in fact, decline – of the regular trader from 1900 to its almost complete replacement by container and roll-on, roll-off ships in the last decades of the twentieth century. The field is so large that it is convenient to consider steam and motor ships separately.

Although the major technological change in this period was the complete replacement of steam engines by diesels, the change often came later than in the more competitive bulk trades. Liners spent proportionally more of their time in port, and were – thanks to a conference system – often less subject to competition from other shipping (it came from rail and later road transport), so that economical machinery was not an overriding priority. Conservatism among owners was also a factor (some were still building steamers after the Second World War), as was the larger average size and speed of the regular trader, for which sufficiently powerful and reliable diesels were late in developing.

Technological change was felt most notably in the development of cargo gear. There was a trend away from complete reliance on masts and derricks, because these were supplemented and at times completely replaced by deck cranes. Time in port does not earn money, so provision of fast and efficient cargo handling equipment helped reduce this down time, although the whims and vagaries of dock labour had a major effect on turnaround time. In a ship built for a route in which shoreside gear could be relied upon, elimination of on-board cargo gear both saved on initial costs and crew time as cargo gear, exposed to the elements and often worked by semi-skilled operatives, needed constant maintenance.

What becomes apparent in this chapter is the consistency of design of the steamers involved, regardless of where built and their intended trade. Smaller craft, in general, were of the bridge-amidships, engines-aft configuration, whilst the larger ones – usually over 220 ft in length – had engines and most accommodation amidships. As will be seen in Chapter 13, this consensus on how a coastal liner should look ended once steam was replaced by diesel machinery.

An asterisk in a caption indicates the vessel shown in the photograph.

Coastal steamers of Coast Lines

The largest UK group operating coastal liner services was Coast Lines Ltd, and indeed it claimed to be the largest such operation in the world. Its routes were divided between cross-Irish Sea and British coastal services.

Taking its name in 1917, Coast Lines Ltd was the result of a 1913 amalgamation of three companies trading on England's West Coast. Powell, Bacon & Hough Lines Ltd connected London and Liverpool with many intermediate ports on the English, Welsh and Irish coasts. Acquired by the hugely ambitious Owen Philips, later Lord Kylsant, Coast Lines pursued his goal of absorbing as many companies as possible. Many of these had lost considerable tonnage during the First World War, and saw much of their trade taken by railways, with the connivance of the government, which wanted coastal ships to be deployed on war service. To many owners, rebuilding their fleet and trade looked a daunting task, and they were pleased to offload their surviving assets at a time of inflated prices.

*Durham Coast** came into the Coast Lines fleet in 1918 upon acquisition of the Kirkcaldy-based Stocks, Turnbull & Co Ltd, for which she had been built at Goole in 1912 as *New Abbotshall*. The 783-grt, 215-ft steamer was unusual in having a flush deck, with rails rather than bulwarks for much of its length. The photograph shows the aftermath of a collision with the tanker *Sunoil* in the Mersey on 7 June 1924. Despite this, *Durham Coast* was repaired and remained in the Coast Lines' fleet until 1946, when sold to India as *Rama-Raja*. She was broken up in 1957. *(J and M Clarkson)*

Acquiring a very heterogenous fleet, Coast Lines attempted to standardise, partly through buying five of a group of shelter-deckers ordered by the British government during the First World War. *Kerry** had been launched as *War Spey* by the Caledon Shipbuilding & Engineering Co Ltd at Dundee in February 1919. Of 1391 grt and 282 ft, she was completed in April as *Lady Patricia* for a Coast Lines subsidiary. In 1936, she became *Kerry*, and just prior to the Second World War was transferred to Coast Lines Ltd as *Kerry Coast*.

In March 1944, *Kerry Coast* had a bizarre accident that potentially impacted on building craft for the invasion of France. Colliding off Liverpool's Prince's Landing Stage with the Norwegian motor vessel *Mosdale* and holed in the engine room, *Kerry Coast* drifted slowly up the River Mersey and, after her crew had been taken off, was nosed by tugs into the beach just off the Number 6 Slipway of Cammell Laird's shipyard. This was not a wise move, because the hulk was in the way of landing craft that were about to be launched. Fortunately the shipyard could slew their launching ways so the landing craft could clear the wreck. Not without considerable difficulty, *Kerry Coast* was refloated by the Mersey Docks & Harbour Board in May.

Kerry Coast went to Dublin for repair by the Liffey Dockyard, which was a surprising move in view of Ireland's neutrality, but a condition of it accepting the work was that steel be provided by the UK. Resuming the name *Kerry*, she is seen during September 1956 in the colours of Burns & Laird Lines. She was broken up near Cork in 1959. *(World Ship Society Ltd)*

In the early 1920s, Coast Lines also ordered several steamers to its own designs, all from the yards of Harland & Wolff with which Kylsant was closely associated. In 1920, its yard in Glasgow delivered the 1097-grt *Somerset Coast**, while the subsidiary company A & J Inglis Ltd of Pointhouse built *Eastern Coast* and *Northern Coast*, all to the same length of 240 ft. All had a profusion of derricks, but none were exact sisters, and *Somerset Coast* was distinguished by a pair of kingposts ahead of her bridge and a single kingpost just ahead of the poop.

Coast Lines was notorious for moving its ships between subsidiaries as trades altered: one of the few strengths of this ponderous organisation. *Somerset Coast* moved less than most, however, and in 1950 came her only transfer, to the Belfast, Mersey & Manchester Steamship Co Ltd of Liverpool, which renamed her *Mountstewart*. She carried general cargo between the ports in this company's title until November 1955, when she arrived at Troon to be demolished by the West of Scotland Shipbreaking Co Ltd.

Although Coast Lines was reasonably successful despite depressed trading conditions, the desperate state of the finances of Lord Kylsant's Royal Mail Group meant that money for fleet renewals was in short supply. The rebuilding programme largely ground to a halt after the ships described above were completed, and it was over ten years before it was resumed. *(J and M Clarkson)*

For Coast Lines' acquisitions

Matthew Langlands & Co of Glasgow was bought by Coast Lines in 1919 and was one of the few subsidiaries for which a fleet replacement programme was begun. Two ships for Langlands' important Glasgow to Liverpool and Manchester trade were almost certainly ordered by the still-independent company, and were intended to carry the Langlands' names *Princess Caroline* and *Princess Dagmar*. However, these were launched in 1920 as *Redbreast* and *Gorilla*: changes of name were to be a recurring feature of the careers of these four sisters. Both were registered in the ownership of G & J Burns Ltd, and were initially operated under the title Burns-Langlands Line.

Two sisters to this distinctive, if not enormously attractive, 774-grt and 201-ft shelter-deck design followed in 1922, the second completed in November as *Lurcher*. But in 1925 Coast Lines decided to transfer all four to the parent company, and *Lurcher* became *Scottish Coast*. The four sisters were then dispersed away from their intended routes, and *Scottish Coast* became *Ulster Coast** in 1938. She is seen in the cover photograph transiting a tranquil Manchester Ship Canal on the service of owners Belfast Steamship Co Ltd.

The four reached the end of their Coast Lines' careers in the mid-1950s, and in 1954 *Ulster Coast* was sold to owners in Montreal and renamed *Ahern Trader*.

The ageing steamer was wrecked at South Fogo Island, in Gander Bay, Newfoundland, during January 1960 after she had broken adrift during a snowstorm. She was carrying a cargo of hay. *(World Ship Society Ltd)*

Among the later companies acquired by Coast Lines was Fisher, Renwick & Co's Manchester-London Steamers Ltd. Initially from Newcastle, Fisher and Renwick were attracted by the plans for the Manchester Ship Canal, and having interests in ship building and repairing on the Tyne saw the potential of repair facilities at the new port of Manchester, which they developed as Manchester Dry Docks Ltd. In return, the Manchester Ship Canal Company agreed to a Fisher, Renwick liner service connecting Manchester with London. This commenced in 1892, even before the Canal was fully open, using the area known as Saltport at the junction of the Weaver Navigation and the Ship Canal. Cargoes included timber, grain, pottery, iron and, naturally for the area, salt.

The interesting thing about this service is the distance sailed by the ships compared with that between its two terminals by road, which was less than 200 miles. Indeed, Fisher, Renwick also noticed this, introduced a fleet of heavy lorries and in 1939 sold its remaining three ships and the marine operations to Coast Lines Ltd. The ships sold included *Sapper**, built by William Dobson & Co at Low Walker in 1923, of 1036 grt and 231 ft. Coast Lines renamed her *Avon Coast*, but quickly lost interest in the Manchester to London service, transferring the ship to their Belfast Steamship Co Ltd subsidiary, which renamed her *Ulster Star*. She then served on the Irish Sea until broken up at Briton Ferry in 1954. *(F W Hawks)*

Between Scotland and London

Coast Lines never managed to achieve the same dominance on east coast routes as it did on the west of the UK, and independent companies handled much of the important trade from London to north-east England and Scotland. Here, passenger carrying was significant and offered a cheaper alternative to rail travel, but much of this trade was lost when long-distance motor coach services were introduced in the early 1930s.

The senior company on the east coast was Dundee, Perth & London Shipping Co Ltd, an amalgamation in 1826 of companies formed from 1798 onwards. Built by Hawthorns & Co Ltd, Leith in 1921, *London** was its last ship completed with significant passenger accommodation: thirty in first class (reduced to twelve in winter) in cabins amidships with second class in temporary berths in her 'tween decks. Together with *Perth* of 1915, the 1491-grt, 251-ft *London* offered twice-weekly sailings between Dundee and London. Cargo was significantly more important than passenger carrying, as evidenced by the need for a third ship on the route, the *Dundee* of 1934, which carried just twelve passengers.

London had a unique wartime role. In 1942, she was requisitioned and converted to a pipe layer to help prove the feasibility of under-sea pipelines, a concept that proved itself as 'PLUTO' in supplying fuel to the armies invading France in 1944. Initially renamed HMS *Holdfast*, in 1946 she was transferred to the Ministry of Transport, and as *Empire Taw* recovered the pipeline she had laid beneath the English Channel a few years previously. Her work done, and now thirty-two years old, she was broken up at Cork in 1953. *(Ships in Focus)*

During the Second World War a number of companies in the Scotland to London trade began planning how they would develop services when peace returned. The outcome was a new company, London Scottish Lines Ltd, to run cargo-only steamers from Leith to the Thames. Initially, the four lines holding shares in the company provided tonnage, but in 1946 a 'tween-deck steamer was bought and renamed *London Merchant**. Of 733 grt and 215 ft overall length, she had been built by Swan, Hunter & Wigham Richardson Ltd in 1935 as one of the last steamers for the Tyne-Tees Steam Shipping Co Ltd of Newcastle as *Craster*, and was sold after her owners had been taken over by Coast Lines. Her accommodation for twelve passengers was not needed post-war.

London Merchant was one of four vessels needed to maintain London Scottish Lines' thrice-weekly services. Initially the line was a success, and loadings grew year on year. Among cargoes carried southbound were beer from William Younger's brewery in Edinburgh and paper from the numerous mills in eastern Scotland. From 1953, however, trade declined, not assisted by the unhelpful practices of London dock workers. A series of dock strikes reduced the confidence of customers, who transferred much cargo to rail and road. As a result, the service was terminated in early 1959 and *London Merchant* laid up awaiting sale. The buyer was a company based in Colombo, which renamed her *Maldive Crescent*. In June 1967, she stranded on the Burma coast, and her crew set off inland, reaching Rangoon after a march of several hundred miles. But the wreck could not be relocated, and not until 1981 did insurance underwriters pay out on her loss.

From London to the Netherlands

General Steam Navigation Co Ltd was the oldest steam ship company in the world, and its diversity of routes and services, although very much centred on the Thames, meant that a variety of sizes and designs of ship was necessary. A distinctive feature of its steamer fleet were the adoption of deck cranes: once more we are seeing the importance of fast and extensive cargo gear in the regular short-sea trades. Two steamers built by Ailsa Shipbuilding Co Ltd at Troon, *Groningen* of 1928 and *Leeuwarden* of 1929, relied entirely on their eight deck cranes. The departure from General Steam's policy of using names of birds was because the pair was built for a service between London, Amsterdam and Rotterdam operated jointly with Batavier Line of Rotterdam.

The flush-decked *Groningen* was 256 ft overall and had a modest gross tonnage of 1205. Sister *Leeuwarden* had the misfortune to be sunk by a stray mine 18 miles north of Dieppe on 24 February 1946, but *Groningen* sailed on. In 1958, she took the name *Philomel**, because of transfer away from the Dutch routes. She continued running into the Thames, where the accompanying photograph was taken, and on 24 April 1961 was beached in that river following a collision. She was quickly despatched to the ship breaking yard of T W Ward Ltd at Grays, where she arrived one month after the collision. *(Ships in Focus)*

One of *Groningen*'s running mates would have been *Batavier I*, built in 1915 by Maatschappij Fijenoord at Rotterdam for local owners and in 1923 transferred to W H Müller & Co, operators of Batavier Line. This line had originated in 1829 with the Rotterdam to London sailings of the paddle steamer *De Batavier*, which represented the first foreign-owned steamship service into the Thames. The original operators, Stoomboot Maatschappij Nederland, sold the service to Müller in 1895, insisting that the Batavier Line name be retained. Müller ordered new ships from Dundee, and developed the service to the extent that from 1899 there was a departure from London every day of the week except Sunday. The Batavier Line service continued until 1958, latterly running from a pier at Gravesend.

With dimensions of 235 ft and 1013 grt, *Batavier I* was slightly smaller than *Groningen* and had a mixture of deck cranes and conventional derricks. After a number of inconsequential changes of her registered owner's name, she was renamed *Sandenburgh** in 1937, signifying transfer away from the London to Netherlands route. *Sandenburgh* survived the war to be broken up at Hendrik-Ido-Ambacht in 1954.

Müller had several shipping interests besides the Batavier Line, including the iron ore trade from Norway and Sweden to the Netherlands. In the 1900s the company ordered some large 'turret' type steamers, which are candidates for being pioneer bulk carriers.

Four rival near-continental services

Hollandsche Stoomboot Maatschappij (Holland Steamship Company) operated short-sea services from Amsterdam to a number of English, Irish, Scottish and French ports as well as deep-sea ships to West Africa. Photographed in the Mersey, *Zaanstroom** of 1920 was one of a number of ships that the company built in Dutch yards, financed partly out of the healthy profits that the company, along with other Dutch ship owners, had made during the First World War. Unfortunately, profits disappeared until 1936, thanks to the general depression in trade, and fierce competition from a rival British company.

Of 1646 grt and 263 ft registered length, *Zaanstroom* had accommodation for twelve passengers. Her cargo gear consisted of six conventional, three-ton capacity derricks, one capable of lifting 10 tons and a pair of 2-ton deck cranes mounted on her quarterdeck.

Zaanstroom was away from Dutch waters during the German invasion in May 1940 and spent the war in British service, initially working around Iceland, but then being sent to the Mediterranean to support the Allied operations in North Africa and Italy. She was returned to her owners late in 1945 and continued with them until 1950, when sold to DDG 'Hansa' of Bremen as *Hundseck*. Further owners in Germany and Greece followed until 1960 when she was broken up at Perama. *(J and M Clarkson)*

The line whose competition hurt Hollandsche Stoomboot Maatschappij was British & Continental Steamship Co Ltd. Although it dated from 1922, it originated much earlier with the Cork Steamship Co Ltd of 1843. British & Continental's *Egret** (1391 grt) was delivered by Burntisland Shipbuilding Co Ltd in March 1937 and – apart from the unpleasantness between 1940 and 1945 – seems to have led a blameless existence on the company's routes until 1957. British & Continental's steamers ran from the UK to Amsterdam, Rotterdam, Terneuzen, Ghent, Antwerp and Dunkirk. The line's main base was Queen's Dock, Liverpool but ships also called at Manchester, Glasgow, Belfast, Barrow-in-Furness, Southampton and occasionally Ellesmere Port on the Manchester Ship Canal, where they loaded chemicals. General cargo was usually carried outwards from the United Kingdom, with a variety of mainly bulk cargoes homeward: steel bars from Belgium to Ellesmere Port, silver sand for glassmaking from Antwerp to Liverpool, flax and cotton waste to Belfast. With so many ports the crew were kept busy: it was not unusual to enter ten different ports during a round trip of two to four weeks.

After a career confined to European waters, *Egret* sailed out East in 1957, first running for African Coasters (Pty) Ltd of Durban as *Reef*, then in 1966 continuing to Timor in Indonesia to become *Ainaro*. She was broken up in Hong Kong during 1967. British & Continental just survived her, their last ship, their only motor ship which also carried the name *Egret*, was sold in 1972. *(World Ship Society Ltd)*

Dundee-built for the Irish sea

Irish companies were important early operators of steam ship services both across the Irish Sea and from their home ports to continental Europe. In the twentieth century they were somewhat eclipsed by British mainland operators, especially because Liverpool-based Coast Lines Group bought several major Irish operators.

A notable survivor was Limerick Steamship Co Ltd, whose vessels had to endure the wild seas off the exposed western coast of Ireland. Founded in 1853 by the Malcolmson family of Waterford as the London & Limerick Steamship Company, the name Limerick Steamship Co Ltd was adopted when services expanded to Liverpool, Bristol and continental Europe.

As part of its expansion following Irish independence, the company took delivery of *Clonlara** from the Caledon Shipbuilding & Engineering Co Ltd at Dundee in 1926. At 1203 grt and 253 ft, she was followed from Dundee in 1928 by the very similar *Lanahrone*, also intended for the Limerick to Liverpool cattle trade. The pair was not confined to this trade, and in November 1935 had refrigeration equipment installed to open a service from Ireland to Spain and Spanish Morocco, principally loading potatoes and cattle out and fruit homeward.

Clonlara continued voyages to the Iberian Peninsula during wartime, and was outward bound from Cardiff to Lisbon with coal on 22 August 1941 when she was torpedoed by the German submarine *U 564*. Although technically neutral, *Clonlara* was sailing in an Allied convoy when attacked. She sank almost immediately, the few survivors being picked up by escorting Royal Navy corvettes. *Lanaharone*, by coincidence in the same Gibraltar convoy in which *Clonlara* was sunk, survived to be broken up in the Netherlands during 1960.

(J and M Clarkson)

Ireland's other major short-sea liner company was Palgrave Murphy Ltd, which was even older than the Limerick company, having been founded in Dublin in 1835. It dropped out of ship owning after heavy losses during the First World War, and when it resumed business in 1926 rebuilt its fleet largely with second-hand vessels. Representative of this policy, the example shown is *City of Cork**, acquired in 1947 when already thirty years old.

The 1586-grt, 270-ft steamer had been completed by Caledon Shipbuilding & Engineering Co Ltd in May 1917 as *Goodwin* for the Clyde Shipping Co Ltd, and was immediately requisitioned by the Admiralty as a submarine decoy or 'Q' ship. After further naval service in the Second World War, as a guard ship and later a convoy rescue vessel, *Goodwin* was sold in 1946 to a Belfast company, which in little more than a year sold her on to the Saorstat & Continental Steamship Co Ltd as Palgrave Murphy had designated its shipping operation. *City of Cork*, as she became, was sold to breakers in Dublin during 1955.

The long histories of Palgrave Murphy and of Limerick Steam came to an unfortunate end. In 1969, the two companies merged to form the Hibernian Transport Group. But in little more than a year the new concern was in financial trouble and went into voluntary liquidation.

Cross-Channel railway ships

Railway companies were significant owners of ports in the United Kingdom, and several had important fleets of cargo and passenger ships on short-sea routes.

Created in 1923, the Southern Railway inherited a motley collection of war-weary freighters from its predecessor companies, and began a replacement programme by ordering ten 230-ft overall cargo steamers from D & W Henderson & Co Ltd, Glasgow. The 755-grt *Ringwood** of 1926 was intended for use from Southampton to the Channel Islands and to Le Havre, St Malo, Honfleur, Caen and Cherbourg. With several others of the group, she was given relatively basic cargo handing gear, with a derrick at her foremast and two aft supported by kingpost/ventilators. The mainmast seen in this photograph was a later addition to support a navigation light. *Ringwood* also had four double-berth passenger cabins, something of an extravagance given that her owners also had passenger ships, but probably provided for services to smaller French ports. The larger part of the order for these ships was intended for use out of Dover and Folkestone, and in these the derricks aft were omitted. At least one of the group had stalls for horses.

All of the ships were rendered temporarily redundant at the fall of France, but had useful naval careers. *Ringwood* was first used as a netlayer at Scapa Flow, and continued in a passive anti-submarine role during 1945, laying lengths of floating cable intended to snag on the schnorkels of patrolling U-boats. In 1946, she returned to the railway company, mainly working between Weymouth and the Channel Islands until withdrawn for breaking up in 1959. *(Ships in Focus)*

Of the four railway companies formed at the grouping of 1923, the Great Western had the smallest shipping fleet. Its major routes were from South Wales to southern Ireland and Weymouth to the Channel Isles. For the latter route, in 1925 it took delivery of the 776-grt, 210-ft overall flush-decked cargo steamers *Roebuck** and *Sambur* from Swan, Hunter and Wigham Richardson Ltd of Newcastle-upon-Tyne. Their intended length was 230 ft but, as this would have caused berthing problems, about 20 ft was saved by eliminating a fourth hatch, giving them a rather odd, truncated appearance. Derricks were initially fitted, but quickly found to be unnecessary and removed. Extensive 'tween deck space was provided in view of the extensive fruit and vegetable traffic from the Channel Isles. Twelve passengers were accommodated in a small saloon on the main deck, used mainly by salesmen, or commercial travellers as they were known.

Both ships were actively engaged in the May and June 1940 evacuations of the British Expeditionary Force from France. *Roebuck* was at Dunkirk as part of Operation 'Dynamo' and later St Valery-en-Caux in Operation 'Cycle', coming under heavy fire during the latter operation. During the later part of the war both sisters were used as barrage balloon vessels to help protect east coast convoys. *Roebuck* returned to the Channel Islands almost as soon as the islands were liberated in May 1945, resuming a twice-weekly service from Weymouth until withdrawn for breaking up in 1964. Her photograph was taken at Weymouth on 9 July 1956.

Low-air-draught steamers

In a parallel with the up-river colliers described in Chapter 6, a number of low-air-draught general cargo steamers were built, principally to trade up the Rhine or from London to Belgian and French inland ports.

*Ringdove** is seen late in her long and varied life. She was built and engined as *Badenia* by F Schichau at Elbing for Rhein und See-Schiffahrts Gesellschaft of Cologne, which, as its name suggests, ran services up the Rhine, also using the Stettin-built sister *Borussia*. By 1931, both steamers were operating for Rhein-London Linie GmbH, also of Cologne, but managed by General Steam Navigation Co Ltd of London. At 221 ft and 921 grt, *Badenia* was of a size with contemporary 'flat-iron' colliers, and like them her funnel and masts would hinge to clear bridges. Unusually for a short-sea trader, she had twin screws, to minimise draught because low water is a recurring problem for ships working on the Rhine.

By the end of the Second World War the two ships, by now named *Titania* and *Timandra*, were taken over by the United Kingdom, and by 1947 were running for General Steam as *Ringdove* and *Woodwren* respectively. Despite their age, photographs show they were kept in good condition, but they did not last long. *Ringdove* went to breakers at Bo'ness in 1950, while *Woodwren* continued working until 1953 when she was converted to a hulk. *(J and M Clarkson)*

A much later incarnation of the low-air-draught general cargo steamer was *City of Brussels** of Brussels Steamship Co Ltd of London, a concern that under various titles had operated steamer services from the Thames and the Humber to Brussels since 1873. In contrast to *Ringdove*, cargo gear was completely absent in *City of Brussels*, and the light masts were hinged, as was the funnel. She had two holds, with a second deck worked into the after hold.

Of 691 grt and 180 ft overall, *City of Brussels* had a basic triple-expansion engine, supplied by her builders John Lewis & Sons Ltd of Aberdeen. This machinery was a surprising choice for a ship built as late as 1947, because up-river collier builders and owners had realised that – as well as its other advantages – a more compact diesel engine gave greater hold capacity than a steamer with its paraphernalia of boilers and coal bunkers.

Notwithstanding obsolete machinery, her career was lengthy. Renamed *Barbihalis* following her sale in 1964, it was even felt worthwhile rebuilding her when a stranding in September 1965 led to insurance underwriters declaring her a constructive total loss. As the motor ship *Capitão Bismarck*, she traded until 1969 when laid up at Bilbao. She was broken up at nearby Santander in 1972.

The low-air-draught motor vessel was to become much more common, as later chapters will illustrate. *(Ships in Focus)*

North Sea traders

Denmark's major coastal shipping company, Det Forenede Dampskibs-Selskab (DFDS), resulted from a merger in 1866 of a number of small companies operating both domestic and international services, the latter including routes to the UK, Antwerp, Norway, Iceland and Baltic States. DFDS has continued as major player in Baltic and North Sea services, having successfully moved into roll-on, roll-off.

Alexandra of 1931 represents the DFDS cargo steamers, built by the Helsingørs yard as Elsinore and of 1463 grt and 280 ft overall. *Alexandra* initially served mainly on the route from Esbjerg to Grimsby. In 1939, as a neutral ship, she had prominent Maltese crosses applied to her hull and a large DANMARK painted beneath her name (something of a Danish tradition was to carry a ship's name in large letters amidships). For a few wartime months she varied her route out of Esbjerg by circumnavigating the UK to call also Newcastle, Glasgow, Manchester and Tilbury. The German invasion of Denmark put an end to this and during the subsequent five years, when not laid up, she made a few wartime voyages into the Baltic.

Post-war voyages out of Esbjerg and Copenhagen were more varied and she ran on most of the DFDS services to UK east coast ports, Antwerp and Le Havre until 1964. Surprisingly, she retained coal firing until 1956. Her post-DFDS career was short: sold to Greek owners without change of name in December 1964, after less than three months she was damaged by stranding off Tripoli and was subsequently broken up at Piræus. *(World Ship Society Ltd)*

Wilson Line of Hull had an extensive network of services, mostly out of its home town, to ports around the North Sea and in to the Baltic. Its smaller steamers included *Salerno** of 870 grt and 227 ft overall, designed to work mainly on routes to Norway.

The Wilson Line and its owners had prospered from the trade of Hull, and the family was wealthy enough to buy a local shipyard when its owners, Earle's Shipbuilding & Engineering Co Ltd, had been put into liquidation in 1900. Wilson Line itself was sold in 1917 to Sir John Ellerman, who renamed it Ellerman's Wilson Line Ltd, but the interest in Earle's shipyard was retained by the Wilson family. Nevertheless, the yard continued to build for the company, completing *Salerno* in 1924.

During the Second World War, *Salerno* suffered from the attention of both sides. She was running from Hull to Bergen in April 1940 when captured by the German navy, but a few weeks later was sunk by RAF aircraft. Raised and repaired, she worked for the Germans as a torpedo testing vessel. After these events, Ellerman's Wilson had some problems re-establishing ownership when, at the end of the war, she was recaptured by British forces.

Sold out of the fleet late in 1956, she became the Greek *Taxiarchis*, but a grounding on Kos in December 1958 sealed her fate and she was broken up at Perama during 1959.

Scandinavian local steamers

Norway remains a stronghold of coastal shipping, thanks to poor land connections to some of its more remote coastal communities. Many of the distinctive small steamers that served on its routes had extensive passenger accommodation, and in illustrating these, this book makes a necessary exception to its self-imposed concentration on pure cargo carriers.

The elegant *Vikingen* was delivered in 1900 by Trondhjems Mekanisk Værksted for Hardanger Sunnhordlandske D/S of Bergen, a company formed in an 1880 merger of two operators serving the area between Bergen and Haugesund. Of 421 grt and 150 ft registered length, the passenger capacity of *Vikingen* is not known, but a considerable number of souls can be seen on deck or the after deckhouse. There are two cargo holds, and at least one car on her foredeck. The photograph shows her in later years, probably after a rebuild in 1937, and with a considerably extended midships house.

The steamer gave up her name to a new motor vessel in 1957, but carried on, first as *Vøringen* and later *Tyssedal* mainly in a reserve capacity until September 1959 when she was broken up at Arendal.

Steamers similar to *Vikingen* were built for local routes on the Swedish coast. In 1912, *Svanen* came from the yard of Lindholmens Varv at Gothenburg for Hallands Ångbåts A/B, a company based at Halmstad on Sweden's west coast. After several changes of manager, and service as an auxiliary gunboat for the Swedish navy between 1939 and 1941, she was sold in 1946 to Det Stavangerske Dampskibsselskab and transferred to services in the south-west of Norway as *Kong Olav**. She was somewhat larger than *Vikingen* at 180 ft overall and 790 grt, but basically similar with two cargo holds and accommodation for what were probably unberthed passengers amidships and aft.

In 1959 she moved to very much warmer waters when sold to owners in Jeddah to become *Om El Kheir*. A stranding at her new home port in December 1968 left her fit only for scrap and, after a long and at times exciting career, the fifty-six-year-old steamer was broken up locally.

Baltic traders

Routes into the Baltic employed vessels very similar to those used on the North Sea – indeed, some vessels would be used on both services. However, some distinctive features emerged, especially for Finnish owners that specified ice-strengthening and an ice-breaking bow. Of 1909 grt and 310 ft overall, *Aldebaran** was completed in 1938 for Finska Ångfartygs A/B of Helsinki by local yard Sandvikens Skeppsdocka & Mekaniska Verkstad, which also provided her triple-expansion engines. The company's first new ship for some years, she was a development of the same yard's *Orion* of 1935, longer, with extra kingposts aft and a cruiser stern.

Finland suffered through being associated with the German cause through their 1939–40 war with Russia, begun when their huge neighbour attacked them without warning, and Finland subsequently lost many ships. Although *Aldebaran* was briefly held by the Germans in late 1939, she survived and became an important unit of the company's post-war fleet, serving routes from Finland to the UK and western Europe and to the Mediterranean. The steamer was sold in 1967, when she went to Greek owners, and as *Antonios* worked in the Mediterranean until sold to Turkish shipbreakers in 1972.

Regular traders for Swedish owners are represented by *Belgia**, built by Nya Varvs A/B Öresund at Landskrona for Förnyade Ångfartygs A/B Götha of Gothenburg in 1930. The 2023-grt, 287-ft compound-engined steamer had a relatively short but eventful career. She was bombed and sunk near the Sunk Light Vessel in January 1941 while on a voyage from London to Sunderland with general cargo: clearly, her Swedish owners were reluctant to return her to the Baltic, where trading opportunities were distinctly limited. *Belgia* was salved, repaired and returned to service under the auspices of the British Ministry of War Transport, which renamed her *Empire Bell*. But her reprieve was short: on 25 September 1942 she was torpedoed and sunk by the German submarine *U 442* while on a voyage from the Tyne to Reykjavik with a cargo of coal for the Allied forces occupying Iceland.

From the Baltic to the Mediterranean

Although rarely out of sight of land, the vessels that voyaged between ports in the Baltic and the Mediterranean are at the limit of what can be considered as coasters. Nevertheless, steamers such as the 1829-grt, 287-ft *Livorno** were not significantly different from those that ran on shorter routes, such as those across the North Sea. Owned by Robert M Sloman Jr of Hamburg, *Livorno* began her life on the Baltic in January 1924 when completed at the yard of AG 'Neptun', Rostock. Her end came in the Mediterranean seventeen years later when torpedoed by a British submarine twenty-four miles north of Benghazi on 11 September 1941. The submarine responsible was HMS *Thunderbolt*, probably better known as HMS *Thetis*, which had sunk with heavy loss of life on her trial trip in June 1939 but was later salvaged and refitted.

One of the ultimate Baltic steamers was the 'Hansa A' type, the most numerous German standard ship of the Second World War with sixty-nine examples built in yards in Germany and occupied countries. Their initial trading was, perforce, mainly in the Baltic because few North Sea routes were open to them. With the Allies' decision to take over most German tonnage in 1945, the class was dispersed, but some did eventually return to the German flag.

Fangturm was completed in December 1944 by Deutsche Werft AG in Hamburg for operation by DDG 'Hansa' of Bremen. Damaged by bombing towards the end of the war, in May 1945 she was taken over by British forces at Kiel and sent to Methil in Scotland to be renamed *Empire Gallop* under the control of the Ministry of War Transport. In 1947, she was bought by United Baltic Corporation Ltd and renamed *Baltonia* for services from London to the Baltic. A change of naming policy saw her renamed *Baltic Oak* in 1953, and in 1957 she returned to German ownership as *Palmyra** for Deutsche Levante-Linie GmbH of Hamburg. She now became a Mediterranean trader, and was in fact on a voyage from Hamburg to Istanbul when she collided with the British tanker *British Mariner* off Ushant in March 1962 and sank. The tanker came off little better, and was declared a constructive total loss.

Australian coasters

The similarity between Australian coastal steamers and those of Britain was easily explained: they mostly came from the same Scottish yards. Australian shipbuilding had a brief flowering during the First World War, but inability to compete with European yards caused it to make little contribution in terms of coastal ships until war broke out again.

The 1910 *Canonbar**, built by the Ardrossan Dry Dock & Engineering Co Ltd, was an example of a smaller steamer, employed on the coasts of New South Wales and later Queensland. Its original owner was North Coast Steam Navigation Co Ltd, formed in 1891 to serve the rich agricultural lands north of Sydney and Newcastle, where it quickly achieved a dominant position. The size of *Canonbar*, 708 grt and 186 ft registered length, reflected that the company's trade involved frequent services to relatively small ports on the rivers of New South Wales.

In 1927, *Canonbar* was sold to John Burke Ltd of Brisbane which moved her north to serve the Queensland coast trade. This was just the start of *Canonbar's* wanderings as, following requisition by the Australian Government during the Second World War, she had a variety of owners in Hong Kong, Singapore and Manila, taking the names *Rosita* and later *Valiente*. Under the latter name she became involved in the Vietnam war, going missing after leaving Singapore on 14 March 1966 with a cargo comprising cement and stores for the US base at Danang. It was subsequently established that she had been sunk on 16 March 1966 by artillery of the North Vietnamese Army. *(Warwick Foote)*

The longer Australian coastal services evolved in similar ways to those in Europe, so that steamers which could carry both passengers and cargo gradually gave way to dedicated passenger and pure cargo carriers, the transition taking place after about 1900. Long distances meant relatively large ships, typified by the 2459-grt, 296-ft steamer *Kooliga** of McIlwraith, McEacharn Ltd, and by no means the largest built for inter-state cargo services. Facilities for handling cargo at all but the biggest ports were rudimentary, only gradually improving after the First World War, and comprehensive cargo gear was essential for ships like *Kooliga*. In contrast to European 'tween-deck steamers in the liner trade, she had a single deck, suggesting that bulk cargoes such as coal were important aspects of the inter-state trade.

One of about ten operators eventually involved in the inter-state trade, McIlwraith, McEacharn began as shipping and insurance agents in 1875. Its business quickly expanded to run ships between the United Kingdom and Queensland under the patriotic title Scottish Line, and after establishing a Melbourne base it became involved in coal carrying and the inter-state trade. Its roots meant that Scottish yards enjoyed its patronage, and *Kooliga's* 1928 builder was Caledon Shipbuilding & Engineering Co Ltd of Dundee. Photographed at Burnie, Tasmania, she appears to have had a blameless career, and was sold directly from the McIlwraith, McEacharn fleet to Japanese shipbreakers in 1953. *(Winter's Studio)*

CHAPTER

13

Coastal Motor Liners

Even in two chapters it is difficult to illustrate the enormous diversity of ships that plied on coastal and short-sea liner routes. Examples have been picked that are generally typical of their owners, their builders, their period and of their services. Several fleets were large enough to develop individualistic styles, and this chapter gives some prominence to such major players. It will become apparent that there were fewer consensuses on the design of these motor ships than for their steam predecessors. This chapter has therefore been organised somewhat differently from Chapter 12, and reflects the design approach of different nations' owners and builders (it is often difficult to tell which of these parties had the most influence on design).

In the liner trade, cargoes were usually suited to stowage on a number of decks, for example, foodstuffs, package goods, or (less conveniently) timber. The ships built for this trade were mostly shelter-deckers or 'tween-deckers, distinct from single-deck ships in having an extra deck worked into their hull. With a shelter deck, a small opening to the outside was carefully arranged so as not to compromise a ship's seaworthiness, and could be closed by a relatively straightforward modification. Tonnage regulations allowed that, in the 'open' configuration, the space within the shelter deck did not count towards the tonnage on which harbour and other dues were paid. Because it did not seriously reduce cargo capacity, the shelter-deck design was thus particularly attractive to many owners, including those Europeans specialising in trades such as timber, and it also made the vessel suitable for a charter to liner operators. Several such ships were illustrated in Chapters 10 and 11.

This chapter completes the story of the regular coastal and short-sea trader in the twentieth century. It is possible to say 'completes' because this type of ship has been almost completely supplanted by vessels specialising in carrying cargo that has been either stuffed into containers or loaded into road vehicles. The period covered has seen the virtually complete elimination of purely coastwise regular cargo services, thanks partly to rail competition but mainly to the growth of road haulage. The dominance of road transport, with its ability to offer almost door-to-door delivery, also helped drive the regular trader off short-sea routes in favour of the roll-on, roll-off vessel and the container ship, the latter serviced by rail or more frequently road vehicles.

An asterisk in a caption indicates the vessel shown in the photograph.

Coast Lines motor ships

Coast Lines' management was among the first in British coastal shipping to see that the motor vessel was the way forward. It was helped by a gradual return of its business to profitability, an improvement that allowed Coast Lines to unravel itself from the other companies in the now-moribund Royal Mail Group and return to independence in 1936. Its first new motor ship was *Fife Coast* of 1933, a relatively basic single-deck, raised quarterdeck ship with no more cargo gear than the average bulk-carrying coaster.

More sophisticated in hull arrangement and cargo gear was the *Antrim Coast**, completed by the Coast Lines-owned Ardrossan Dockyard Ltd in 1937, and seen here off Alfred Dock, Birkenhead in March 1950. A 646-grt shelter-decker with an overall length of 210 ft of which 23 ft was accounted for by her forecastle, she was broadly typical of vessels entering the fleets of Coast Lines and its growing number of subsidiaries over the next two decades.

The inevitable transfer came only in 1964, when she became *Sark Coast* of subsidiary British Channel Islands Shipping Co Ltd, London. Only three years later she was sold to Greek owners who registered her in Beirut as *Miltiadis*. Before she was broken up at Perama in 1973, the Greeks squeezed another six years of work out of her now-ageing oil engines that had been made by J G Kincaid & Co Ltd, Greenock.

A few of Coast Lines' routes still offered passenger facilities in post-war years, including that between the Thames and Mersey. Compared with a three-hour train journey, this was hardly a convenient way to travel between the capital and the north-west of England, and Coast Lines began to market it as a cruise. Four passenger-cargo motor ships built for this service included *Ocean Coast** of 1934. Although there were obvious stylistic links with the contemporary cargo-only motor vessels, she was a size larger at 1173 grt and 263 ft overall, and had a grossly enlarged amidships superstructure to accommodate her twelve passengers. Oil engines by British Auxiliaries Ltd, Glasgow drove twin screws. With Ardrossan Dockyard busy on her sister, *Pacific Coast*, Coast Lines went to Henry Robb Ltd of Leith for *Ocean Coast* and two smaller cargo-passenger vessels, named *British Coast* and *Atlantic Coast*.

The original *Pacific Coast* was lost on Admiralty service in 1939, but with further cargo-passenger ships delivered post-war the service resumed and continued into the 1960s. *Ocean Coast* went in 1964, flag-of-convenience owners naming her first *Effy* and later *Anna Maria*. In February 1969, she stranded in heavy weather in the Black Sea on a voyage from Hamburg to Romania.

Coast Lines was successful in that it became very large, with operations in South Africa as well as Britain. But once coastal and short-sea liner traffic began to decline, the company seemed unable to cope with the challenges. It attempted containerisation and carrying trailers across the Irish Sea, but failed to benefit from what were to become the most important types of short-sea trades. Instead, it meekly retreated, abandoning one service after another and selling its ships.

Dutch gladdekkers

Hollandsche Stoomboot Maatschappij began building motor ships for its short-sea routes with *Amstelstroom* and *Ystroom*, completed in January and November 1936 respectively. With each successive ship the design was enlarged slightly, eventually giving the *Eemstroom** of 1940. This flush-decker – gladdekker in Dutch – was typical of Dutch vessels built for the liner trades. *Eemstroom* had three holds, that furthest aft being refrigerated, and above all of them – from the engine room right forward – was a shelter deck. In the open configuration, with its so-called tonnage openings, the shelter deck did not count towards the ship's gross tonnage, hence the modest figure of 399 grt for a 207-ft overall ship.

Compared with the typical Dutch coaster described in Chapter 8, cargo gear was enhanced with twin 2.5-ton derricks at the foremast and twin 4.5-ton derricks at the main. The derricks are not attached to the masts, but – in order to achieve lateral separation – to very short posts alongside. Note also the unusual cradles in which the derricks rest. Builders were E J Smit & Zoon's Scheepswerven at Westerbroek and, unusually for a Dutch coaster, she had a Sulzer rather than a home-grown diesel engine.

Eemstroom was launched in October 1940, but completion was delayed by the war until July 1941, when she almost immediately entered German service. On return to her owners in August 1945, she was reconditioned and put into the service for which she was intended, primarily on routes from the Netherlands to London and the Bristol Channel. In 1963, she was sold to Groningen owners as *Accres*, spending almost a year on charter to Lamport & Holt's Metric Line under the name *Hecto*. Sold to Singapore owners in 1968, she resumed the former name *Accres* and under this name was broken up in Indonesia in the late 1980s.

With the honourable exception of Coast Lines, British companies in the coastal and short-sea liner trades were reluctant to buy motor ships in the years before the Second World War, and when they did, they turned to Dutch yards. In 1937, Tyne-Tees Steam Shipping Co Ltd, Newcastle-upon-Tyne, went to J Koster Hzn Scheepswerf 'Gideon' at Groningen for *Lowick* (596 grt and 196 ft overall), and accepted *Sandhill* from the same yard in 1938. Flush-deckers, these differed from *Eemstroom* largely in having three masts with a derrick at each.

Formed in 1903, the Tyne-Tees company was an amalgamation of several lines operating services along the east coast of the United Kingdom and to near-Continental ports. At the time of ordering *Lowick*, Tyne-Tees was still independent but Coast Lines took over in 1943 and, once wartime regulations on renaming were relaxed, *Lowick* became *Frisian Coast**. In 1967, after thirty years of steady service, she went to the almost inevitable Greek owner as *Agia Eleni*. She was wrecked at Mandraki, Rhodes when her moorings parted in heavy weather during November 1977.

The last engines-amidships designs

At first, the availability of reliable and sufficiently powerful diesel engines simply meant that liner companies could build to layouts they had used for their steamers. The engines-amidships design was perpetuated, and in several fleets this meant a distinctive style could be retained. Clyde Shipping Company built its first motor ships in 1947, a 254-ft overall class of four comprising *Toward*, *Beachy*, *Copeland* and *Goodwin** all from the Caledon Shipbuilding & Engineering Co Ltd of Dundee. Twin-screw ships, these were built for the service between Glasgow, Belfast and London and, recognising that the cattle that had formerly been carried on the hoof, were now sent as carcasses, had refrigerated spaces in their holds. The treatment of the hances – where bulwarks change levels between decks – gave the class a distinctive appearance.

The 1271-grt *Goodwin* was sold in 1962, initially to Dutch owners that renamed her *Hardenberg*, and later to United States owners that renamed her *Patrician* and finally *Mary Anna* before she was broken up in 1975.

Goodwin and sisters were not quite the last engines-amidships design for Clyde Shipping, however, for after a number of smaller, engines-aft motor ships *Tuskar* emerged as late as 1962. With a similar hull form, but with deck cranes providing her only cargo gear, she was to be the last vessel built for Clyde Shipping's regular cargo services, and lasted just six years before her sale.

As the largest British operator of near-Continental short-sea services, General Steam Navigation Co Ltd demands a place in this chapter, as it did in Chapter 12. Following the successful twin-screw *Laverock* and *Seamew* of 1947, a total of seven engines-amidships single-screw motor vessels were built for the company during 1953–57. The series began with the 249-ft overall *Whitewing* and *Ringdove** from Ailsa Shipbuilding Co Ltd at Troon. Contemporary with these was the larger *Adjutant*, and they were followed by the near-sisters *Gannet*, *Woodlark* and *Heron* and the one-off *Sandpiper*, variations mostly involving masts and details of superstructure. The ships were designed to be suitable for near-Continental routes and for the company's trades to Bordeaux and to Oporto. In contrast to *Groningen*, illustrated in Chapter 12, the 1102-grt *Ringdove* and her contemporaries had no cranes, and cargo gear comprised six 5-ton and one 15-ton derricks, the latter at the foremast. Midships accommodation had grown and a neat motor ship funnel had replaced the tall smokestack. No passengers were carried, most of the amidships accommodation comprising single-berth cabins for the officers and crew. As with many shelter-deckers, the hull was flush-decked. On sale in 1967, *Ringdove* was registered in the Bahamas as *Horizont*, later moving to Yugoslavia where, as *Otok*, she was broken up on 1983 at Rijeka.

Post-war Dutch variations

Although still an important force in coastal shipping, the Dutch began to give way to others in the 1960s, including the Danes and particularly the Germans, who began building standardised coasters in series. A sign of this was that Dutch owners began, almost for the first time, to buy or build outside of the Netherlands. However, one relatively large Dutch design achieved considerable success, finding buyers not only at home but especially among British and Danish owners. The most prolific builder of the type was E J Smit & Zoon's Scheepswerven NV at Westerbroek, which delivered the 1599-grt, 262-ft overall shelter-decker *Jytte Danielsen* to Copenhagen owners in 1970.

Other Dutch yards and at least one in Spain were involved in construction of the type, and not surprisingly there were several variations on the theme, including modification of the hull shape right aft and in the length of the accommodation block. Nevertheless, the overall hull shape, the tall conical funnel and inward sloping bridge front made them readily recognisable, even in later examples for which cargo gear was omitted. London-based Shaw, Savill & Albion Co Ltd and associates of Turnbull Scott were good customers for early and late models, while the Turnbull Scott-managed Coronet Shipping Ltd had three built under licence by Astilleros Construcciones SA at Vigo in Spain.

In 1976, *Jytte Danielsen* was bought (along with sister *Cairntrader*) by Rotterdam owners, Van Nievelt, Goudriaan & Co and she was renamed *Situla*.* She was sold in 1981 to become *Asuncion*, her last known owner being Chinese, which bought her in 1987 and renamed her *Jiu Long*. *(G Monteny)*

Low air-draught

Following their success with small, single-deck ships in the 1920s and the 1930s, Dutch shipyards began building shelter-deck type vessels. Clearly hoping to emulate the success of its *Gideona* type (see Chapter 8), the Koster yard at Groningen introduced the 'New Koster' type. Almost unique among Dutch-built coasters, both bridge and engines were placed amidships. Alas, the design was nowhere near as successful as its predecessor.

Perhaps ironically, given the rivalry between the British and the Dutch coaster owners, a major customer was London's General Steam Navigation Co Ltd, which took delivery of three in 1938: *Alouette**, *Kingfisher* (both 276 grt, 158 ft overall) and the larger *Drake* (531 grt, 193 ft overall). The low tonnage of the first pair was because these were shelter-deckers, the upper deck being disregarded for purposes of tonnage measurement.

Alouette largely worked on her owner's services from London to Belgian ports and up the Rhine given her folding masts and relatively low air-draught. She was sold to Greece in 1966 along with *Drake* and as *Olympos* was broken up in 1982. *Alouette*'s sister, *Kingfisher*, had been torpedoed off Beachy Head in June 1940. *(Ships in Focus)*

The ability to lower top hamper to clear bridges on inland waterways was common to Dutch craft, and little modification was needed to give a true low-air-draught coaster. As well as routes from the Netherlands to London described in Chapter 12, Wm H Müller & Co NV of Rotterdam ran services up the River Seine, known as the 'Parisvaart'. *Seine* of 1929 set the standard design for these craft, with a relatively low wooden wheelhouse amidships, engines and crew accommodation aft, a low forecastle and poop, plus masts for each hold. The layout seems to have been successful, because almost two decades later, in 1947, *Escaut** was built by Haarlemsche Scheepsbouw Maatschappij for the same owner. Of 393 grt and 161 ft overall, the major external differences was that *Escaut* had a steel wheelhouse amidships and a gently raking bow.

Escaut was sold in 1965 to a Channel Islands-based company associated with the Dundee, Perth & London Shipping Co Ltd, which continued to use her as *Grouville* on sailings to Paris from London and on other routes. This lasted for three years until it became clear that road transport and roll-on, roll-off shipping could offer a faster and more convenient service. *Grouville* was sold with the rest of the small fleet of Channel Shipping Ltd. Under the Maltese flag and various flags-of-convenience, she carried no fewer than nine further names from September 1968 until January 1985 when she stranded after breaking adrift from a lay-up berth in Limassol harbour. *(Fotoflite/Skyfotos)*

Post-war Bristol-fashion

Ships from the Bristol Steam Navigation Co Ltd, one of the UK's oldest shipping companies, illustrate the immediate post-war design trends in British motor ships for the short-sea and coastal trades. Seen in her natural habitat of the River Avon, *Juno** of 1949 followed the rather conventional bridge-amidships, raised-quarterdeck layout. The major distinction from the many similar bulk carriers is her enhanced outfit of derricks and heavier masts. *Juno* and her contemporaries with this layout, *Ino*, *Cato* of 1946, and *Pluto* of 1950, were all single-deck ships, Bristol Steam disdaining the 'tween-deckers favoured for the liner trade elsewhere. Builders of *Juno* and *Pluto* were the owner's local yard, Charles Hill & Sons Ltd, with the former having an overall length of 224 ft and a tonnage of 969 gross.

In 1967, *Juno* was sold to Greece as *Enarxis* and, as so often happened, remained in the western and northern European trades. But not for long, because in December 1968 she struck rocks off St Jean de Luz while carrying maize from Bayonne to Leith. Declared a constructive total loss, she was broken up at Bilbao in 1969.

For their next order, Bristol Steam returned to the Hillhouse yard of Charles Hill & Sons but design went from the conventional to the avant garde. At 991 grt and 224 ft overall, *Milo* of 1953 was of a size with *Juno* but had her superstructure aft and a radical treatment of the wheelhouse and funnel, which shared a casing. The shape of this unit was echoed in a small deckhouse aft. Another major departure was to omit cargo gear altogether, with the tripod mainmast positioned well aft. What owners and builders could not bring themselves to do in this single-deck ship was to move away from the traditional raised-quarterdeck layout.

In 1969 came sale to J & A Gardner & Co Ltd of Glasgow, which renamed her *Saint Angus* and used her for six years in its coastal tramp trades. She then went out to the Maldives as *Lady Maria*, but her tenure in the Indian Ocean was brief. In August 1976 she was wrecked on the coast of Somalia.

Swedish style

Silvia demonstrates her credentials as a liner trade vessel by exporting a deck load of caravans from London. Owners were Rederi-A/B Svenska Lloyd of Gothenburg, known in the UK as Swedish Lloyd, and once the premier company operating regular services from Sweden to Britain, but which faded away in the car ferry era. An ice-strengthened shelter-decker of 490 grt and 216 ft overall, *Silvia* was built for Svenska Lloyd in 1955 by Uddevallavarvet. Cargo gear consisted of a hybrid mixture of two conventional 5-tonne derricks fore and aft with two deck cranes forward of amidships.

In 1965, *Silvia* was sold to Norway as *Nordstad*, and began a long saga of sales and at least nine name changes that saw her progressing through further Norwegian, then Lebanese and finally Syrian ownership. She was re-engined in 1968 and in 1982 converted into a livestock carrier while under the name *Al Taher I* and the Syrian flag. After more changes of name, she was last reported as *Almina I*, the name that she was given in 1995. There have been no reports of the vessels for several years and it is thought that at best she is out of service and at worst has been scrapped or sunk.

Ice-classed Finns

In 1956, Finska Ångfartygs A/B of Helsinki took delivery of *Mira*, an ice-classed shelter-decker from a yard in Norrköping, Sweden. Thirteen sisters were delivered over the next five years by the Swedish builder and by three yards in Finland, the penultimate vessel being *Titania** of 1961 (1422 grt and 292 ft overall). The builder was Rauma-Repola O/Y at Rauma, which fitted her with a Finnish-manufactured Sulzer diesel. Minor variations in the class mainly affected the ample outfit of kingposts, which supported a total of nine derricks including a heavy-lift variety just aft of the bridge. The ships ran from the Baltic to western Europe, *Titania* being photographed in a South Wales port, but were quite capable of trading further afield, especially after the later batch of six were lengthened to 330 ft in the early 1970s.

In 1977, *Titania* was sold to Yick Fung Shipping & Enterprises Co Ltd of Hong Kong, which renamed her *Tabi Shan* under the Panamanian flag. In 1980, like most Yick Fung ships, she was transferred to her real owners, the People's Republic of China, which renamed her *Tai Yung Shan*. She was deleted from *Lloyd's Register* in 2008. *(J and M Clarkson)*

The cargo gear of the short-sea traders of Finnlines, Finland's other major operator of worldwide liner services, evolved steadily through the post-war years. Conventional masts gave way to bipods (which reduced the need for staying) or goalpost masts (which facilitated stowing long items on deck) and finally to deck cranes. A quartet with mainly cranes that was built by Wärtsilä koncernen Crichton-Vulcan at Turku/Åbo in 1964 and 1965 comprised *Finnseal*, *Lotila* (later *Finntube*), *Rekola* (later *Finnstrip*) and *Finnfighter**, all intended for services from Finland to the UK and western Europe. These measured 300 ft overall, with *Finnfighter* having a gross tonnage of 1682 as an open and 2727 as a closed shelter-decker.

The variation in names of the ships arose because the umbrella of O/Y Finnlines Ltd covered a number of ship-owning subsidiaries, *Finnfighter* being owned by Enso-Gutzeit O/Y of Kotka, a state-owned forest products company. Paper-making companies were also under this umbrella, indicative that pulp and paper products comprised much of Finland's exports.

The trend towards ships becoming more quickly obsolescent thanks to development of roll-on, roll-off traffic and containerisation led to *Finnfighter*'s sale after just ten years' service, becoming *Lun Shan*. Registered owners were associated with Yick Fung Shipping & Enterprises Ltd of Hong Kong, which in reality was a front organisation for the Government of the People's Republic of China, which at the time seemed reluctant to buy directly from Western shipowners. As with the former *Titania*, she eventually moved to mainland Chinese companies, becoming *Wan Fu* on transfer in 1986. She was deleted from Lloyd's Register in 2002. *(J and M Clarkson)*

French Mediterranean traders

French ship designers went their own way in the early 1950s, turning out a series of distinctive short-sea traders with long well decks forward on which were two of their three hatches. Although single-deck ships, those shown were heavily rigged with masts and derricks and had good turns of speed to suit for services from French Atlantic ports to the Mediterranean.

Penhir was completed in 1952 by Ateliers et Chantiers de Bretagne SA, Nantes, for local owner Compagnie Nantaise des Chargeurs de l'Ouest. Measuring 272 ft overall and 1672 grt, she had a licence-built MAN engine capable of propelling her at 13 knots. She was photographed in June 1953. Renamed *La Manche* in 1961 by owners in Concarneau, she went to Greek owners in 1965 as *Grigorousa* and to Italians in 1970 as *Quovis*. Under the last name she was converted to a hopper, probably losing all her gear in the process, but this extended her life to 1991 when she was broken up at Porto Nogaro.

Isée also started life with owners in western France, Société Navale Caennaise, and was later sold to Mediterranean owners. Described as a motor reefer, she too was a single-decker, also 272 ft overall length and 1317 grt. She was also completed in 1952, by SA des Anciens Chantiers Dubigeon, and the coincidence of their being, like the previous ship's builders, in Nantes might explain the very considerable external similarities to *Penhir*. In 1961, *Isée* was sold to Compagnie Tunisienne de Navigation, Tunis, which renamed her *Tabarka** and would use her in trans-Mediterranean trades, and quite probably added the circular tank seen immediately ahead of her bridge, quite possibly to carry wine. *Tabarka* is reported to have been broken up in November 2004.

Australian motor ships

Australian coastal operators were not slow to embrace the diesel engine, and the Australasian United Steam Navigation Co Ltd took delivery of *Babinda** from Scott & Sons, Bowling in April 1936, not long after Coast Lines in the UK had taken their first motor ship. In many respects, this 181-ft overall, 659-grt coaster was similar to her coal-fired forebears with a raised-quarterdeck configuration, a straight stem and a large funnel. Typical of many ships built for Australian coastal trades, cargo gear is substantial and derricks are so long that they require tall masts and upright stowage.

The 9.5-knots, single-deck *Babinda* was one of a succession of cargo ships built mainly for the trade from the sugar plantations of Queensland to Brisbane. Her funnel colours of black with two white bands reflect the role of British India in establishing the Australasian United Steam Navigation Co Ltd in 1887. The company sold its last ships in 1961.

Babinda herself was sold in 1955 and traded around the Pacific under her old name, eventually being sold, via Singapore owners, to Indonesia where she was eventually renamed, first as *Tamiang* and later as *Bintang Samudra IV*. With her continued existence being in doubt, she was deleted from *Lloyd's Register* book in 2006 *(Warwick Foote)*

Babinda was of quite modest size but, as mentioned elsewhere, running coastal and short-sea services in Australasian waters usually involved much longer distances than in Europe, and required bigger ships. At 305 ft overall, the 2437-grt *Karoon** is at the upper limit of what Europeans then regarded as coasters, yet she was typical of ships built for Australia. She and sister *Kootara* were built in 1951 and 1952 respectively for the Union Steam Ship Company of New Zealand Ltd by the New South Wales Government Engineering & Shipbuilding Undertaking at Newcastle. Australian shipbuilding had been encouraged during the Second World War, but its competitiveness was fragile, and this pair was an isolated example of the New Zealand giant deserting its usual Scottish suppliers, possibly because the ships were for use on Australian coastal routes. Union Steam Ship clearly had its own ideas on design, and with her tall masts, kingposts, winch houses and other details, *Karoon* had a strong family resemblance to others in the fleet, a style that dated from the Glasgow-built motor ship *Kauri* of 1936. The sisters had Australian aborigine names, *Karoon* simply meaning 'Number 1' and *Kootara* 'Number 2'.

After leaving the New Zealand-owned fleet in 1968, *Karoon* had a long, though ultimately somewhat tragic career first with Sydney owners who renamed her *Lisa Miller*, then in Malaysian ownership as *Southern Cross* and finally *Southern Glory*. In December 1993, she was on voyage from Muara to Singapore with sawn timber when she developed a heavy list and, after her engines became disabled, was abandoned by her crew and sank.

CHAPTER

14

Container Coasters

Containerisation has been the most significant development in shipping since the application of steam power. It has reduced costs while at the same time speeding up the movement of goods and improved their security while in transit. Its contribution to globalisation, the spread of manufacturing, has been enormous.

Coastal shipping has both gained and lost through containerisation. Ship owners that have been prepared to invest in specialised tonnage (and renew it regularly) have benefited from the development of container feeder services, which is a consequence of the size of mainline container vessels and their concentration on routes connecting a small number of hubs. In contrast, the coastal and short-sea cargo liners described in Chapters 1, 12 and 13 have been all but driven to extinction by container carriers and roll-on, roll-off ferries. Arguably road transport has gained most from containerisation, through the ease and speed with which a container can be lifted off a deep-sea ship and placed on a trailer. This has been to the detriment of short-sea shipping in reducing the range of ports that offer trading opportunities. Perhaps the classic British examples are Manchester, which has all but died since containerisation, and Preston from which the earliest European container services were launched, but which has since closed. Other ports once extremely busy with coastal and short-sea shipping, including London, Liverpool and Glasgow, have seen massive declines in this sector, while hitherto insignificant ports such as Felixstowe have blossomed. Similar trends can be seen across Europe and beyond, with hubs such as Rotterdam and Hamburg reducing other ports, for example Copenhagen and Gothenburg, to the shipping equivalent of branch-line termini.

This sector has seen a major alteration in ownership patterns, with few feeder ships now belonging to the container lines, and most being chartered in, often from relatively small owners that may have but a single ship. Short-term chartering gives the operator considerable flexibility to adjust capacity to demand and, as a result, such vessels often carry a string of different names as various charterers exercise their naming options.

Despite the significance of containerisation, this chapter is short. This reflects the relatively brief period in which the container has been a major factor in shipping, the speed with which the feeder ship developed, and the relative lack of variety in the design of recent vessels. Containerisation is, however, an unfinished story. The container feeder ship is testimony to the economy and flexibility that small ships can offer, and it offers much potential for development of new short-sea and perhaps even coastal routes.

An asterisk in a caption indicates the vessel shown in the photograph.

Railway enterprise

Although containerisation as a system developed only in the 1950s and the 1960s, the idea of packing goods in a large box is much older. European railways began using containers on a small scale between the world wars. The British variety, employed to carry items such as furniture, was small, designed to sit on a typical short wheelbase flat truck, and little attempt seems to have been made to standardise containers between countries. The design of British railway containers, with arched roofs derived from rail van practice, precluded them from being stacked one upon another. Given what has developed, this was a serious missed opportunity.

Typical rail containers can be seen on the deck of *Brest** approaching Newhaven in June 1965. This 1038-grt, 238-ft overall, twin-screw motor ship was owned by the French state railways, Société Nationale des Chemins de Fer Français, for which she had been completed in May 1951 at the Penhoët shipyard at Grand Quevilly. *Brest* was one of three near-sisters for the Dieppe to Newhaven service operated jointly with a British railway. The first pair *Nantes* and *Rennes*, had been ordered in 1939 but construction was halted in June 1940 and these were not completed until 1946 and 1947, respectively. Their holds were designed to carry motor cars, which were craned on and off at their terminal ports.

Following her sale in 1967, *Brest* followed the familiar route to Mediterranean ownership, initially with a Greek gentleman as *Lassi IV*, and later with Beirut owners. Her final Lebanese owner, which renamed her *Mahdi* in 1971, went out of business about 1985, and the vessel was deleted from *Lloyd's Register* in 1995. *(World Ship Society Ltd)*

The railways had long carried a significant proportion of Irish Sea cargoes, and were anxious to share in the growth of traffic as containerisation began to take off in the 1950s. In 1958, British Railways took delivery of two ships each capable of carrying forty-seven 20-foot units. Although basic cargo ships, to emphasise their capacity for boxes – modest though it was – they were named *Container Enterprise* and *Container Venturer**.

Completion at Troon by Ailsa Shipbuilding Co Ltd gave the pair an interesting connection with some of the first steam coasters on the Irish Sea, because this builder's predecessors, S McKnight & Company, had commenced building these in 1883. The 1958 sisters were somewhat bigger (982 grt and 263 ft overall), but their Glasgow-built British Polar engines propelled them at a similar speed of 10 knots.

Intended service was between Heysham in Lancashire and Belfast, and the pair remained on this service for almost two decades, although *Container Enterprise* is known to have had a spell on British Rail's Fishguard to Waterford route in 1972.

On sale in 1979, *Container Venturer* was put under the Panamanian flag and suffered the multitude of name changes to which old cargo ships are often condemned. She was last heard of as *Jeanny Cay II*, apparently owned in land-locked Bolivia, but was deleted from *Lloyd's Register* in 2006. Her sister gravitated out to the Caribbean, and was owned in Miami as *Freedom Express* until in September 2003 the authorities scuttled her after deciding that she had been abandoned by her owners in the Miami anchorage. *(World Ship Society Ltd Collection)*

Early Irish Sea adaptations

In British waters, containerisation first made an impact on Irish Sea routes. Anglo-Continental Container Services Ltd opened a service in 1950 between Preston and Larne, ports that already had a roll-on, roll-off service. This and many later services used chartered ships, and initially this was tonnage which was cheaply adapted to conveying boxes.

Typical of the adapted motor vessels was the Dutch *Trinitas** of 1951. When built at Foxhol by Gebroeder Bodewes, Scheepswerf 'Volharding' as *Prior* she was a conventional raised-quarterdeck coaster of 499 grt and 167 ft overall. After sale to members of the Klugkist and Kalkhuis families of Delfzijl and renamed *Trinitas* in 1963, her hinged mainmast amidships was removed and this left just light poles fore and aft, and her conventional hatch covers modified. The deck cargo in this photograph, taken as she approached Preston from Belfast, are typical non-standard early containers. The angle at which containers are stowed on the well-deck hatch also illustrates why purpose-built container ships dispensed with sheer, and why the raised-quarterdeck layout quickly disappeared. Funnel colours are those of charterer Atlantic Steam Navigation Co Ltd, which had taken over Anglo-Continental Container Services Ltd in 1960. Her pioneering role over, *Trinitas* was sold to Belgian shipbreakers in July 1972. *(J and M Clarkson)*

Although not designed as container ships, the 228-ft Type 33 of J J Sietas Schiffswerft at Hamburg-Neuenfelde became familiar on the Irish Sea and elsewhere in the early days of containerisation. A total of twenty-nine were built between 1964 and 1968 to several variants that differed mainly in their provision of cargo gear, and the ten vessels of the Type 33e had no more than a pair of kingposts aft. At 499 grt, the tonnage of these shelter-deckers was just within the regulations that permitted the minimum size of crew.

The largest group of the Type 33, and with a generous provision of gear, is represented here by the 1965-built *Hasselwerder* belonging to Walter Bartels of Hamburg. She is seen on the River Ribble during her 1966–67 charter to the short-lived Hibernian Transport Group (see Chapter 12) as *City of Le Havre**.

After reverting to *Hasselwerder*, the ship was sold to Danish owners in 1974 to become *Karen Silvana*, and has since been through a succession of renamings and reflaggings and in 2011 was under the Greek flag as *Mema*, her eleventh name. *(J and M Clarkson)*

It was not just motor coasters that participated in the Irish Sea unit-load services: the steam coaster survived into the container era in the shape of the 191-ft registered length, 766-grt *Loch Linnhe**. Built in 1928 by Goole Shipbuilding & Repairing Co (1927) Ltd as *Anna* for Belgian owners, she was bought by John Rainey Ltd, Larne, in 1955, renamed and converted from coal to oil burning. In the photograph on the River Ribble she is in Rainey's colours and her derricks have been landed. She must have been one of the very few steam coasters to have carried a radar mast.

Initial employment as a unit load ship was between Londonderry and Preston for Anglo-Irish Transport Ltd, but this ended in 1964 when Coast Lines ships took over sailings. From March 1965 *Loch Linnhe* was chartered by Greenore Ferry Services Ltd to run between Greenore and Preston. Replaced by the purpose-built *Owenro* in October 1965, she changed hands briefly before being sold to breakers to be demolished at Troon. *(J and M Clarkson)*

Coast Lines Ltd's subsidiaries once dominated general cargo services on the Irish Sea but were followers rather than pioneers of containerisation. Its initial entry was through subsidiary Link Line Ltd, which began a Liverpool to Belfast service in January 1959 with the motor vessels *Spaniel** and *Pointer*. These names reflected the long-discontinued practice of G & J Burns Ltd, predecessors of Burns & Laird Lines. Link Line owned the containers and flats, but the two ships belonged to Coast Lines.

Spaniel and *Pointer* had been built in 1955 and 1956, the former by George Brown & Co (Marine) Ltd of Greenock as *Brentfield*, both for the Coast Line's subsidiary Zillah Shipping Co Ltd. At 1263 grt and 224 ft overall, these were considerably bigger than the ships usually operated by this coastal tramping company, and proved an expensive mistake. The coal trades for which they were intended were shrinking rapidly and similar-sized vessels were chasing too few cargoes. The Zillah board turned to its parent to help bail it out of what was becoming an acute predicament, requesting the ships to be redeployed elsewhere in the group and in November 1958 they were converted to become Coast Lines' first container ships.

In 1962, the purpose-built container ships *Bison* and *Buffalo* entered Link Line's Liverpool to Belfast service and *Spaniel* and *Pointer* were transferred to a Larne to Ardrossan service. The pair soldiered on for some years under various company titles, including P & O Short Sea Shipping Ltd. *Spaniel* was sold in 1963 but remained on the Irish Sea running for the Isle of Man Steam Packet Co Ltd as *Conister*. She was broken up at Aviles, Spain in 1981. *(J and M Clarkson)*

First cellular container ships

The first cellular container ships – in other words fitted with cell guides – built in the United Kingdom were *Sea Freightliner I* and *Sea Freightliner II**, completed in 1967 and 1968 by John Readhead & Sons Ltd for British Rail. They were substantial ships, of 4034 grt and 388 ft overall and capable of 13.5 knots, but undeniably short-sea vessels, giving the lie to any definition of coastal and short-sea craft that relies on size alone. These were intended for the services between Parkeston Quay near Harwich and either Zeebrugge in Belgium or Rotterdam. The ships could turn round in the then-unprecedented time of five hours, enabling daily services to be operated. They worked steadily on these routes for almost two decades, moving to ownership by Sealink UK Ltd in 1979 when the British government hived off British Rail's successful shipping ventures preparatory to selling them off to private bidders. By 1987, the ships' capacity of just 148 containers was far outclassed, and both quietly went to Taiwan to be scrapped.

An inauspicious trend inaugurated by these two ships was a bland, corporate and mechanistic naming scheme that continues to rear its head from time to time, as if owners of container carriers disdained any echoes of poetry or resonance in naming their craft. Only such soullessness can explain names such as *Sea Freightliner I*, *ACT I*, and *Containerships IV*. *(W J Harvey)*

Hamburg-Neuenfelde builder J J Sietas Schiffswerft has been the most successful German shipyard in recent decades, thanks to its ability to economically build standard designs that have proved highly popular with German owners large and small.

Type 67 was the yard's second design for a 'pure' container carrier, fourteen of which were built for German owners during 1970–72. It had a modest container capacity of 150 TEUs on an overall length of 290 ft and a remarkably consistent tonnage of 999 gross. Note the cavity at main deck level in the superstructure into which the steel hatch covers fold, allowing containers to be lowered into the cell guides immediately ahead of the bridge. Despite absence of cargo gear, styling of details such as the superstructure and hull form is still quite traditional, certainly compared with what was soon to happen to such features.

Owner of the 1971-built *Nautic** was Hans Beilken of Brake on the River Weser. The funnel colours in the photograph are those of the inevitable charterer, probably Oldenburg-Portugiesische Dampfschiffs-Rhederei, although the absence of this company's containers suggests she has recently come off charter but has yet to be repainted. German container ship owners have tended to sell on ships quite quickly, ensuring that they have as modern a fleet as possible, and in 1982 *Nautic* went to Finnish owners that briefly renamed her *Pepilo* before restoring *Nautic*. This became a pattern: a spell as *Elmwood* from 1987 to 1990 ended with her reverting to *Nautic*. Since 2006 she has been sailing as *Miraj*, registered in Georgia.

Self-sustaining

Comparison of *Nautic* with another Sietas standard ship illustrates the development of the container ship into the 1980s. The Type 111a was only a little longer, at 89 metres overall, but capacity has grown to 256 TEUs. Gross tonnage has shown an even more dramatic leap, to 3120 grt, but this reflects new and more sensible measurement procedures rather than an enlargement, and shows what owners have been getting away with for years. The 1984-built *Calypso** was described as self-sustaining, in that the trend to eliminate cargo gear has been reversed. The two 30-tonne cranes are cunningly mounted at the extreme port edge of the deck to maximise space for container stowage on the hatches. The cranes also offer considerable flexibility to load other items of deck cargo. Compared with *Nautic*, superstructure design has been revolutionised and it now begins to resemble a tower block. This shot also emphasises the highly flared bow.

Owners of *Calypso* from 1984 to 1993 were members of the Heinrich family of Hove, and she was managed by Paul Heinrich of Hamburg; note his familiar funnel markings. In 1985, she became *Band Aid Hope* for five months to carry relief goods to Africa for a charity. Since 1992, she has carried a variety of names for German and Danish owners and in 2010 was renamed *Tiger I* for unknown owners for which she flies the flag of Georgia.

Design matures and enlarges

WEC Canarias ghosts along a New Waterway lit by a December sun in 1990, demonstrating just how large the coastal and short-sea container ship had grown, at 94 metres but only 1400 grt. She was built in 1980 by Maritima del Musel SA at Gijon as *Ana Del Mar*, part of a flowering of Spanish container-ship building.

Features typical of her breed include a long, totally flat deck, complete absence of gear and a superstructure extended upwards rather than fore and aft to maximise the length of deck available for carrying boxes. Service speed is quoted as 13 knots, similar to that of the short-sea cargo liners which this type of ship replaced.

WEC Canarias was owned by Ibercargo SA, and charterers were WEC Lines, a Netherlands-based container line specialising in services to the Iberian Peninsula. When the charter ended in 1992, she reverted to *Ana Del Mar*. In 1995, she went to Malaysian owners as *Giswee*, and in 2009 to United Arab Emirates as *Shaheen*. On 17 September 2009 she stranded on Kermagad Island, off the west coast of India, after dragging her anchor. Refloated and taken to Mumbai, at the time of rewriting her fate had not been decided. *(Author)*

At 142 metres overall, the unimaginatively named *Containerships IV* shows how far Sietas has pushed the feeder ship concept. At 7550 grt, it also demonstrates how this once-small yard has expanded the size of its offering and, of necessity, its premises at Neuenfelde just below Hamburg on the Elbe, the river on which *Containerships IV* was photographed outbound in September 1998. Her capacity is 749 TEU, 248 in her four holds and a massive 501 on deck. Fifty of the containers could be refrigerated.

She was completed in March 1994 as *Containerships IV*, having been laid down as *Spica* for Hans Peter Wegener, Hamburg. Charterers were Containerships Ltd of Helsinki, which operate a network of routes stretching from the Baltic to the eastern Mediterranean. In 2003, the ship was briefly renamed *Melfi Italia* for another charterer, before reverting in 2004 to *Spica*, as which she remained in service with her original owner in 2011. *(Author)*

Open holds

On the principal that a ship earns money only when it is on the move, speed is of the essence when loading and discharging containers. To improve turnaround time, a radical innovation in container ship design has been to omit hatches. The designers convinced themselves, and certain users, that with a reasonable load of containers the amount of seawater or rain entering the holds could easily be dealt with by bilge pumps.

However, the open hold concept has not been enthusiastically embraced by the shipping industry. The stacking height of containers is limited by the ability of those at the bottom to bear the weight of others in the stack, and in larger ships load-bearing hatch covers extend this height. In any case, opening the hatch covers is not greatly time-consuming.

Sietas has not received as many orders for its Type 160 open-hatch ship, such as *Yvette**, as for its conventional container carriers. The 6362-grt, 121-metre *Yvette* was completed at the Hamburg-Neuenfelde yard in June 1996 as *Partnership* for a company managed by Heinz Georg Vöge, Hamburg, whose funnel markings she wears, and in September 1996 was renamed *Yvette*. After several name changes and sales, in 2011 she was owned in Stade, Germany and was in service as the Cypriot-flagged *WEC Rubens*.

Unconventional features of this 700-TEU vessel include the long raised forecastle, reminiscent of the Dutch half shelter-deckers. The 'wall' across the deck and the heightened coamings to the hatch immediately abaft this structure are also of note. This three-quarter aft view in Antwerp during May 1999 emphasises the offset exhaust and the high, short superstructure to maximise deck space. *(Author)*

Low air-draught

A low-air-draught container ship is almost a contradiction in terms, as operators' economics depend on having boxes several stacks high on deck. Nevertheless, some owners have decided that they must have pillar-mounted wheelhouses that can retract to clear any low bridges encountered, and these include the operators of *Pride of Braila**, which was photographed off Goole on 20 May 2001. At 110 metres, she was almost the maximum size for this port, and was preparing to move stern first from the River Ouse into the Ocean Lock so that she could manoeuvre to the container berth. As her name suggests, the Veere-registered, 2077-grt *Pride of Braila** along with her sister *Pride of Veere*, was built by Santierul Naval Braila SA in Romania, and both ships were completed in 1988. Twin screws help achieve a shallow draught of 3.6 metres. Owners were Braila BV, and remained so in 2011, with managers Rhein Maas-und See-Schiffahrtskontor GmbH.

All of the ships included in Chapter 8 on Dutch coasters were built or extensively converted in the Netherlands. *Pride of Braila* has been included partly to illustrate that Dutch builders have been losing the monopoly of supplying Dutch coaster owners. Indeed, with the notable exception of the Sietas yard, most western European coaster builders are experiencing serious and probably life-threatening competition from yards in eastern Europe and the Far East. *(Author)*

The main challenge to the current orthodoxy that bridge and superstructure shall always be aft has come from builders of container ships. A full load of containers on deck seriously restricts forward vision, yet the rules of classification societies and national authorities insist that watch-keepers must see objects in the water at a modest distance ahead as an essential aspect of safe navigation.

Among the very few Soviet-built ships exported when new were *Cast Bass* and *Cast Salmon**, built in 1991 by the Nevskiy Shipyard at Petrokrepost near St Petersburg. These were originally members of the 'Nevskiy' class, which included two quite distinct variants, one with conventional superstructure aft and a low air-draught version with bridge forward. Soon after completion as the bridge-forward *Nevskiy-37* and *Nevskiy-36*, these went to Werkendam and Gdansk, respectively, to be converted into container carriers, emerging with a capacity of 200 containers, a length of 109 metres and a tonnage of 2264 gross. The conversions were destined for a container feeder service from ports on the River Rhine to Zeebrugge, from where Cast Shipping of Canada ran a transatlantic container line.

The photograph shows *Cast Salmon* with wheelhouse raised passing the Hook of Holland during May 1995. The mast above the bridge and that aft with its cluster of navigation lights fold for passing under low bridges.

After the Cast service collapsed, the two ships, which were chartered from a Belgian operator (although under the Cyprus flag), moved on to other charters, *Cast Salmon* becoming *AKN Pride* in 2005. In 2011, she is running under the flag of Paraguay as *Dona Veronica*. *(Author)*

CHAPTER

15

Asian Assortment

A heady mix of vessels has operated the equivalent of coastal and short-sea services in Asiatic waters. Historically, this assortment has included a number of ships built in British and Dutch yards, many of which were intended for or which gravitated to services in former possessions or dominions of these colonial powers. As builders in other European countries joined and indeed surpassed these two pioneers of coaster construction, German and Scandinavian yards made a contribution, and the mix was made even more interesting by a seasoning of wartime-built ships from the United States. More recently these have been joined by growing numbers of locally built vessels, initially from Japanese and Hong Kong yards, but more recently from Singapore, Korea, China and Turkey. Indeed, yards in Asia look set to dominate shipbuilding worldwide, not just in short-sea cargo vessels but in large and highly sophisticated ocean-going ships. The tables have been turned and the Asian nations that once bought their ships from western Europe are now the major suppliers of tonnage to that continent.

It is almost impossible to single out typical characteristics of an 'Asian' coaster, any more than a 'European' type. A large number of those shown are at anchor off Singapore or Hong Kong, and while some are undoubtedly waiting for scarce berths or an improvement in freight rates, transshipment of cargo at anchor is important, requiring a good outfit of cargo gear.

The trends apparent elsewhere in the world of small cargo ships are apparent: increasing size, more sophisticated cargo gear and a growing emphasis on container friendliness, often with detriment to their aesthetics. However, beyond this it is impossible to generalise and this chapter roams widely in both geography and time in attempting to give a flavour of the small vessels at work in the East. Ships are arranged generally by country of origin. Those featured were designed for use in the East or built by yards in Asia, not vessels that simply went there from Europe, North America or Australia, and which have been represented in earlier chapters.

An asterisk in a caption indicates the vessel shown in the photograph.

China coaster

British involvement in trade from Shanghai up the Yangtze River and along the coast of China grew after Alfred Holt pioneered direct steamer services to China. Holt had an important supporter in John Swire, whose company, Butterfield & Swire, was soon appointed Holt's agent in China, responsible for providing Holt's homeward cargoes. Local steamer services to feed the deep-sea ships were a natural development, and in 1872 Swire floated the China Navigation Co Ltd on the London Stock Exchange. Within a few years, it was trading from Manchuria down to Hong Kong in the south.

Given the length of its routes, China Navigation's 'China coasters' were substantial ships. Delivered from three Scottish yards in 1946 and 1947, *Soochow* and her sisters, *Sinkiang*, *Szechuen* and *Shansi*, were 321 ft overall. They were China Navigation's last ships for their traditional trade between Shanghai, Tsingtao, Amoy, Swatow and Hong Kong. Soon, China's civil war led to a blockade of Shanghai and eventual victory by the communists, which first disrupted China Navigation's routes and later deprived it of much business. The company successfully refocused, seizing other business opportunities in the Far East.

The 3152-grt *Soochow*, completed by A & J Inglis at Glasgow in 1947, was gainfully employed until 1967, when sold to Pacific International Lines as *Kota Ratu*. She is seen under her final name, *Sang Fajar**, adopted in 1975 when acquired by the Malaysian Shipping Corporation. She was reportedly used as a troop transport, and possibly in connection with this her after well was plated in and awnings erected over the after deck. *Sang Fajar* was broken up at Kaohsiung in 1984. *(R J Kittle)*

Built in Hong Kong and Singapore

Some of the earliest shipyards in the Far East to construct sea-going steamers were in the British colony of Hong Kong, and these were also the earliest to compete on reasonably equal terms with European yards. Interestingly, the Taikoo Dockyard & Engineering Co Ltd at Quarry Bay was building motor ships as early as 1913, well before most European yards. The *Ah Kwang* was a 612-grt, 218-ft overall, Bolinders-engined, twin-screw craft for the Asiatic Petroleum Co (North China) Ltd of Shanghai, which was the Asian marketing arm of Shell. She was a dry cargo vessel rather than a tanker, and probably carried oil and paraffin in cans. She managed to survive the Second World War in the Far East – no mean feat for a British ship – and came into full Shell ownership soon afterwards, renaming as *Playaran* in 1951 coinciding with her being based in Singapore. She was sold to other local owners in 1955 and converted to single screw. Quite likely her bridge and other details were modernised at the time, and the photograph depicts her as trading in the late 1960s under the Thai flag as *Sri Thai**, owner a Madame Poonsri Sutharom of Bangkok. Her fate is not known. She was deleted from *Lloyd's Register* as early as 1961 (before this photograph was taken), but there were reports of movements as late as 1992. *(R J Kittle)*

The predominant local shipping company in Singapore while it was a British colony was Straits Steamship Co Ltd, founded by the trading house of Mansfield & Company in 1890.It expanded to such an extent that by 1932 it had fifty-five steamers and motor ships, and served seventy-eight ports in Malaya, Thailand and what is now Indonesia. Its Second World War losses amounted to thirty ships, and – although the company's great days were over – new ships were urgently needed. British war-built coasters were bought in large numbers, but more specialised passenger-cargo ships were needed. The company had for some years favoured placing the bridge and part of the accommodation right forward, and in *Petaling** of 1953 this gave a very distinctive profile, although those steering from such a forward position required a pole mounted on the bow. Built by Taikoo Dockyard, the 1359-grt, 211-ft overall motor ship was followed in 1954 by two slightly larger vessels which were externally identical, *Perak* built at Blyth and *Perlis* at Dundee. All had substantial cargo gear to serve their two holds, a necessity when working cargo at anchor.

Petaling was transferred several times between Mansfield subsidiaries, but retained the black, blue and white funnel of Straits Steamship until sale in 1983. Renaming *Lin Petaling* in 1986 was brief, as she was broken up in Singapore in mid-1987. *(R J Kittle)*

Despite their total lack of colonies, enterprising Norwegian owners also ran large coasters around China and elsewhere in the Far East. Delivered to one of these owners by Taikoo Dockyard in 1953 was the large motor ship *Henrik*. Built for Bruusgaard, Kiøsterud & Co, *Henrik* measured 1702 grt and 277 ft overall, and shared with *Petaling* a substantial cargo gear and a massive bridge and accommodation block, although the latter was not placed so far forward.

Henrik was sold 1964 to another Norwegian owner who renamed her *Sletholm*, and she traded around Papua New Guinea until 1972.That year she was sold to Guan Guan Shipping (Private) Ltd, a company founded by a Chinese family in Indonesia, but who were encouraged to leave that country by the racial policies of its dictator General Sukarno. The family migrated to Singapore and built up a substantial fleet of predominantly second-hand ships, expanding into ocean-going cargo ships. Guan Guan had traded to the People's Republic of China when other nations' ships had been forbidden to do so by their governments, and as a result the company gained significant trading privileges from the communists.

The former *Henrik* was renamed *Golden Eastern** and repainted into Guan Guan's unusual colour scheme in which masts were painted the same blue as the lower part of the funnel. Note also the letters 'GG' neatly painted on the bow crest. Transferred to a Guan Guan subsidiary in 1975, *Golden Eastern* traded until 1984 when she passed to shipbreakers at Jurong. *(R J Kittle)*

Singapore was some way behind Hong Kong in establishing its shipbuilding industry, but with its impressive industrial and financial growth following independence it quickly surpassed its Asian rival. *Asean Pioneer** was built by Singapore Slipway & Engineering Co (Private) Ltd in 1975, a workmanlike cargo ship of 1579 grt and 69 metres in length overall with two 12.5-tonne cranes serving its two holds that shows she means business. A trend seen in contemporary European coasters is to minimise the length of the superstructure, symptomatic of dwindling crew sizes. A German oil engine gave her a fairly modest 9 knots. Owners were Straits Maritime Leasing (Private) Ltd of Singapore, although she was registered in Panama. In this late 1970s photograph, she is working for the unrelated operator, Pelangi Line.

In 1981, she was renamed *Ocean Pioneer*, and further renamings soon followed to *Helen* and then *Minibok*. On 17 September 1988, she foundered in the Indian Ocean.

Singapore continues to have a thriving shipping industry, although its shipyards have not aimed to compete head-on with other Asian yards but have specialised in sophisticated repair and conversion work. *(R J Kittle)*

Japanese coasters of the 1940s

Japan was the first Asian nation to establish a major shipbuilding industry, stimulated in part by orders received from Great Britain during the First World War. Japan entered the Second World War with a strong merchant fleet, the majority built at home. The massive expansion of Japan's empire in 1941 and 1942 was predicated on a large fleet, but the Imperial Japanese Navy's signal failure to protect merchant ships against the onslaught of US and Allied submarines was an important factor in Japan's downfall.

Like the majority of pre-war ships, the steamer *Mishima Maru* of 1940 became a war loss, mined off Kobe on 15 May 1945. Such was Japan's shortage of ships that she was raised and repaired after the war, retaining the triple-expansion engines made by her builders, Tsurumi Seitetsu Zosen KK of Yokohama. Only in 1964 were these replaced with diesels.

The photograph depicts her under the Panamanian flag in the early 1970s owned by Ednasa Co Ltd as *Angelina**, the third name carried since her sale to this Hong Kong company in 1967. Her acquisition of a diesel engine has made no difference to her steamer-like appearance: she still sports an impressively tall funnel. A recurring feature of Asian craft is the extensive cargo gear, including a heavy-lift derrick at her chunky main mast. Her overall length was 285 ft and tonnage 1972 gross.

She underwent a further sale, this time to Singapore owners, which renamed her *Wing On* in 1978. But soon after leaving Madras on voyage to Brunei with a cargo of barytes on 28 May 1978 she sprang a leak in heavy weather and sank for a second time. *(R J Kittle)*

Hishi Maru No 3 was an uncommon example of a Japanese ship that survived the war. The 193-ft registered length motor ship was completed by Mitsubishi Jukogyo KK at Shimonoseki in January 1944 and was surrendered to the British at Singapore in August 1945. It took until 1947 before she was given the name *Empire Tenby* in the series allocated to captured and surrendered ships, suggesting that she might have needed substantial repair work. She quickly became *MTS No 7*, the initials presumably standing for 'Ministry (of) Transport, Singapore'.

The Ministry disposed of her in 1949, and she was renamed several times as she passed through different hands. In 1954, she became *Tong Thay* of Kie Hock Shipping Co Ltd of Singapore, but even then was subject to several renamings, moves to subsidiaries, reflagging to Panama and lengthening in 1957 before becoming the 830-grt *Fajardo**, as seen at Singapore, in 1967. Registered in the ownership of subsidiary Compania Naviera Thompson SA, Panama, she yet flies the Kie Hock house flag and wears their badge on stem and bridge front, conveying some pride in ownership. Despite this, she was broken up at Hong Kong in July 1976, not long after she was photographed in Singapore.

It is interesting to speculate just where the new section was inserted in 1957. It may have been responsible for the abrupt change in sheer forward of the foremast, but equally this may result from the urgency of her building in 1944, when so many Japanese ships were being lost. As with any Japanese post-war survivor, we are looking at a ship which has been much modified since completion. *(R J Kittle)*

Evidence from remaining Japanese coasters suggests that there was little standardisation, at least between yards, during wartime. *Hisatsu Maru* was completed in March 1944 by Nippon Diesel Zosensho KK of Osaka, who not surprisingly also built her oil engine. At 842 grt and 212 ft overall, she is larger than she looks at first glance, her compact bridge disguising her size. The counter stern is somewhat surprising in a motor ship built as late as 1944.

She remained with her original owners, Osaka Shosen KK until 1956, and passed through various Japanese hands as *Dai-Ichi Mutsu Maru* until 1967 when Hong Kong owners put her under the Panamanian flag. By the late 1970s, when photographed at Singapore, she carried the name *South Star** and was registered in San Lorenzo, although like a myriad other Honduras-registered ships she had never been anywhere near Central America. An interesting touch is that she flies a house flag, the letters 'PO' which also appear on her funnel denoting owners Penta Ocean Maritime SA. *South Star*'s fate is unknown. *(R J Kittle)*

Conclusions about the original design of *Isalina**, the fourth example of a 1940s Japanese-built coaster, need to be drawn tentatively as this photograph of her in Singapore Roads under only her second name was taken after re-engining and possible rebuilding in 1954. She was completed as the steamer *Tokai Maru* by Okamoto Zosen Tekkosho KK of Kobe in December 1945. Evidently work on her was so far advanced on the Japanese surrender that the occupation forces, who strongly regulated Japanese maritime activity, allowed her to be completed.

Her triple-expansion engine was replaced by a diesel in 1954. The vessel's entry in *Lloyd's Register* indicates that she was lengthened at this point, but retains the original dimensions, 163 ft and 606 grt, maybe because the new dimensions had not been notified. *Lloyd's Register* also does not indicate her new owners following sale in 1965, when she took the name *Isalina* under the Panamanian flag. However, the owner apparently did not wish to remain anonymous, because it provided the ship with a house flag displaying the letters 'CA' which she flies aft.

Unlike a number of east Asian coasters, however, her fate is known. On 17 July 1976 *Isalina* sprang a leak and sank off Miri in eastern Malaysia while on voyage from Singapore to Kudat in Sabah. *(R J Kittle)*

Born in the USA

In the 1940s, only the United States could have thought of a ship 339 ft long as a short-sea vessel, yet today this length of ship is common in coastal and short-sea trades. The C1-M-AV1 type originated from the US Maritime Commission's recognition in 1943 that a vessel smaller than its ocean-going standard types would be needed. A particular requirement was for short-sea vessels of relatively shallow draft capable of using smaller harbours, especially those in the Pacific where dislodging the Japanese from the many islands they had occupied was a priority. In introducing these ships, the Maritime Commission was mindful of peacetime needs, and chose a size suitable for trading on the US coast. This thinking resulted in a proportion of the 239 built being given names beginning *Coastal*.

Although some transferred to the British government and a handful ended up with British deep-sea operators, in peacetime these ships mostly found their way to operators elsewhere in western Europe, in Central and South America and, increasingly, in the Far East. *Tong Lam** was one of the twenty two lent to the British Ministry of War Transport as *Hickory Glen*, and between 1947 and 1960 did run for Lamport & Holt Line as *Sheridan*, mainly working south from New York but occasionally crossing the North Atlantic. As *Tong Lam*, her owner from 1964 was a Hong Kong-based subsidiary of Kie Hock Shipping Co Ltd, Singapore. On 22 October 1970, *Tong Lam* stranded on Scarborough Reef in the China Sea and was abandoned, later breaking up when hit by a typhoon. She was carrying pig iron from North Korea to Chittagong. *(Ships in Focus)*

Smaller ships than the C1-M-AV1s were needed by the US Army and its Transportation Corps ordered 180-ft freighters with the designation 'FS' for 'freight and supply'. Towards the end of the war, twenty were contracted with the Albina Engine & Machine Works at Portland, Oregon, but were cancelled on Japan's surrender. The builder immediately offered the ships for sale, and quickly found a buyer in the Government of the Dutch East Indies where the war was responsible for massive losses of ships which the war-damaged industries of the Netherlands were in no position to replace. The series was delivered from November 1945 to July 1946 and managed for the government by the Amsterdam-based NV Koninklijke Paketvaart Maatschappij (KPM), who later took over the fleet.

Seroei was the fourth of the class, completed in December 1945 and recorded with a length of 171 ft; subsequent deliveries being noted as 180 ft, yet all had an identical tonnage of 556 grt. *Seroei* was renamed *Lariang*, remaining in KPM ownership until 1959 when sold to a subsidiary of Guan Guan Shipping Ltd of Singapore who renamed her *Pulau Mas* under the Panamanian flag. Although she underwent three further changes of name, culminating in *King Sun**, Guan Guan are believed to have maintained control at least until 1979 when she was renamed *Seaking*. She was deleted from *Lloyd's Register* in 1998.

Although the design of these ships was not Dutch, it was distinctive and neat, and rather unAmerican. They all had the light foremast-cum-ladder right forward and a form of crow's nest on the main mast. *King Sun* and several others had awnings fitted over their winches. *(R J Kittle)*

British wartime designs

Anticipating a long campaign against Japan, in 1944 the British designed three classes of dry cargo coasters for the Far East, plus the tankers described in Chapter 6. The most numerous and easily the ugliest were the prefabricated 'Shelt' type, cousins of the *Empire Fabric* coasters for European waters, and of 522 grt and 148 ft overall. Straits Steamship Co Ltd of Singapore was chosen as manager and either liked them or could get nothing better, and eventually eighteen out of the twenty-three 'Shelts' passed though its ownership.

Two Yorkshire yards built the Shelts; the Goole Shipbuilding & Repairing Co Ltd completed eleven and Henry Scarr Ltd finished twelve at Hessle. For delivery to the Far East, the Shelts and other coasters were formed into convoys with the larger coasters being fitted with radios. The first convoy, including nine Shelts, sailed from Falmouth at the end of July 1945, just a few days before the war with Japan ended.

None therefore saw operation in their intended area during wartime, but proved useful to replace extensive losses in the Far East. Scarr's sixth, *Empire Seabreeze* completed in June 1945, was one of those taken over by Straits Steamship, which renamed her *Senai* in 1947. In 1962, she moved on to Hong Kong owners and within a few months was wearing the Panama flag as *Mene** of Cosmos Shipping Co SA. In 1983, she was sold again and became *Mercury*. But changing her name was not propitious, and on 23 December 1984 *Mercury* sprang a leak and foundered off Tumpat in the Gulf of Siam while on a voyage from Songkhla in Thailand to Singapore. *(R J Kittle)*

The wartime 'C' type shelter-decker came in two varieties. The British-built variant had its bridge and officers' accommodation forward, the Canadian version had it conventionally aft. The Canadians were all delivered in 1946, and *Maystar** was not even given her intended 'standard' name, *Ottawa Maystar*, being launched for the Maystar Shipping Co Ltd of Montreal in October. Builder was St Lawrence Metal & Marine Works Inc at Quebec, dimensions 342 grt and 151 ft overall length.

Only a minority of the twenty built in Canada are known to have reached the Far East, and several, including *Maystar*, remained in North American waters, at least initially. These were eventually to be joined by several of the CHANT and *Empire Fabric* type, which found their last owners on the eastern seaboard of Canada. *Maystar* did cross the Atlantic, however, at least in terms of ownership, because in 1954 she became the Groningen-owned *Pia-Geerto*. Later names with Dutch owners were *May*, *Westerhorn* and *Triad*. Extensive rebuilding took place, probably while under the Dutch flag, and the two masts gave way to one mast placed between the hatches, bulwarks were fitted alongside the holds, bridge wings fitted and davits modified. In 1958, ownership moved back to Canada with a Quebec owner renaming her *Brion*. On 4 August 1976, she sank after stranding near Kegaska in the Gulf of St Lawrence. *(Fotoflite/Skyfotos)*

The third group of dry cargo motor coasters, and the largest in size at 224 ft length overall, was the prosaically named 'B' type shelter deckers which were also built in both Britain (eight in four yards) and Canada (fifteen in four yards), and again were too late to see war service. Henry Robb Ltd of Leith did not deliver any 'B's for British Government account, but in 1946 completed two for Union Steamship Company of New Zealand Ltd, the 942-grt *Kanna* and *Katui*, which were used for services between the North and the South Islands.

In 1967, *Kanna* was sold to Panamanian owners and renamed *Luna Marina**, as photographed at anchor off Singapore in the 1970s. The design was unusual, with the forward pair of kingposts built into the bridge, with crosstrees running fore and aft to serve sets of derricks both ahead and abaft of the bridge (a modest structure compared with other eastern designs). Derricks had capacity of 5- and 10-tonne safe working load. The hull was also unusual in having a forecastle and bridge deck but no poop.

Luna Marina was put under the Panamanian flag but later hoisted that of Malaysia, owned by Apollo Shipping & Trading Sdn Bhd of Kuching: note the letter A on funnel and houseflag. In 1981 these owners renamed her *Seng Giap* and she continued trading between Singapore and eastern Malaysia until 30 December 1983 when she grounded at Tanjong Datu at the western end of Borneo while on a voyage Sibu in Sarawak to Singapore. Salvaged but declared a constructive total loss she was broken up locally. *(R J Kittle)*

Post-war Japanese designs

The two large Japanese-built motor coasters featured here were completed just five years apart, but design shows considerable evolution.

The 273-ft, 1588-grt *Kashiwaharu Maru* was built by Onomichi Zosen at Onomichi in 1960 for Kashiwa Kisen Sangyo KK, Tokyo, but there is little to single her out as Japanese-built. The compact bridge and superstructure, with few openings below the boat deck, and upright funnel could be to a British or Swedish design. The cargo gear – though extensive with four 5-ton and four 10-ton derricks – was of the two masts and kingpost arrangement that Dutch and German builders often used. An oil engine by Niigata Engineering Co Ltd drove her at 11.5 knots.

Sale in 1971 saw her become *Asia Mariner*, owned in Hong Kong but flying the Panamanian flag. She is shown under her last name, *Gulf Prosperity**, adopted after being acquired in 1975 by Sharjah Shipping Co Ltd of the United Arab Emirates: its stylised 'S' design appears on her funnel in this Singapore photograph. She was not to survive long, however, and on 2 August 1979 she foundered during a cyclone in the Indian Ocean while on a voyage from Penang to Bombay with general cargo. *(R J Kittle)*

*Chin Dar**, originally *Seiyo Maru* built by Kurushima Dock Co Ltd at Imabari in 1965, has an altogether more 'modern' appearance than the rather upright *Gulf Prosperity*. A number of factors contribute, including a slightly beaked, strongly raked bow, rounded funnel, more 'open' superstructure and kingposts substituted for conventional masts. One of the few features that marks her out as characteristically Japanese are pyramidal lattice masts, one right aft for radio aerials, and one on the forecastle. Having a paired set of these right aft became an almost universal feature of Japanese bulk carrying ships. Almost exactly as long as *Gulf Prosperity* at 271ft, she had the considerably higher gross tonnage of 1999.

Original owners were Kokudo Sangyo KK of Osaka, who sold her in 1971. Owners of *Chin Dar* were the Horng Dai Navigation Co Ltd, officially of Panama (whose flag she flew), but whose masters were probably Taiwanese. She was broken up in Taiwan late in 1984. *(R J Kittle)*

Dutch designs for the East Indies

The Dutch empire in south-east Asia comprised much of what is now known as Indonesia, including many islands and much territory where land transport was difficult, requiring a large fleet of small ships to maintain communications and trade. The major operator of these craft was NV Koninklijke Paketvaart Maatschappij (KPM) of Amsterdam.

The ships of KPM came in various shapes and sizes, but were generally distinctive. The motor ship *Toboali* was completed in 1930 by Werf Gusto Firma A F Smulders of Schiedam, and was larger than other Dutch coasters at 211 ft overall, but of a modest 984 grt. Her two sets of kingposts with ample provision of derricks are more reminiscent of ocean-going ships than coasters, and probably indicate that she carried logs. Her straight stem and counter stern were something of an anachronism for 1930.

Toboali was bombed on 10 January 1942 in the Malacca Strait when making for Singapore, attempting to escape from the invading Japanese. The blazing ship was put aground and was thought worthy of salvage when the Japanese themselves were becoming short of ships in July 1944. Naturally, the returning Dutch recovered the renamed *Api Maru* after the war, and she arrived back in Batavia (now Djakarta) in June 1946 to resume service as *Toboali*.

Sale in 1958 saw *Toboali* passed around among owners in the Far East, under the Singaporean and later the Panamanian flag. She is seen at Singapore under the last of the eight names she carried in her long career, *King Moon**, owned by King Line SA, a subsidiary of Guan Guan Shipping of Singapore. She went to breakers in Singapore in 1977. *(R J Kittle)*

The out-of-scale superstructure block amidships to provide accommodation for officers was a feature of several Dutch Far Eastern ships built to replace losses in the Second World War. The motor ship *Bakongan* came from NV Rotterdamsche Droogdok Maatschappij in 1948, and although operated by Koninklijke Paketvaart Maatschappij she was actually owned by the Government of the Netherlands until 1952, when KPM assumed ownership. Sold in 1960, she was owned by various subsidiaries of Guan Guan Shipping Ltd as *Kali Mas*, *Bona* and *San Blas*.

She is seen in the ownership of King Line Private Ltd of Singapore, where she is working cargo in the anchorage with her extensive cargo gear. Again, she is untypical of contemporary Dutch coaster building practice, with, for instance, a stern design that disappeared elsewhere around 1930. The huge midships house tends to disguise the fact that she is comparatively large at 227 ft overall and 1331 grt. The ports in her side indicate a strength deck below the uppermost light awning deck.

*King Lion** was her final name, taken in 1966. The port of registry on her stern indicates that the photograph was taken some time after 1975 in which year her owners reflagged her from Panama to Singapore. She was broken up at Jurong in 1984. *(R J Kittle)*

Larger Dutch ships for the Far East had engines amidships, but otherwise shared several features with their smaller brethren, including a box-like superstructure, tiny upright funnels and the anachronistic stern. *Kalianget* was another product of the post-war rebuilding, again financed and owned by the Netherlands government for management and eventual ownership by KPM. Her builder in 1948 was NV C van der Giessen & Zonen's Scheepswerven at Krimpen a/d Yssel, a few miles upstream of Rotterdam, and she measured 277ft and 2164 grt. In this view at Singapore late in her career she has a varied mix of boats and extensive awnings both fore and aft. These and an array of ports below her awning deck suggest that she carried unberthed passengers on her weather deck.

Her post-KPM career involved the usual mix of Far Eastern owners and flags of convenience, with a Singapore owner registering her in Panama during 1960 as *Fama*. In 1962, she returned to Indonesia as *Ogan**, as seen here. Her owner was PT Pelajaran Nusantara Sriwidjaja Raja of Djarkata. She looks somewhat forlorn in this photograph taken in a Singapore anchorage: no one appears to be on board, suggesting she is laid up, perhaps awaiting the next pilgrimage season? Her fate is unknown and she was deleted from *Lloyd's Register* in 1993. *(R J Kittle)*

The motor ship *Soon Bee* was also built in the Netherlands, by Scheepswerf 'Piet Hein' at Papendrecht in 1953, but for a Singapore owner, Heap Eng Moh Steamship Co Ltd. Again, the bridge structure appears out of proportion to her relatively modest overall length of 158 ft. Her even more modest tonnage, 373 gross, indicates that she is an open shelter-decker, an arrangement confirmed by her entry in *Lloyd's Register*. The cover on her forecastle (it is too substantial to be called an awning) plus the large openings beneath her bridge wings suggest that she was expected to carry unberthed passengers on deck and the ports fore and aft that others were accommodated on her main deck. The officers on her bridge certainly enjoyed a panoramic view.

Unusually for a Far Eastern ship of her period, sales did not see her renamed. The letter T on her funnel identifies the date as during 1974–76, when owner was Tunas Private Ltd of Singapore. In 1976, she moved on to Malaysian owners, carrying the name *Soon Bee* to her grave in the scrap yards of Singapore, where she arrived for demolition in July 1987. *(R J Kittle)*

European ships for Indonesia

As Dutch rule came to an end, Indonesia began to exercise its independence by banning KPM ships from trading in its waters, and also by buying its ships from elsewhere than the Netherlands. *Empoh* was completed for the national fleet, PT Pelajaran Nasional Indonesia, by Schiffswerft August Pahl in Hamburg during 1958. At 167 ft and 504 grt, she was in many respects typical of contemporary West German practice, with her well deck forward and sharply raked bow. Less usual was the doubling of derricks, and a many-windowed wheelhouse that extends right across the superstructure. Particularly unusual was her machinery; not the expected German or even Dutch diesel, but a unit made in 1951 by the Enterprise Engineering Company of San Francisco. Providing a modest 350 bhp, this four-stroke engine gave an equally modest service speed of 8 knots. *Empoh* remained in the same Indonesian government ownership throughout her career. She was broken up in Indonesia, at Tandjung Priok, in 1983. *(R J Kittle)*

The Indonesian *Iramuar** came from Norway, the yard of L H Salthammer Batbyggeri at Vestnes completing her in 1978. Owner of this 751-grt, 60-metre motor ship was the National Fleet Development Corporation, known to the Indonesians as PT Pengembangan Armada Niaga Nasional, mercifully shortened to PANN.

State ownership and other evidence points to her being partly supplied as Norway's commitment to overseas aid. Norway in 1978 was not the cheapest place to build ships, but that year at least two similar ships came from other Norwegian yards for the same owners, a sister to the *Iramuar* named *Ikaguri* from Sandnessjøen Slip & Mekanisk Verksteds and the similar-sized passenger-cargo vessel *Irimawa* from Hasund, Smie & Sveiseverk at Ulsteinvik. All remained in Indonesian government ownership, although under a slightly different company title, until broken up. *Irimawa* was delivered to breakers in Chittagong during March 2005, *Iramuar* and *Ikaguri* following her to this fate in April 2005 and January 2006, respectively.

European practice of the 1970s is apparent in her practically sheerless hull and in the cargo gear, with the three hammerhead derricks that are slung from two points on the crosstree of the mainmast and from the pair of kingposts aft. Numerous aerials point to sophisticated electronic communication and navigational equipment. Only the substantial awning on the forecastle suggests she was destined for the Far East. *(R J Kittle)*

The Greco-Japanese 'Minis'

Greek owners have preferred to acquire second-hand coasters from northern European or, more recently, Japanese sources rather than order new coasters. A spectacular exception to this rule has been George P Livanos, who worked with the Hakodate Dock Company to produce a design for a small, twin-screw bulk carrier to carry 3200 tonnes of cargo on a draught of under 5 metres and a length of 65 metres. Livanos ambitiously planned to build 200 of these and, although his plan was scaled back to produce about fifty-five, this was nevertheless an unprecedented achievement for a Greek owner of coasters. In peacetime, classes of such as size have only been built for state-controlled enterprises in Eastern Europe.

The series was built between 1969 and 1975 by eight Japanese shipbuilders, with Hakodate producing the lion's share, a total of twenty-one at three different yards. There were variations from vessel to vessel: some had just two hatches, in others hatches were paired athwartship to give a four-hatch configuration. Some had a single 8-tonne electric crane set between the two hatches or groups of hatches, others had a pair of 15-tonne cranes, and a couple had no cargo gear at all. The original pair of 500 bhp Daihatsu engines fitted was superseded by 750 bhp units.

The 'Mini' ships found employment working to the river ports around the Indian sub-continent and the Caribbean, where they were often used for transhipping grain and other bulk cargoes from deep-drafted ships for delivery to up-river or other ports with shallow water. They proved particularly useful on the Mississippi and Missouri rivers. Although some have found their way into the Mediterranean and Black Sea, they have been rare birds in other European waters.

Two variants are shown here, both photographed in the Mediterranean, and both in the blue and white funnel colours used by the single-ship companies controlled by George P Livanos. At 1355 grt, *Mini Lance** has a single 8-tonne crane and flies the Liberian flag, and is registered in the ownership of Elmini Lance Inc. The starboard quarter view emphasises the sheerless hull with its cutaway section aft. She was built by the Hakodate Dock Co Ltd at Muroran in 1969. Sale in 1989 saw her become *Sea Sabah*, and she has since worked out of Bahrain under the Honduras flag.

The 1592-grt *Mini Lass** was also built at Muroran but in 1970 and with twin cranes rated at 15 tonnes each, although the crane bodies appear smaller than the single, 8-tonne crane of *Mini Lance*. She flew the Greek flag in this overhead view at Malta in which the four-hatch configuration and the broad beam are clearly seen. *Mini Lass* was later transferred to the Caribbean, and was broken up in New Orleans during 1993.

This was one of the most radical redesigns of the coaster yet seen, but the lack of any further development of the concept and the failure to replace the ships when they were sold or scrapped suggests that the success of one of the most numerous types of coaster ever built other than for state-owned concerns was limited.

Turkey resurgent

Turkish owners were once noted for taking coasters which had become redundant in northern European waters, repairing them, often fitting new engines, and extracting the maximum life from a basically sound hull. Gradually, Turkey's own coaster-building industry has developed, initially building basic vessels purely for local owners in local trades. The town of Tuzla has a particular concentration of building and repairing yards, and it was here that *Omer Bey* was completed in 1982 by Torgem Gemi Insaat ve Sanayii. In 1993, she became *Ilke Mete* and in 1997 *Hilmi-K** for Fuden Dinizcilik Ticaret ve Sanayi, Istanbul.

The 1923-grt, 81-metre *Hilmi-K* was photographed during October 2008 in the Kartal anchorage, possibly awaiting the northbound convoy through the Bosphorus, or perhaps just waiting for a cargo, because her hatches are partly uncovered. With her modest sheer, almost a clipper bow and a 'wing' on her funnel she has a certain style which suggests Turkey has the potential to rival east Asian countries as an exporter of coasters if only its shipbuilding industry can match the quality and reliability of delivery which the best Japanese, Korean and Chinese yards can offer. *(Martin Wright)*

Turkish shipbuilding has advanced to the point where relatively sophisticated vessels are produced, in some cases indistinguishable from those built by more mature shipbuilding nations. Symbolic of this was an appearance by a Turkish coaster on the Mersey in May 1988 when the *Ayca** turned up at the port of Garston. *Ayca* sailed on an early morning tide, which provides the best opportunity to photograph ships off this port, whose approach channel runs north east to south west.

The 1533-grt, 82-metre *Ayca* was yard number 1 of Desan Deniz Insaat Sanayi of Istanbul in 1984. Unfortunately, the yard did not prosper, and ceased work after building four general cargo ships and a ferry. Many Turkish coasters use eastern European diesels, and *Ayca* was fitted with a nine-cylinder Skoda oil engine made in Prague. Also typical of most Turkish coasters, she has four 5-tonne derricks serving her two holds.

Owners were Gepa Gemi Nakliyat Sanayi ve Ticaret AS, which sold *Ayca* in 1991. She has since carried the names *Naica*, *Icaro*, and *Phoros*, and in 2011 is still under Turkish ownership as *Seher Yildizi*, but now registered in Kingstown, capital of St Vincent and the Grenadines. *(Author)*

Modern Chinese coasters

Even the meteoric rise of Japan and Korea as shipbuilding nations is likely to be surpassed by the People's Republic of China, and its industry threatens the remaining coaster-building yards in Europe. A relatively early example of Chinese coaster building, and of a Chinese-built ship classed by *Lloyd's Register*, was *Marine Jade*. She was completed for Singapore owners in 1994 by the Zhejiang Shipyard at Ningpo, south of Shanghai and fitted with a standard Chinese diesel engine.

In 2003, sales began that were to see her stray way beyond her original restricted range. First she became *Paradise*, still owned in Singapore, and in 2006 *Nermin N*, owned in Turkey. The name *Bluemarine**, under which she was photographed in the Bosphorus off Istanbul in November 2008, was adopted in 2007 when she passed to Cenker Denizcilik ve Ticaret of Istanbul. In 2011 she is still under Turkish ownership as *Zeybe*.

Unusually for a Turkish coaster, *Bluemarine* has lost the four derricks originally fitted to her stout mainmast. This may be a temporary measure because the winches remain in place and apparently functional on their platform. The twelve navigation lights in a cluster on her radar/signal mast would seem a little excessive. The tonnage of the 72-metre overall, two-hold ship has remained at 1511grt over the sixteen years since she was built. *(Martin Wright)*

The unusual feature of *Zhi Xian 38** in having her bridge right forward merits the inclusion of this photograph, although alongside views have been shunned where possible in this book. She was loading pipes at Shanghai in September 2007, and was registered as owned locally by Shanghai Zhixian Transport Shipping. *Zhi Xian 38* was completed by the Zhejiang Tenglong Shipyard at Wenling in 2006, has machinery from the Chinese Diesel Engine Factory and measures 86 metres and 2220 grt.

Chinese state ownership and her newness have not saved *Zhi Xian 38* from the apparently arbitrary changes of flag and owner that have afflicted many ships in recent years. Currently she is officially owned in Hong Kong yet since 2006 she has flown the flag of Tuvalu. It takes a good atlas to locate this state, which consists of nine coral atolls in the South Pacific with a total area of 10 square miles. It can only be guessed as to why a ship owned by a country where everything is under state control should need to fly such a flag of convenience. *(Martin Wright)*

CHAPTER

16

Specialised Coasters

Neither bulk-carrying tramp ships nor dedicated to a given route, there are a number of interesting dry cargo coasters built or modified to suit a particular cargo or trade. These include ships with refrigerating equipment for meat or fish, or – less critically – to provide the right conditions for moving fruit or vegetables. For markets in which live animals are preferred to refrigerated carcasses, dedicated livestock carriers have been provided. Ships have also been adapted or built to carry particularly heavy items of cargo. It is not only the vessel that has to be specialised, the officers and often the crew as well have to fully understand the requirements of the trade and increasingly to have the appropriate certificates.

These ships again beg the question as to the definition of a coaster, because their cargoes may well require long hauls. Again, the answer must come down to size, with most of those described here having bigger brothers intended for ocean routes.

In acquiring a specialised ship – and this applies to both those shown here and the gas or chemical tankers in Chapter 6 – the owner is taking a calculated risk. If there is the demand for carrying the particular cargo and little in the way of economic alternatives, a high freight rate can be secured. Against this, the specialist vessel is inflexible compared with a general trader, and difficult or impossible to divert to another trade. With fruit carriers in particular, the seasonality of the trade might require annual lay-ups. A heavy-lift ship might also spend extended periods waiting for suitable work. Financing a conversion may therefore be more attractive than a specialised newbuild, and certainly this is the case when owners are entering a totally new trade. However, an adaptation of an existing hull might result in design compromises and inevitable shorter life-expectancy than would be the case for a purpose-built vessel.

Trading conditions for such ships can alter for industrial, economic, political or even social reasons. Containerisation of chilled and refrigerated cargoes has helped marginalise the reefer. The dedicated livestock carrier has declined in Europe partly through strong popular opposition in the United Kingdom to moving live cattle, and through politically-motivated discrimination against British produce. The heavy-lift ship operator must always depend on the cyclical needs of the heavy engineering industry. The owner of a specialist ship must be, even more than the average ship owner, a risk taker.

An asterisk in a caption indicates the vessel shown in the photograph.

Livestock carrier

In post-Second World War, years some standard dry cargo coasters were converted to dedicated livestock carriers, with stalls and ramps for the livestock and additional ventilation, and losing their now redundant cargo gear. The concept was by no means new, however; the very first photograph in Chapter 1 of this book shows an Irish Sea trader for which a staple cargo was cattle.

Vroon's Handel & Scheepvaart Onderneming NV of Breskens in the Netherlands once specialised in this business, with its trading name Livestock Express reflected in the names of ships such as *Angus Express**, seen here at Malta. The 'Express' was something of an exaggeration: she was capable of a fairly modest 12.5 knots. She had been built in 1950 as the shelter-decker *Ijstroom* for NV Hollandsche Stoomboot Maatschappij of Amsterdam. Vroon bought her in 1970, initially naming her *Holland Express* before she became *Angus Express* later that year. Conversion to a livestock carrier actually reduced her tonnage from 499 gross to 481 gross, and thus another example of the Dutch achieving a tonnage below the magic 500 gross on a substantial, 219-ft hull.

The carriage of live animals by sea attracted the attention of animal rights activists, at least in the animal-loving UK, who argued that – if animals had to be killed – it was more humane to do so locally and export the carcasses. This argument was never likely to gain traction in the Muslim world, which continues to import live sheep from Australia in industrial quantities. *Angus Express* ended her days working for owners in Jeddah, as *Mahmoud* from 1982 and later as *Sultan*. She was broken up at Gadani Beach in 1989. *(World Ship Society Ltd)*

Reefers and fruiters

A number of short-sea traders had some capacity for carrying refrigerated cargoes, but coasters dedicated to the reefer trades were uncommon. The Dutch seized many of the opportunities that were available, constructing some purpose-built vessels, including *Fedala** and *Zeehaan* and converting basic coasters such as *Henry Denny*, *Marathon* and *Prins Bernhard* for the role. A typical trade for these ships was carrying chilled or frozen meat from Ireland to near-Continental ports, while *Fedala* was a frequent sight in the River Thames, where she is at anchor in this photograph.

The builder of the 494-grt, 225-ft overall *Fedala* in 1952 was NV Werf 'Gusto' v/h A F Smulders at Schiedam for NV Dammers & van der Heide's Shipping & Trading Co at nearby Rotterdam. To save space below decks, the large deckhouse amidships housed the refrigeration machinery, and four 2-ton derricks served the adjacent hatches. According to *Lloyd's Register*, she was still in existence in 2011 under the Honduran flag as *Stella Marina*, the fifth name she had carried in a career that apparently stretched for over fifty years. *(World Ship Society Ltd)*

As major exporters of fruit and vegetables, Spain and Portugal owned and built several refrigerated motor vessels. Of 1308 grt and 231 ft, *Madeirense** was completed in 1962 for Empresa de Transportes do Funchal Ltda, of Funchal in Madeira. A sister, *Funchalense*, followed in 1968. Estaleiros São Jacinto at Aveiro, Portugal, built both to Ice Class 3, and since the chances of encountering ice on her regular run to Madeira were minimal, the owners clearly had trades to northern Europe in mind. However, the ships ran to Funchal, functioning almost as ferries: photographs invariably show cars on deck and – usually clustered aft enjoying the sunshine – passengers, of whom twelve could be berthed. *Madeirense* changed owner several times, but throughout her career remained registered in Funchal, and ended her days in her home waters. In January 2000, she was scuttled as an artificial reef off Porto Santo, Madeira. *(Ships in Focus)*

An unusual, and perhaps unique, combination of a Finnish shipbuilder and Cuban owners produced *Anacaona**. She was completed in 1975 by Nystads Varv A/B, Nystad as *Batalla de Santa Clara* for the Cuban government. She was renamed *Anacaona* in 1990 with owners described as Transportes Oceanicos Pibi SA, Habana, another arm of the Cuban state.

A shelter-decker, *Anacaona* has two tonnages – 496 gross in the open configuration and 1327 gross in the closed state, on a length of 74 metres overall. Four hatches serve the two refrigerated holds, worked by eight 3-tonne derricks at the feet of her two bipod masts.

Her trading pattern in the early 1990s involved the expected voyages to Central America and around the Caribbean, and also to Canada, but not of course to the United States, which pursued an economic vendetta against one of its poorest near neighbours. *Anacaona* is a good example of a specialised coaster-sized ship quite capable of crossing the North Atlantic, and her voyages took her to ports in communist countries around the Black Sea, as well as to the Iberian Peninsula, North Africa and western Europe. The by then rather rusty reefer was photographed in Antwerp Docks during March 1993.

She moved to the Belize flag as *Cuban Reefer* in 2002, and was last reported working out of the Canary Islands. *(Author)*

Cabo Frio was not necessarily typical of Norwegian coaster construction (so many yards have been involved that it has proved difficult to pin down a distinctively Norwegian style), but was a brave attempt to build a stylish ship. Experiments such as this with the funnel and wheelhouse block were not uncommon in the 1960s, especially with fruit carriers, but a more economically minded age has since seen such fripperies discarded in place of basic and often austere styles. *Cabo Frio* was a fast ship, with a service speed of 14.75 knots, intended for carrying perishable cargo such as fruit and vegetables, despite her single-deck configuration.

The builder in 1960 was A/S Langesunds Mekanisk Verksted for Ludvig Lorentzen, who, despite being based in Oslo, registered *Cabo Frio* in the port in which she was built, Langesund. Tonnage was 1609 gross and length 245 ft.

Lorentzen sold *Cabo Frio* to an Italian owner in 1969, but the southern-sounding name (it was in fact Spanish) made it unnecessary to rename her. This still held true in 1974, when she went under the Cypriot flag for an operator that was based in London and the name of which, Fruit Transportation (FRUCAS) Ltd gives more than a clue to her role. She traded around the Mediterranean, to continental Europe and to West Africa until 24 August 1982 when she was abandoned by her crew when the engine room flooded as she was approaching Cartagena, Spain while on a ballast voyage from Piræus.

Pallet carrier

Pallet carriers are an exception to the rule that the regular coastal trader has succumbed to the roll-on, roll-off ship and container carrier, although this type has characteristics of both. These ships are a Norwegian specialty, reflecting that the country still has a coastal trade, with ships serving coastal and fjordside towns where sea communication is preferable to long road journeys through inhospitable country. Pallet carriers have also proved useful in the timber products trade, with cargoes such as pulp, paper and board. Features of these ships include bow and/or side doors with ramps for access by fork-lift trucks and side lifts to access lower decks.

Photographed in Oslofjord during September 1996, the ice-strengthened *Trans Vag** was built in 1993 by Loland Verft A/S of Leirvik for an associate of Seatrans ANS, formed in Bergen during 1970. Some of its pallet carriers are dedicated to the paper trade and are painted in the colours of Swedish papermaker Holmen. At 493 grt and 77 metres, *Trans Vag* was unusual in having a 75-tonne derrick aft, necessitating a bipod mast. The capacity of her cargo gear indicates that she was intended more for general cargo than forest products. She is clearly a very flexible craft and can also carry cars and containers.

Sold in 2001, she has since been named *Nordvag*, *Jaxlinn*, *Scan Mina*, *Mina* and in 2011 was listed as the Danish-owned *Vina*. With no rebuilding apparent, her gross tonnage had jumped to 2065 by the year 2005. An increase of 419 per cent purely through changes in international conventions for measuring tonnage demonstrates just how poor an indicator of size gross tonnage can be. *(Author)*

Heavy lifters

Heavy lift ships need substantial deck space combined with exceptional stability while hoisting on board items which may weigh several hundred tonnes. In the extraordinary *Gloria Siderum**, both problems were solved by joining together two coasters.

The two 186-ft hulls combined in this July 1969 to make this catamaran were the 1957-built *Hada II*, which formed the port side and *Hermes* of 1956. Both had been built by NV Scheepbouwwerf v/h de Groot & van Vliet at Slikkerveer, and given identical oil engines by D & J Boot. The port hull retained its masts and pair of 3-tonne capacity derricks, while the starboard side had a massive tripod mast fitted and which could lift 300 tonnes. The masts on the port hull were later replaced to increase deck space. The owner of the 1141-grt *Gloria Siderum* was the Gloria Navigation Line Company of Monrovia, Liberia, and manager was Holscher Shipping of Rotterdam.

Much of the work of modern heavy lift ships has been for the offshore oil and more recently wind-farm industries, and in 1983 *Gloria Siderum* underwent a further conversion to a diving maintenance craft, retaining her big derrick, and given the meaningless name *Multi Service 300*. She seems to have spent an inordinate amount of time in one of the Rotterdam harbours devoted to laying up offshore craft, and drops out of *Lloyd's Register* in the mid-1990s. *(World Ship Society Ltd)*

The heavy-lift vessels *Aberthaw Fisher** and *Kingsnorth Fisher* were both purpose-built and coasters, completed in 1966 specifically to carry heavy items of equipment to power stations located around the British coast. The load was delivered to the ship on a road trailer that was manoeuvred on to a ramp on the ship's after deck, and which could be lowered into the hold. When new, these vessels were based in Pomona Docks, Manchester, at the heart of what was Britain's heavy electrical engineering industry, and were probably the last ships to use this part of the Manchester dock system. Facilities intended for docking the ships were provided at the power stations served, although embarrassingly in one case these facilities proved too narrow for the ships.

Builder of the 284-ft, 2355-grt *Aberthaw Fisher* (seen at Eastham in November 1985) was Ailsa Shipbuilding Co Ltd at Troon, with her sister coming from Hall, Russell & Co Ltd at Aberdeen. Both were owned by a company with long experience of moving heavy loads, James Fisher & Sons Ltd of Barrow-in-Furness, and by which the vessels were chartered long term to the electricity industry. Following privatisation of this industry, *Aberthaw Fisher* was renamed *National Generator* in 1990, and in 1996 was sold for conversion to a diamond dredger for use off Namibia and renamed *Moonstar*. This does not seem to have been very successful because she was broken up in India during 2000. *Kingsnorth Fisher* was renamed *New Generation* in 1990, and remained in service until 2001 when, with her name shortened to *New Gen*, she sailed to Alang and the breakers. *(Author)*

Bibliography

Books

Anderiesse, J H, Kruidhof, E A, and Oostmeijer, J, *Carebeka, 1939–1983*, World Ship Society, Kendal, 1994.

Anderiesse, Jan, and Spurling, Leslie, *Gruno 1937–2002*, De Alk, Alkmaar, 2003.

Anonymous, *N.V. Scheepvaart- en Steenkolen Maatschappij, Rotterdam*, Stegro VOF, Netherlands, n d.

Atkinson, G, *J and A Gardner & Co Ltd*, McCall, Portishead, 2002.

Bent, Mike, *Steamers of the Fjords: Bergen Shipping since 1839*, Conway, London, 1989.

Boerma, A, *Coasters. De laatste 50 Jaren de KHV*, De Alk, Alkmaar, 1992.

Boerma, A, *Coasters. Schepen van de Kustvaart toen en nu,* De Alk, Alkmaar, 1985.

Bowman, A J, *Kirkintilloch Shipbuilding*, Strathkelvin Libraries and Museums, Kirkintilloch, 1983.

Buttkus, Eilhart, Detlefsen, Gert Uwe, and Kramer, Wolfgang, *Deutsche Reedereien Band 23 – VEB Deutsche Seereederei Rostock*, Detlefsen, Bad Segeberg, 2004.

Campbell, Colin, and Fenton, Roy, *Ships in Focus: Burns and Laird*, Ships in Focus, Preston, 1998.

Chappell, Connery, *Island Lifeline*, T Stephenson, Prescot, 1980.

Chesterton, D R, and Fenton, R S, *Gas and Electricity Colliers*, World Ship Society, Kendal, 1984.

Coppack, Tom, *A Lifetime with Ships*, T. Stephenson, Prescot, 1973.

De Boer, Gerrit, *Wagenborgs 100 Jaar: De Schepen van 1898 tot 1998*, De Alk, Alkmaar, 1998.

Detlefsen, Gert Uwe, and Abert, Hans Jürgen, *Die Chronik der deutschen Küstenmotorschiffe 1945–1995* (3 volumes), Verlag Gert Uwe Detlefsen, Bad Segeberg, 1995.

Detlefsen, Gert Uwe, and Abert, Hans Jürgen, *Register des Deutschen Kümos* (2 volumes), Detlefsen, Bad Segeberg, 1999.

Duckworth, C L D, and Langmuir, G E, *Clyde and Other Coastal Steamers*, Brown, Son & Ferguson Ltd, Glasgow, 1939.

Duckworth, C L D, and Langmuir, G E, *West Highland Steamers*, 3rd edn, Brown, Son & Ferguson Ltd, Glasgow, 1967.

Farquhar, Ian, *Union Fleet*, New Zealand Ship and Marine Society, Wellington, 2001.

Farr, Graham, *West Country Passenger Steamers*, T Stephenson, Prescot, 1967.

Fenton, Roy, *Cambrian Coasters*, World Ship Society, Kendal, 1989.

Fenton, Roy, *Mersey Rovers*, World Ship Society, Gravesend, 1997.

Fenton, Roy, *Monk's Navy*, World Ship Society, Kendal, 1981.

Fenton, Roy, *Monroe Brothers*, World Ship Society, Kendal, 1982.

Fenton, Roy, *W S Kennaugh and the West Coast Shipping Co Ltd*, World Ship Society, Kendal, 1979.

Fenton, Roy, and Robertson, Philip, *William Robertson and the Gem Line*, Ships in Focus, Preston, 2009.

Garrett, K S, *Comben Longstaff and Co Ltd*, World Ship Society, Gravesend, 1997.

Garrett, K S, *Crescent Shipping*, Ships in Focus, Preston, 2010.

Garrett, K S, *Everard of Greenhithe*, World Ship Society, Kendal, 1991.

Garrett, K S, *R Lapthorn and Company Limited*, Ships in Focus, Preston, 2001.

Garrett, K S, *Union Transport: 60 Years in Shipping*, Ships in Focus, Preston, 2006.

Garrett, K S, *Weston Shipping*, World Ship Society, Gravesend, 1999.

Gray, Edward, *Lancaster's Little Ships: Robert Gardner's Role in the Coastal Trade 1924–1962*, Gray, Salford, 1996.

Gray, Edward, and Fenton, Roy, *Ninety Years of the Ramsey Steamship Co Ltd*, Ships in Focus, Preston, 2003.

Harvey, W J, *Arklow Shipping*, McCall, Bristol, 2004.

Harvey, W J, and Telford, P J, *The Clyde Shipping Company*, P J Telford, 2002.

Haws, Duncan, *Merchant Fleets: Britain's Railway Steamers* (Volumes 24, 25, 26), TCL Publications, Hereford, 1993.

Huckett, A, *Rowbotham*, World Ship Society, Gravesend, 2002.

McDonald, Dan, *The Clyde Puffer*, David & Charles, Newton Abbott, 1977.

Macrae, J A, and Waine, C V, *The Steam Collier Fleets*, Waine Research Publications, Albrighton, 1990.

McRonald, M, *The Irish Boats* (3 volumes), Tempus, Stroud, 2006.

Mitchell, W H, and Sawyer, L A, *Sailing Ship to Supertanker*, Dalton, Lavenham, 1987.

Mitchell, W H and Sawyer, L A, *The Empire Ships*, Lloyd's of London Press, Colchester, 1990.

Moojen, Willem H, *Zwervend van Kust naar Kust. Nederlandse Kustvaart door de Jaren Heen*, Lanasta, Emmen, 2007.

Patterson, Len, *The Light in the Glens: the Rise and Fall of the Puffer Trade*, House of Lochar, Colonsay, 1996.

Patton, Brian, *Scottish Coastal Steamers 1918–1975: the Lines that Linked the Lochs*, Silver Link, Peterborough, 1996.

Pemberton, Barry, *Australian Coastal Shipping*, Melbourne University Press, 1979.

Pietikäinen, Matti, *The Finnlines Fleet 1947–1997*, Finnlines, Helsinki, 1998.

Pietikäinen, Matti, and Sjöström, Bengt, *The Ships of our First Century: The EFFOA Fleet 1883–1983*, EFFOA, Helsinki, 1983.

Robins, Nick, *Birds of the Sea: 150 Years of the General Steam Navigation Company*, McCall, Portishead, 2007.

Salmon, Anne, *A Sideways Launch*, Meresborough, Rainham, 1992.

Sawyer, L A, and Mitchell, W H, *Victory Ships and Tankers*, David & Charles, Newton Abbot, 1974.

Somner, Graeme, *DP&L: A History of the Dundee, Perth & London Shipping Company Ltd and Associated Shipping Companies*, World Ship Society, Kendal, 1995.

Spargo, O G, and Thomason, T H, *Old Time Steam Coasting*, Waine Research Publications, Albrighton, 1982.

Stammers, Michael, *Mersey Flats and Flatmen*, Terence Dalton, Suffolk and National Museums and Galleries on Merseyside, Liverpool, 1993.

Waine, C V, *Coastal and Short Sea Liners*, Waine Research Publications, Albrighton, 1999.

Waine, C V, and Fenton, R S, *Steam Coasters and Short Sea Traders*, 3rd edition, Waine Research Publications, Albrighton, 1994.

Westerwal, H, *Coasters*, de Alk, Alkmaar, n d.

Papers and articles

Aldcroft, D H, 'The eclipse of British coastal shipping, 1913–21', *Journal of Transport History*, VI (1963), 24–38. Reprinted in Armstrong, J (ed.), *Coastal and Short Sea Shipping*, Aldershot, 1996.

Allen, E E, 'On the comparative cost of transit by steam and sailing colliers, and on the different methods of ballasting', *Proceedings of the Institute of Civil Engineers*, XIV (1854–5), 318–73.

Armstrong, J, 'An annotated bibliography of the British coastal trade', *International Journal of Maritime History*, VII No.1 (1995), 117–92.

Armstrong, J, 'Climax and climacteric: the British coastal trade, 1870–1930', in Starkey, D J, and Jamieson, A G (eds), *Exploiting the Sea: Aspects of Britain's Maritime Economy since 1870* (Exeter, 1998).

Armstrong, J, 'Introduction: the Cinderella of the transport world: the historiography of the British coastal trade', in Armstrong, J (ed.), *Coastal and Short Sea Shipping* (Aldershot, 1996).

Armstrong, J, 'The crewing of British coastal colliers: 1870–1914', *The Great Circle*, 20 No.2 (1998), 73-89.

Clegg, W Paul, 'Irish Sea Unit-Load Services', in *Ships Annual 1967*, Ian Allan, London, 1967.

Fenton, Roy, 'John Bowes: the first bulk carrier?', *Ships in Focus Record* 20 (2002), 253–60.

Fenton, Roy, 'The Clyde Puffer', *Archive* 30 (2001), 49–64.

Fenton, Roy, 'The Innis boats: a reappraisal', *Ships in Focus Record* 26 (2003), 86–99.

Fenton, Roy, 'The slate steamers', *Archive* 64 (2009), 3–14.

Fenton, Roy, and Patterson, Sean, 'Joseph Fisher and Sons Ltd', in Fenton, R S, and Clarkson, J (eds), *British Shipping Fleets* (Preston, 2000).

Robertson, J C, and Hagan, H H, 'A century of coaster design and operation', *Transactions of the Institution of Engineers*, XCVII (1954), 204–56.

Somner, Graeme, 'London Scottish Lines Ltd, Leith', *Ships in Focus Record* 27 (2004), 142–9.

Periodicals

Archive
Coastal Shipping
Marine News
Sea Breezes
Ships in Focus Record
Ships Monthly

Registers

Lloyd's Confidential Index, 1886–1914
Lloyd's Register of Shipping, 1860–1914
Mercantile Navy List, 1870–1914
Miramar Ship Index
Starke-Schell Registers

Index

All ships mentioned are listed, with dates of build for all except warships.